aylor Downing is a television producer and writer. He was
ducated at Cambridge University and went on to become
anaging director and head of history at Flashback Television,
n independent production company. His most recent books
include *Spies in the Sky*, *Churchill's War Lab*, *Cold War* (with Sir
Jeremy Isaacs) and *Secret Warriors*.

S

NIGHT RAID

THE TRUE STORY OF THE
FIRST VICTORIOUS BRITISH
PARA RAID OF WWII

Taylor Downing

940.542142

(ABACUS)

ABACUS

First published in Great Britain in 2013 by Little, Brown
This paperback edition published in 2015 by Abacus

13 5 7 9 10 8 6 4 2

A CIP catalogue record for this book
is available from the British Library.

Map copyright © John Gilkes

ISBN 978-0-349-00025-1

Typeset in Palatino by M Rules
Printed and bound in Great Britain by
Clays Ltd, St Ives plc

Papers used by Abacus are from well-managed forests
and other responsible sources.

MIX
Paper from
responsible sources
FSC® C104740

Abacus
An imprint of
Little, Brown Book Group
Carmelite House
50 Victoria Embankment
London EC4Y 0DZ

An Hachette UK Company
www.hachette.co.uk

www.littlebrown.co.uk

Contents

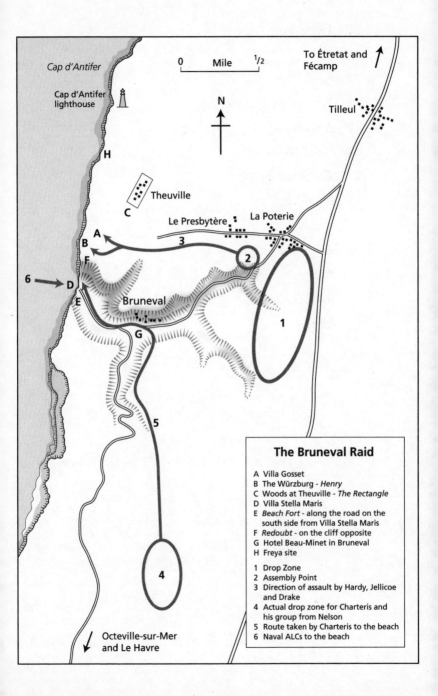

Cap d'Antifer

Cap d'Antifer lighthouse

To Étretat and Fécamp

0   Mile   1/2

N

Tilleul

H

Theuville

C

Le Presbytère   La Poterie

A

B   3

F

6 → D   2

E

Bruneval   1

G

5

6 →

Octeville-sur-Mer
and Le Havre

The Bruneval Raid

A Villa Gosset
B The Würzburg - *Henry*
C Woods at Theuville - *The Rectangle*
D Villa Stella Maris
E *Beach Fort* - along the road on the
   south side from Villa Stella Maris
F *Redoubt* - on the cliff opposite
G Hotel Beau-Minet in Bruneval
H Freya site

1 Drop Zone
2 Assembly Point
3 Direction of assault by Hardy, Jellicoe
   and Drake
4 Actual drop zone for Charteris and
   his group from Nelson
5 Route taken by Charteris to the beach
6 Naval ALCs to the beach

Behind Enemy Lines

It was the silence that amazed him most. No engines. No gunfire. Nothing stirred. He hadn't expected this total, all-embracing silence. The incredible noise inside the aircraft had lasted for two hours and had almost shattered his ear drums. The men had sung songs with a tense, nervous gusto. Some had played cards, mostly pontoon. No one wanted to show the others that he felt scared. Then, as they approached the drop zone, came the shouting of the jump sergeant, straining to be heard above the roar of the Rolls-Royce Merlin engines. 'Action stations ... Hook up ... Stand by ... ' Every man checked that the static line of his parachute was firmly connected to the rail inside the aircraft. Then he checked his neighbour's. After a few seconds of anxious waiting came the scream as the red light went green. 'Number One Go-o!'

He was the fifth out. There was the rushing sound of the slip-stream as he fell through the hole cut in the bottom of the aircraft into 500 feet of cold February night air. The anti-aircraft guns were still firing in the distance. He felt the abrupt pull of the parachute opening, the smooth descent, the force of the sudden landing, the silk parachute collapsing on top of him. He released his harness and with a lot of effort hauled it in and gathered up his chute.

For several minutes everything had been busy, frenzied. Somehow he had imagined that the sound of battle would be the next thing he heard. But there it was. The silence. And the darkness, except for the moon in a clear sky. His eyes took time to become accustomed to the dark, just as his ears did to the quiet. It was uncanny. Then, a dog barked in the distance.

It was Major John Frost's first combat jump. Immediately he felt the elation of having survived the fall and the landing, with nothing broken. Not even any bruises.

The first thing he did was to address a call of nature. Then, in less than thirty seconds, Regimental Sergeant-Major Strachan appeared quickly from the darkness behind the trees. Of course, he had jumped sixth, thought Frost, immediately after him. Strachan would be the nearest to him on the ground. The sergeant was trained to check first that his commanding officer was all right.

They were now behind enemy lines in occupied France. This was no time to hang around and think about the night sky. Paratroopers were at their most vulnerable in the few minutes after they had landed. Suddenly, after the brief pause, everything started to happen at once, as though on a film set where the director had called 'Action'. The rest of the stick of Paras appeared. Their eyes were getting used to the blackness now and they could see each other more easily. They had all landed within a few hundred yards of a line of trees by a gully, in exactly the right spot. Frost reflected that the RAF had done a brilliant job getting them right on to the DZ. It would be some time before he found out that one group crucial to the mission had been dropped miles away and had no idea where they were.

Strachan seemed to take the lead, to do what well-trained sergeant-majors do – rounding up the men and gathering in the canisters of equipment including their guns that had been dropped with them. Strachan checked that every Para had stowed his parachute, gathered his kit and retrieved his weapons. Many of the men had one of the brand new British sub-machine guns called a Sten gun, a knife and four Mills grenades. The officers and senior NCOs had a 4.5 mm automatic pistol.

There was thick snow on the ground. They had only been told about this at the last moment as they were getting on to the transport planes at Thruxton airfield. There was no snow in England. Frost had worried during the flight that they should have brought with them their white smocks, but it was too late. And now they were on the ground it didn't seem to matter much. The snow muted their movement across the fields, but it didn't hold them up. And the enemy would know they were there soon enough.

Once Strachan had got the Paras organised and into battle formation, Frost instructed them to follow him. They had only about six hundred yards to go to their objective. The men set off swiftly into the night, blackened figures moving stealthily across a white landscape. There were no unexpected obstructions. Frost realised how good their briefings had been. From the aerial photographs of their mission's objective a detailed terrain model had been made of the entire location. Every man

had studied this and knew in detail his own part in the operation, exactly what to expect and where to go. From intelligence
gathered before the raid they even knew the name of the
German sergeant in charge of their first objective.

Frost thought how remarkably well prepared they were. If
only the rehearsals hadn't gone so badly. They had never had
a single successful 'dress rehearsal', as he called it. Not a single
run-through of the mission had worked. Something had gone
wrong every time. Sometimes the RAF had dropped the Paras
in the wrong place. Sometimes the Royal Navy had come in to
the wrong beach. Once, they had all ended up in a minefield.
Some of the rehearsals had been a total shambles.

But now it was all going well. It took only ten minutes for the
men to cross the fields and ascend the slope to the strange pre-
war seaside villa perched on the top of the cliffs. Once there,
Frost sent half of his men off to surround the large radar installation about a hundred yards from the villa that was the real
objective of the raid. The boffins back in London needed to
know how this apparatus worked. It seemed unlike anything
that was known about in Britain. The Paras could see the
strange bowl-like shape of its rotating antenna silhouetted in
the moonlight. Everyone had been instructed not to open fire
until Frost gave the signal. Surprise was the essence of any raid
behind enemy lines. With luck, at this point, none of the
German garrison would even know that a team of British paratroopers had landed and were now surrounding them.

Within a few minutes all the Paras were in position. Frost led
his men up to the villa, which they believed acted as the local
German headquarters. There had been much discussion in the
practice runs beforehand as to how he would open the front

door. One bright spark had suggested that he simply ring the door bell. As it was, when Frost reached the door it was wide open. He almost forgot to give the signal but at the last minute he blew a single, long blast of his whistle. This was the sign to the Paras scattered across the cliffs that night. Immediately firing broke out around the radar station a hundred yards away. The raid was on.

1

Radar

On 26 February 1935 two momentous events took place, one in Berlin, the other in a field in Northamptonshire. The consequences of these two events proved to be curiously interrelated. That morning, in Berlin, German Chancellor Adolf Hitler signed a secret document authorising the creation of a new German air force. Under the terms of the Versailles Treaty imposed on a defeated Germany after the First World War, the country was not allowed a military aviation force. Flying in Germany had continued with the state airline, Luft Hansa, and in thousands of private flying clubs up and down the land. But by signing this secret agreement, the Nazi leader was authorising the next stage of Germany's military rearmament with the creation of the Luftwaffe, the third armed force to stand along-side the German army, the Wehrmacht, and its navy, the Kriegsmarine.

The Luftwaffe was to be commanded by the Great War air

ace and senior Nazi Party leader, Herman Göring. Its creation was kept secret so as not to jolt the other European governments into bringing down sanctions on Hitler's regime, which had only been in power for two years. However, the following month, in London, a White Paper announced a new policy of rearmament and the expansion of the RAF. Hitler judged that this was the time to make his plans public, and so he announced national conscription and declared the formation of the Luftwaffe. As Germany's rearmament went up a gear, a new air race was about to begin.

On the same day that Hitler signed the secret decree, in a field at Weedon in Northamptonshire a bizarre experiment took place that attracted very little attention, even from the local farmers. Not far from the large transmitter at Daventry that sent out powerful radio waves for the BBC overseas service, known then as the Empire Service, two men erected a makeshift aerial from a pair of metal cables suspended between wooden poles. They then attached the aerial to a small cathode ray tube oscilloscope set up in the back of a Morris van.

Late that morning, two other men arrived from London in a smart Daimler to observe the experiment. On cue, an RAF Heyford biplane bomber flew overhead at 6000 feet on a roughly prepared course. At first, the men peering at the small screen in the back of the van saw nothing. But when the Heyford turned back to pass overhead again, the little green spot at the centre of the tiny screen began to move and swell into a vertical green line more than an inch in height. Slowly, as the aircraft could be heard disappearing in the distance, the line contracted.

The Heyford made three more passes, and during each one the green dot on the screen lit up and animated with the passing of the bomber. One of the men carried out a quick calculation and concluded that they had followed the movement of the Heyford to a distance of about eight miles. This was the first practical demonstration in Britain of how radio waves could be used to detect and to show the location of an aircraft in the sky, the system that was later called radar.* Robert Watson-Watt, who was to be called the 'father' of radar, turned to his colleague in the back of the van and supposedly uttered the historic words 'Britain has become an island once more.'[1] A new era had arrived.

Although this strange episode in a Northamptonshire field later came to be seen in Britain as the birth of modern radar, scientists had known since the discovery of radio waves that when such waves hit a metal object they would be reflected back, just as the ripples from a splash of water in a pond would reflect back when they hit the bank. The German physicist Heinrich Hertz had shown this in the 1880s. In 1904 a German engineer named Christian Hülsmeyer had laid on a demonstration near Cologne to show that radio waves could be used to locate the presence of a nearby ship in fog, mist or the dark, and by helping to avoid collisions could increase the safety of vessels at sea.

Hülsmeyer patented his invention, which he called a Telemobiloscope, and tried to interest the German navy in it. Admiral von Tirpitz wrote back to him curtly, 'Not interested

*In the early stages of its development and use, the British did not use the word 'radar' but referred to Radio Direction Finding or RDF. The Americans used the word radar, an acronym of RAdio Detection And Ranging. This became the standard term used in Britain from about the summer of 1943. I shall use the word radar throughout this book for simplicity and clarity.

My people have better ideas.' And when Hülsmeyer demonstrated his device to industry he got a similar negative response. The German electrical giant Telefunken told him, 'We have no use for this discovery.'[2]

During the First World War, great advances were made in the understanding and use of radio waves, which could now be sent in more powerful clusters or pulses. Merle Tuve and Gregory Breit in the United States and Edward Victor Appleton in Britain continued this work in the post-war years. Appleton later won a Nobel Prize for his efforts. The huge growth of interest in radio was one of the cultural and technological phenomena of the 1920s, bringing into the business big companies like AT&T's Western Electric in the USA, Telefunken in Germany and the Electrical and Musical Industries group (EMI) in Britain.

This led to the development and mass production of components like the cathode ray tube, which was transformed from an obscure laboratory tool into a device for widespread use. In 1934, experiments measuring the return of radio waves from nearby aircraft or ships took place separately in Washington, at Kiel harbour in Germany, in Leningrad and in primitive forms in Japan and Holland. With the technology racing forward in several places at once, Watson-Watt later acknowledged that there was a 'wide open tool box of ideas from which the weapon of radar might be forged'.[3] A recent historian has concluded more succinctly that it was 'a classic case of simultaneous invention'.[4]

But the story of the development of radar in Britain was different. Not only did it combine brilliant invention with plucky improvisation, but it also developed rapidly because of a profound need. The necessary technology and ideas might have come together in many places at about the same time, but British scientists adopted and turned them into something of real practical value over a remarkably short period. And the need for something like radar did not exist in Britain out of a desire for commercial advantage. It came from the state itself, and from a pressing need to defend the nation's borders.

On 10 November 1932, Stanley Baldwin expressed British government thinking when he proclaimed in the House of Commons, 'I think it is well for the man in the street to realise that there is no power on earth that can protect him from being bombed.' He concluded with the famous phrase, 'Whatever people may tell him, *the bomber will always get through*.' Baldwin was not only stating a fact – at that moment it was impossible to prevent a large bombing force from getting to its target – but he was also seeming to accept that there was no point in trying to defend the country from enemy bombers. Defeatism appeared to have become public policy.[5]

Over the following years the international situation deteriorated. In October 1933, the new German Chancellor, Adolf Hitler, withdrew Germany from the League of Nations. Next year the international disarmament conference in Geneva broke down. Although no one in Britain wanted war, people with vision began to see that one day another war with Germany might be inevitable. This prompted many to become increasingly critical of the government's defeatist attitude.

One of these critics was Frederick Lindemann, an Oxford professor and close friend of Winston Churchill. Lindemann was a distinguished scientist who ran the Clarendon Laboratory in Oxford and through his friendship with

Churchill liked to regard himself as a man of public affairs. A dapper man who dressed very formally with wing collar and tie, bowler hat and umbrella, he always acted the part of the stiff and proper Oxford professor, and was universally known as 'the Prof'. Lindemann liked to be blunt and provocative towards others but was always quick to take offence himself.

In August 1934 he wrote a letter to *The Times* opposing the official policy on air defence. He objected to the fact that 'it seemed to be taken for granted on all sides that there is, and can be, no defence against bombing aeroplanes.' Claiming that it was inexcusable to accept such a defeatist attitude 'until it has definitely been shown that all the resources of science and invention have been exhausted',[6] Lindemann laid down a gauntlet to the scientific community of Britain to come up with a way to identify an approaching fleet of enemy bombers in order to be able to direct the nation's defences against such an attack.

At the same time the man who would become Lindemann's biggest rival entered the fray. Sir Henry Tizard was one of the most dynamic figures of British science between the wars. A tall man with a commanding nature, he got on with almost everyone despite his rather stern appearance, with a pointed chin, a moustache and spectacles. He was a chemist by training who had worked in Germany prior to the First World War in one of the pioneering centres of research under the supervision of Professor Walter Nernst. In the war he had been in the Royal Flying Corps, had learnt to fly and was put in charge of scientific research into aircraft and armaments at Martlesham Heath in Suffolk.

After the war, Tizard moved sideways, away from pure

research, to try to find ways of applying scientific advances to practical problems. He began to work on various government committees and soon earned a reputation as a fine chairman who was skilled in asking the right questions and in finding the right way to go forward. As secretary of the Department of Scientific and Industrial Research and chairman of the Aeronautical Research Committee, he met with many of the leading figures in government. In 1929 he was appointed Rector of Imperial College, London, and from this leading academic position he soon got to know all the leading university research establishments. So, with good contacts in both government and academia, Tizard was in a position to take a central role in co-ordinating scientific developments within the country.

In 1934, like Lindemann, Tizard began to be concerned about predictions that bombers could inflict a devastating attack upon Britain. He wanted to make fighter aircraft and anti-aircraft defences more effective against an air attack. He concluded that the best way would be to seek some form of early warning of an approaching bombing fleet out over the sea before it reached British shores.

Within the corridors of the Air Ministry in Whitehall an official decided it was time to act. A.P. Rowe was a typical civil servant of his day. He was a short man who wore round spectacles, smoked a pipe and had a mind that longed for order and organisation in a sometimes messy and confused world. He worked in a branch of the Air Ministry that dealt with scientific research, and during a quiet spell of work he called up all the papers he could find on the air defence of Britain. There were fifty-three relevant documents and Rowe studied them all. Realising that the nation's scientists had contributed nothing to the development of technology for aerial defence, Rowe did what a good civil servant should do in such a situation. He wrote a memo to his boss, Henry Wimperis, the director of the Air Ministry's scientific research section, pointing out that unless something was done to rectify the situation, Britain was likely to lose the next war.[7]

Henry Tizard discussed his own thoughts separately with Wimperis, who had by now received Rowe's memo. Together they resolved to form a committee 'to consider how far recent advances in scientific and technical knowledge can be used to strengthen the present methods of defence against hostile air-craft'.[8] The committee was duly formed, with Tizard as its chairman and two distinguished professors with experience of the armed forces, Patrick Blackett and A.V. Hill, as members. Blackett, a physicist at Birkbeck College, London, had been an engineering officer in the Royal Navy in the First World War and had taken part in the great naval battle at Jutland in 1916. He worked with Ernest Rutherford's famous nuclear research team at Cambridge and had already completed the work that would win him a Nobel Prize after the war. He was in his late thirties and became an energetic member of the new committee. A.V. Hill was an older man who had been an artillery officer in the Great War, and had already won a Nobel Prize as a physi-ologist at Cambridge. Wimperis also joined the committee to represent the Air Ministry, and the bespectacled Rowe became its secretary.

While this team was being recruited, Wimperis had a con-versation with another luminary in the world of British science. Robert Alexander Watson-Watt was a short, round-faced and slightly chubby Scotsman. He ran the Radio

Research Station of the National Physical Laboratory, based at Ditton Park near the Berkshire town of Slough. Watson-Watt had served in the Great War at the Royal Aircraft Establishment in Farnborough detecting the approach of thunderstorms, which offered a serious threat to the fragile biplanes of the day. Having designed a basic radio direction-finder to establish when storms were approaching, he continued to develop and improve this after the war, when sealed cathode ray tubes first became available. Having constructed a simple device to locate the existence of thunderstorms, he went on to explore other atmospherics that might threaten aircraft in flight. His Radio Research Station became a centre of expertise in direction finding using cathode ray tubes and in studying the atmosphere using radio waves. Watson-Watt was a lively, enthusiastic man, a great chatterbox with the ability to out-talk anyone. 'He never said in one word what could be said in a thousand,' wrote one of his colleagues later.[9] Partly due to his verbosity, partly to his humble Scottish background and partly to the rarefied nature of his research, the widely respected Watson-Watt was still something of an outsider to the English scientific establishment.

On 18 January 1935, Wimperis met Watson-Watt to discuss a phenomenon that had attracted much interest without so far yielding any real science. Inventors kept pestering the Air Ministry with proposals for a death ray that could be used to shoot down an aircraft, or at least kill a pilot at some distance. In bizarre consequence, the Ministry had publicly offered a reward of £1000 for anyone who could come up with a death ray gun that could kill a sheep at a hundred yards. Wimperis asked Watson-Watt if it would ever be a scientific possibility to kill a man at a reasonable range with a ray gun. Watson-Watt said he thought it highly unlikely but that he would investigate.

Watson-Watt asked his junior colleague back at Slough, Arnold Wilkins, to calculate the force that would be necessary to boil a man's blood at a distance of three miles. Wilkins was easily able to show that the immense amount of force that would be needed was far beyond any technology of the day. Watson-Watt responded by saying, 'Well, if the death ray is not possible how can we help them?'

Wilkins thought for a moment and remembered an observation he had recently heard from Post Office engineers who were in charge of short wave communications, that when an aircraft passed their transmitters they picked up interference on their receivers. The two scientists speculated that it might be possible to use this as a way of detecting an approaching aircraft. Wilkins again went off to do the mathematics and came back with the daunting conclusion that the energy returned from a radio wave that had hit a metal object and bounced back was likely to be less than a million, million, millionth part of that sent out; in mathematical terms 10^{-19} of that transmitted.[10] Whether it was feasible to measure such a tiny amount would entirely depend on the power of the transmitter and the sensitivity of the receiver.

Watson-Watt reported back to Wimperis that calculations showed that a death ray was impossible but that 'attention is being turned to the still difficult but less unpromising problem of radio-detection as opposed to radio-destruction'. His note appeared just before the inaugural meeting of Tizard's new Committee for the Scientific Survey of Air Defence on 28 January 1935. After considering various other options such as the deployment of barrage balloons, the use of infra-red, the deployment of toxic gases to harm an aircraft's crew, and the construction of huge 200-foot 'sound mirrors' to hear the approach of enemy aircraft, the gentlemen of the committee seized upon Watson-Watt's suggestion and asked for more details.

Accordingly, Watson-Watt and Wilkins carried out a more detailed study of the possibilities. To their enormous relief, it seemed that with the very latest technology a radio wave with a length of 50 cm should produce a detectable echo of an object flying at a height of 20,000 feet at 10 miles distance. In a state of great excitement, Watson-Watt hurriedly wrote a memo, 'Detection of Aircraft by Radio Methods'. He argued that by using the latest radio pulse generators and the most sophisticated cathode ray displays, it should be possible to calculate the length of time between the transmission of a radio wave and the reception of its return echo. As radio waves moved at the speed of light, roughly 186,000 miles per second, in one microsecond a wave would have travelled 0.186 of a mile or 328 yards. An echo received ten microseconds after being sent would have travelled 3280 yards, or nearly two miles. The metal object from which it bounced back would therefore be located at half this distance, as the radio wave had to travel there and back. In other words it would be one mile away.

Watson-Watt concluded that the calculations were quite favourable, but that 'I am still nervous as to whether we have not got a power of ten wrong but even that would not be fatal' with the current state of technology. He pointed out that any detection scheme would have to incorporate a way of distinguishing between friendly and enemy aircraft and that it would be better to use shorter wavelengths, which were less vulnerable to atmospheric interference. He even wrote that it would be important to add height and bearing as well as range to the measurements. In only four typed pages, Watson-Watt laid out in this historic memo most of the principles of what would come to be called radar.[11]

When the Tizard committee met for its next session, its members could barely believe their luck. They had been assigned one of the toughest defence problems of the day and here, almost at the beginning of their deliberations, the solution seemed to have dropped into their lap. Tizard invited Watson-Watt for lunch at his club, the fashionable Athenaeum, and was suitably impressed. He agreed to pass the memo on to the head of research and development in the Royal Air Force, Air Marshal Sir Hugh Dowding. A stiff, prickly man whose nickname within the RAF was 'Stuffy', Dowding, despite his reputation, was also outward looking and interested in new ideas as long as they were practical and delivered results. As desperately concerned about air defence as anyone else, he was keen to find a solution. He would go on to lead Fighter Command in the summer of 1940 when the results of this experimentation would be put to a critical test. But at this point, Dowding was still sceptical of new theories. He wanted proof that the concept was no more hare-brained than some of the other ideas that crossed his desk and he wanted a demonstration to see if the complex calculations that meant little to him on paper had any substance.

So it was that on 26 February, Watson-Watt and Wilkins found themselves in the Northamptonshire field staring into a cathode ray tube. It had not been possible to quickly find a way of generating powerful enough radio waves and so the scientists 'borrowed' the waves that were being sent out by the BBC from their transmitter at Daventry. The RAF agreed to provide the Heyford bomber for the experiment and the pilot, who knew nothing of what was happening below, was told simply to fly a course up and down past the transmitter four times. Accompanying Wilkins was a handyman from the Radio Research Station named Dyer, who helped to construct the equipment needed for the experiment. And along with Watson-Watt, who drove out from London in his prized Daimler, came A.P. Rowe to observe and report back to Tizard's committee.

After this successful experiment, things began to move at high speed, reflecting the urgency that was widely felt in the need to establish some form of air defence. Dowding was sufficiently impressed to commit £10,000 to further development – a sum large enough in 1935 to fund a full year of staff and equipment costs. A new unit was set up to report to the Air Ministry with a small team of four scientists seconded from the Radio Research Station. Watson-Watt selected a remote strip of land on the extreme east coast of Suffolk called Orford Ness as a location for the intense phase of testing and development that was now called for. The shingle and marshes that made up this promontory, often wrongly referred to as an island, had been a test site in the First World War, and the RAF still owned the land and used it as an experimental centre. It was an extraordinary and isolated coastal strip only accessible by ferry. Some, like A.P. Rowe, described it as 'one of the loveliest places in the world'.[12] Others were less keen on its wild, windswept, godforsaken feel. Its location was ideal as it was, as Watson-Watt put it, 'not too far from London for administrative convenience and yet too far for administrative interference'.[13] And, being so remote, all the work carried out there could be done in total secrecy.

A few weeks later, a small team set off from Slough on a delightful spring morning in two private cars, backed up with two RAF lorries to carry the equipment. This was offloaded onto a small ferry at the village of Orford. The team manhandled it across to the promontory and, using an old fire engine that was a relic of the Great War, installed everything in a set of huts also left over from the war.[14] The weather changed dramatically as the small team transported their equipment across to Orford Ness. The heavens opened, and the scientists were met with hail and sleet along with a howling easterly gale. They had the impression they had left the warmth of civilisation to work in an Arctic wasteland, an impression which took some time to wear off. Nevertheless, on 14 May 1935 Britain's first radar research station opened for business.

The four scientists working on Orford Ness included Arnold Wilkins, who was forever optimistic about the possibilities ahead, and a twenty-four-year-old Welsh physicist named Edward Bowen, nicknamed Taffy, who had been specially recruited to join the team. He had just finished his Ph.D. research and had spent time at Slough, where he had come 'under the benign influence of Watson-Watt'.[15] Conditions on the station were spartan in the extreme but the men stayed in digs in the small fishing village of Orford. Their cover story was that they were studying the ionosphere, part of the outer atmosphere of the earth which is ionised by solar radiation. On most Friday evenings, Watson-Watt would come up and discuss progress with the team in the Crown and Castle pub. Often these sessions went on late into the night, to the puzzlement of the locals who could not fathom what 'the Islanders', as they called them, were up to.

The purpose of the first experiments was to get a primitive transmission system and a separate receiver up and running. To speed up development, it was decided to operate on a frequency of 6 MHz and a wavelength of 26 m. This involved building large 75-foot towers and the construction of powerful transmitters using borrowed silica transmitter valves from the navy. Getting the system to work involved putting more and more power through the transmitters to increase the energy of the waves. The engineers calculated that they needed to transmit 100 kW of energy in order to produce a powerful enough return signal for the receivers to pick up. They soon realised that the most efficient way to concentrate the waves was to send them out in bursts or pulses. A second set of pulses would only be sent out when the first had been received back. Using components largely purloined from discarded X-ray equipment, they had to build receivers capable of the maximum sensitivity in order to record the echo of the radio waves and generate a line across a screen on a cathode ray tube.

So keen was everyone to see what was going on that the Tizard committee made the trek out to Orford Ness one weekend barely a month after the researchers had set up shop. Although the equipment failed to detect a passing RAF aircraft, the committee seemed happy with the progress that was being made. On the Monday after the committee had returned to London, Watson-Watt and the team had another go and this time the equipment clearly detected a Scapa flying boat that had taken off from Felixstowe. They were so excited that

Watson-Watt rang up the station commander at Felixstowe and asked him to tell the pilot to fly the same route again, and for an hour the team followed its passage up and down the coast with great delight.

Despite the primitive conditions, progress at Orford Ness was swift. As they managed to generate more power in the transmitters, so the range at which they could detect aircraft increased to 40 miles in September, 80 miles by the end of the year and 100 miles in early 1936. Edward 'Taffy' Bowen remembers this period of excitement and challenge as 'one of the happiest periods of my life'.[16] It was a time of great achievement and very obvious progress and none of the young team working there minded the lack of refinements.

In December 1935 the success of the experiments prompted the Air Staff to commission the building of five stations to provide an air warning network around the Thames estuary. It was still less than a year since the first demonstration in the Northamptonshire field. But the decision to build the first chain of radar stations was recognition both of the advances being made and of the growing urgency of the need for a system of defence. From this a far bigger plan would soon follow.

2

Bawdsey Manor

By early 1936 it was clear that the primitive research station had outgrown its location on the marshes of Orford Ness. A new site was quickly found a few miles south at Bawdsey, where the Air Ministry bought the local manor and about 180 acres of grounds for £23,000. By April everything had been transferred from Orford Ness, and for the next three and a half years Bawdsey Manor was to be at the centre of British radar research and development, becoming a sort of radar laboratory.

Bawdsey was another ideal site for top secret research – remote and very much at the end of the line, far from the prying eyes of locals or other interested parties. It was on the coast, so radar experiments could be conducted over the sea, and there was a slight hill that helped raise the height of the towers. Furthermore, Bawdsey Manor was a magnificent Victorian mansion built by Sir Cuthbert Quilter, who had made a vast fortune out of the early telephone industry. It had two large wings, parts of the interior were lined with fine wood panelling and there were eight acres of gardens and lawns. Its terrace was bursting with lavender and had terrific sea views. The luxury provided a marked contrast to the bleakness of Orford Ness.

This time Watson-Watt himself moved to the site, and he and his wife, Margaret, took up residence in a large flat overlooking the sea. Most of the men who were single lived in the Manor. The mansion had two capped towers, one of which, the White Tower, and the stable block became the first laboratories, and 240-foot masts were built on the hills behind the Manor. The site was soon busy with a growing staff and the buzz of ideas and construction. New recruits, often young physicists straight from the universities, joined the team. By the summer of 1936 there were about fifty scientists and engineers working at Bawdsey Manor.

An air of pioneering optimism pervaded the research station, and although everyone worked immensely hard it was not unusual for the men to break off for a swim in the sea before lunch or a quick game of cricket on the magnificent lawn before dinner. In the eastern wing of the grand house there was a splendid billiard room with a large billiard table that the previous owner offered to sell to the new incumbents. Taffy Bowen bought the table with his own money and donated it to the Bawdsey mess. The atmosphere at Bawdsey Manor was often compared to that of an Oxbridge college where a small community of men (there were no female scientists at Bawdsey at this time) living and working apart, and dining together, dedicated themselves to research and development. Discussions about new ideas often went on late into the night in the grand timbered hall, sitting around a table in front of a roaring fire, just like in a college common room of the day. It was a heady atmosphere, and life at the new research laboratory was good.

However, progress was not continuous or smooth. In September 1936 a set of trials held at Bawdsey nearly put a stop to the whole development programme. The RAF ordered a fleet of its aircraft to fly out to sea and then approach Bawdsey. The radar operators were not told when to expect them or from what direction they would arrive. For the first couple of days, the trials proved to be a disaster. In front of a host of dignitaries, including Tizard and several RAF chiefs, who had been invited to view progress, the planes came so close that they could be heard overhead before the scientists saw any sign of them on their screens. Dowding himself was present at the fiasco. He was not impressed. Tizard wrote to Watson-Watt with the rebuke that 'unless very different results are obtained soon, I shall have to dissuade the Air Ministry from putting up other [radar] stations.'[1]

Watson-Watt was furious. So many changes and developments were being carried out at the same time in the rush for progress that the equipment was just not ready. However, with a bit of improvisation and the recalibration of some of the transmitters, the trials continued after a four-day delay. This time everything worked perfectly and Bawdsey reported sighting the RAF aircraft with great accuracy.

It was not clear to Tizard, Watson-Watt and the others what conclusions to draw from these trials. In practical terms the results had varied from dismal failures to great successes. But the Chief of the Air Staff, Sir Edward Ellington, who was desperately keen to get a radar network up and running, having

heard the arguments for and against pronounced himself sat-
isfied that the radar system was 'already proved'.[2]

In fact, it was not until further totally successful trials had
taken place in April of the following year that the government
took the momentous decision to build a chain of radar stations
along the east and south coasts of Britain, as a shield facing
towards Germany. In the summer of 1938 the full go-ahead was
given for the first ever national radar system, known as the
Chain Home system.[3] The Treasury allocated the vast sum of
£1 million to the project. In times of limited government spending this was another sign of the enormous importance that was
attached to radar defence. The cost would increase regularly
over the next few years, but there now began a race to get a
system in place before war came.

Despite the immense difficulties, the technology was advancing all the time. The team at Bawdsey developed a new type of
receiver using a goniometer, a control knob which allowed the
operator to determine the direction of the returning radio
echoes and the height of objects. With this came a dramatic
improvement in measuring height, range and bearing. But it
called for a redesign of the layout of the Chain Home stations.
Some scientists were worried that the whole system could be
jammed, and so it was decided to build four transmitter towers
each capable of operating on different frequencies to avoid the
problems of one or even two frequencies being jammed. The
Air Ministry predicted that the Chain Home system would not
be ready until spring 1940. But would that be soon enough?

The task of finding twenty locations for a radar station, each
about forty miles from the next, taxed the minds of many in the
Air Ministry in the summer and autumn of 1938. Each site had

to be high, near the coast, large and flat. Watson-Watt and his team had final informal approval over each one. When a site was finally selected, power supplies had to be laid on, supply roads built and the station itself, consisting of four 350-foot steel towers and four 240-foot wooden towers, constructed. At the same time, the transmitting and receiving houses had to be built, along with an emergency back-up generator supply house and a home for a full-time warden. Arguments about the design of the wardens' houses with the Treasury, who wanted to keep costs down, went on for nearly a year. Finally, telephone cables had to be laid by the General Post Office, air raid shelters built, earth revetments constructed to absorb blast, and anti-aircraft defences installed. Meanwhile the clock was ticking and although of course no one knew it at the time, the moment when Britain would be at war again was approaching fast.

When all of these issues were resolved, opposition to the RAF's plans came from an unexpected source. The Council for the Protection of Rural England was a powerful body in 1930s Britain and had led the fight against the siting of many of the giant pylons that were planned to carry electricity for the new National Grid, arguing that such constructions were a scar on the face of the countryside. Now they objected to some of the new RAF sites with their huge towers. What was more, several landowners proved unwilling to sell, including local councils who had set the coastal land aside for leisure use. No one was told exactly what the towers were for, although the Air Ministry put out the line that they were radio stations vital for the nation's defence.

The Ministry wanted to keep their construction as low key as possible, avoiding publicity. So they were willing to give in to

local objections in order to avoid a public row. One planned site
was never built and a couple of others were relocated following
local objections. The Ministry even wrote into the specifications
that the choice of a site 'should not gravely interfere with the
grouse shooting'.[4] This phrase is often quoted to illustrate how
fuddy-duddy the men from the Ministry were at the time. In
fact, it was put in so as not to alienate the powerful landown-
ing classes and to avoid creating a public row.

Constant changes to specifications, redesigns and reactions to
local objections slowed the construction of the Chain Home
sites to a snail's pace. And then, in December 1938, the weather
struck. An icy spell with heavy snow and bitterly cold winds
closed down many of the high, exposed construction sites. It
was a near miracle that by April 1939, seventeen Chain Home
stations had been built, their equipment installed and calibrated, and were ready to go into operation. The next few
stations to complete the link were constructed through that
summer. Although ready, the system was never complete, as
the Ministry constantly called for new stations and upgrades
were repeatedly made to existing stations. But at least the basic
Chain Home network was up and running, with a series of
radar stations from northern Scotland to the Isle of Wight, in the
nick of time when war came in September 1939.

The development of the science behind radar and of the technology to use it was, however, only one half of the problem of
defending the skies above Britain. Unless effective intelligence
could be drawn from the information provided, the Chain
Home system would remain a scientific wonder but a practical
irrelevance. Watson-Watt realised the need to assess and assim-
ilate the mass of information coming in so as to iron out the

slightly different interpretations of height, bearing and distance of enemy raiders produced by the various stations. He proposed the use of filter rooms to turn the radar sightings into usable intelligence.

For this next stage, Sir Henry Tizard once again came to the fore. He oversaw a series of experiments at Biggin Hill airfield in 1936 and 1937 to introduce a largely sceptical group of senior RAF officers to the new technology. Tizard realised that the detailed intelligence gained from radar could provide officers on the ground with a continuous visual display to reveal the distance, height and bearing of aircraft approaching the coast of Britain. This would give them the vital minutes needed to get their fighters in the air and directed towards the approaching bombers. In the Biggin Hill exercises a squadron of RAF Hawker Hind bombers were instructed to approach Britain on various routes at different times and a squadron of Gloster Gauntlet biplane fighters were ordered to try to intercept them. Before long the fighters were achieving an almost 100 per cent success rate in locating the bombers. So far, so good.

The first set of exercises were, however, somewhat artificial as the bombers flew on a straight course as they approached Britain. It was highly unlikely that enemy bombers would be so obliging. Therefore, the bombers were told to change course at repeated intervals. This made it much more difficult for the ground controllers to direct the fighters into their path. Again, Tizard's fertile brain came up with the solution. Knowing that fighters always fly faster than bombers, and using simple geometry, he realised that all the ground controllers had to do was to draw a line between the fighters' position and that of the bombers and to use this as the base line of an isosceles triangle.

The bombers' new flight path formed the second side of the triangle, and the best interception route for the fighters to take formed the third. The angle at which to direct the fighters was frequently referred to as the 'Tizzy Angle' for some years to come.[5]

During the course of these experimental exercises the basic working pattern emerged for RAF Fighter Command that was to become familiar during the Battle of Britain. Ground controllers employed large maps laid out on tables and plotters marked the position of approaching aircraft, while fighter aircraft were sent up to intercept them. These too were represented by discs on the map. Officers in a ground control room could as a consequence control an entire aerial battle.

Although this system of command and control might seem obvious today, it was revolutionary at the time. Pilots were used to flying under their own initiative, and where and how they thought best. They had now to surrender this privilege to ground controllers who would, in RAF parlance, 'scramble' them and 'vector' them straight to the 'bandits' – that is, order them to take off and provide the course for them to steer to the enemy aircraft. This transition did not happen easily or without objection from the pilots. It was fortunate that in Tizard, the RAF had found an exponent of this new form of aerial warfare who had been a flying officer in the First World War. He was able to talk to the crews in their own language. They accepted him not as an outsider but as one of their own. And it was Tizard's way always to collaborate closely with those he was working with, to understand their perspective and to persuade rather than instruct.

Gradually the new ideas took hold. During 1936 and 1937,

the RAF developed a completely new command and control system for the fighter defence of Britain. The science and technology of radar was married to the requirements of an operational programme and the wizardry of radar was turned into a fighting tool to defend the country.

But there was still one major problem. While the Chain Home system would provide early warning of the approach of enemy bombers in daytime and could guide fighters to the point at which they could visually identify the enemy bombers, the RAF recognised that it did not have the accuracy to guide fighters close to enemy aircraft if they chose to attack at night. Even with his eyes attuned to the dark, a pilot would never be able to see an enemy aircraft at night even if he flew within a thousand feet of him. Poor weather would reduce night visibility still further. Some sort of airborne radar would be essential to guide the night fighters accurately to their enemy.

But this posed awesome challenges. The transmitting masts for the Chain Home radar were 240 feet in height. The transmitting equipment weighed several tons. The receiving equipment bristled with valves, control knobs and indicators requiring the interpretation of a highly skilled operator. Bringing all this down to a size that could be fitted inside a fighter aircraft's fuselage and able to run off the plane's 500 volt electric supply seemed an impossibility. The sort of miniaturisation that we are familiar with today with microchip technology is a far cry from the use of the large and heavy valves of the 1930s. Nevertheless, Taffy Bowen was told to study how airborne radar might be developed. It was a daunting task.

However, around the world technology was developing fast and Bowen managed to obtain some powerful 'doorknob' transmitting valves from Western Electric in the United States. The introduction of television in Britain by the BBC was taking place at the same time as that of radar and this too was based on the cathode ray tube. Companies like Pye were designing tubes that only weighed a few pounds. With these new devices, Bowen came up with a viable system operating on a wavelength of 1.25 m, and in August 1937 the first airborne radar was given its test flight. The RAF provided aircraft for Bowen to experiment with and these flew out of the nearby airfield at Martlesham Heath. Although the early systems were not sensitive enough to identify aircraft, they proved capable of locating large vessels at sea and became known as Air-to-Surface Vessel or ASV radar.

Bawdsey expanded rapidly during 1937 and 1938. The RAF established a training school there and its graduates became the first operators of the Chain Home system. As the potential military use of radar spread, army officers arrived to study how radar could be used to assist the targeting of anti-aircraft guns, and naval specialists arrived to study the use of radar to identify enemy ships at sea. The historian David Edgerton has estimated that the total investment in research and development of radar before the war amounted to roughly the same as the cost of building of a battleship, a considerable sum.[6] When Watson-Watt moved on to work directly for the Air Ministry, A.P. Rowe replaced him. In charge at Bawdsey he issued a spate of instructions to keep the station run on what he saw as neat and orderly lines. Needless to say, his view on what was acceptable behaviour rarely coincided with that of the boffins who were working there. When Rowe upbraided one scientist for shooting a rabbit by telling him that he could not shoot game on RAF property, he was met with the contemptuous rebuff, 'Rabbits are not game, they are vermin.'[7]

In June 1939, Air Marshal Dowding, who was by now commander-in-chief of Fighter Command, visited Bawdsey to inspect the new air-to-air interception radar that Bowen and his small team had finally come up with. In the back of a Fairey Battle aircraft, a plank of wood was placed across the seat behind the pilot where the observer usually sat. Bowen and Dowding squeezed themselves into this tiny space in the cockpit, with no room to be strapped in or to put on parachutes. They covered their heads with a black cloth so they could see the cathode ray tube screen.

The aircraft flew to 15,000 feet and the demonstration began with Bowen and Dowding's plane making approaches to another Fairey Battle from various angles. When the last interception had been made, Dowding asked for the black cloth to be removed so he could see how near they were to the target aircraft. Bowen pulled off the cloth and Dowding looked around but couldn't see the other plane. Bowen pointed out that it was only a few feet directly above them. 'My God,' exclaimed Dowding, 'tell him to move away. We are too close!' The pilot broke away and headed back to Martlesham Heath. The Fighter Command chief announced that he had been greatly impressed by the demonstration.[8] An order for thirty airborne radar sets followed – far too big an order for the tiny research establishment to fulfil.

Work at Bawdsey Manor ended with the declaration of war on 3 September 1939. Rowe believed that the site on the edge of the North Sea, with its tall radar masts and test towers, was too obvious a target for enemy bombers. He sent out a panicky prediction that German bombs would soon flatten all of Bawdsey. The staff, amounting to about 250 people, were evacuated on the day war was declared and the massive amount of equipment they had built was shipped out. Their new location was to be in Dundee and Perth, where Watson-Watt had arranged with the head of his old university to house the research team. It would prove to be a difficult move and a disastrous location. Radar research came almost to a halt just as the war began and demands upon the technology grew exponentially.

However, almost unimaginable progress had been made at Orford Ness and at Bawdsey in the four and a half years since Watson-Watt and Wilkins had stood in a field at Weedon and watched the cathode ray tube come alive as the old RAF bomber flew by. A network of radar stations had been set up around the eastern and southern coasts of Britain. An understanding of how to calculate range, bearing and even height had been made. Strides had taken place in the development of airborne radar. The army and the navy were now aware of the opportunities this new science offered them. But as the research scientists packed their bags and left Bawdsey, there were still questions for the rest of the scientific establishment in Britain to ponder: had the Germans developed their own radar system? Was there a German version of Bawdsey Manor also working somewhere in great secrecy? And if so, did the enemy have anything equivalent to the operational radar system now in place in Britain?

3

Freya and Würzburg

Robert Watson-Watt had been working tirelessly for more than two years on the development of radar when, in the early summer of 1937, he decided to take a holiday. He and his wife Margaret planned a walking tour in a remote part of what was then called East Prussia, the easternmost part of the German Reich. They were both interested in ecclesiastical architecture and liked Germany and the Germans. Equipped with suitable walking gear and heavy boots, along with a wooden mount and paper for his wife to sketch on, and what looked like a small pocket torch, they set off. After a few days in Berlin going to concerts and movies, they moved east and checked in to a hostel in Neukirchen. It was a remote spot. Not a single foreigner had signed the hostel register for five years.

Although Watson-Watt and his wife intended to enjoy a brief break from the demands of creating a new technology for the defence of Britain, there was rather more to their walking holiday than might be supposed. The British intelligence service, known as the Secret Intelligence Service (SIS), had picked up stories of an establishment similar to Bawdsey in the Grosses Moosbruch, a remote forested moor in eastern Germany. The SIS wanted someone to go out and see what was happening. Who better than the chief himself, who would be sure to identify anything resembling radar towers under construction?

So, under the guise of a walking holiday, Watson-Watt and his wife headed off on their spying mission. The SIS kitted him out. The 'torch' he took was a tiny telescope-and-microscope. Margaret made sketches not only of local churches but also of high-tension pylons. And they even had a cover story if interrogated that they were looking for the grave of a great-grandmother called Brücker – in fact the name of the German grandparents of Watson-Watt's secretary at Bawdsey.

Watson-Watt took his spying responsibility seriously and systematically covered the region in question, walking through woods and climbing church steeples to gain good views of the local countryside. At one point he and his wife thought they were under surveillance from a man disguised as a peasant who repeatedly rode past them on a bicycle. But the man on the bicycle really was a local peasant busy on an errand. And there were no signs of any towers, for radar use or otherwise. Watson-Watt concluded that the SIS had been taken for a ride. He came home after a pleasant break and reported that there was no evidence to suggest the Germans were developing any form of radar.[1]

Watson-Watt's walking holiday had significant consequences for British science. It became the established view within Britain that while this country had developed a sophisticated radar system and was in the process of integrating it into an effective command and control system for national defence, the Germans had developed no such system. When the war began the prevailing wisdom within the British establishment was still that the Germans did not have radar. Nothing could have been further from the truth.

German scientists had been aware from the late nineteenth century that when radio waves hit a metal object they bounced back. Even after Christian Hülsmeyer's failure to interest the German navy and industry in his Telemobiloscope, other scientists and engineers had played with similar ideas during the First World War, although no progress was made in developing a practical system of radar for military use. The key figure in the next stage of radar development in Germany was a brilliant young experimental physicist named Dr Rudolf Kühnhold. He was a passionate and serious young man, sometimes impetuous and very sensitive to the impression others had of him. Kühnhold had done his postgraduate work at the University of Göttingen and was only twenty-five years old when in 1928 he joined the NVA, the Experimental Institute of Communication Systems, which was a part of the German navy in the port town of Kiel. As in Britain, the Germans were experimenting with the use of audio signals to pick up the presence of vessels at sea, and with sonar, underwater acoustics, to follow vessels below the surface. Kühnhold grew frustrated with this line of research and decided that the future lay with the electromagnetic study of radio waves rather than acoustics. In 1931, Kühnhold was appointed Scientific Director of the NVA and his appointment ushered in a new era in German science.

In Germany, the impulse to develop a system for identifying

objects at a distance came not from defence, from finding an early warning of the approach of enemy bombers as in Britain, but from offence. The German navy was keen to find better ways of targeting its guns on enemy ships and to find an improved system for range finding and location, a two-dimensional problem, in contrast to Britain's need. So Kühnhold began a series of experiments using short wave transmitters to detect the presence of vessels at sea. He started working with the Pintsch company using directional antennae. As this system was intended for use on board ship, there was no possibility of constructing 350-foot towers like those Watson-Watt and his team were to build on the Suffolk coast. Everything had to be smaller in scale, and German radar research therefore went off in an entirely different direction to the work that would follow in Britain. Instead of a system that covered a broad field of action, as it were floodlighting a large area of the sea in its search for enemy aircraft, Kühnhold developed a system that would be far more focused and directional, more like a searchlight seeking out a specific object. But he and the Pintsch company kept coming up against the problem that would dog the early development of radar. Using a wavelength of about 50 cm, he simply could not generate enough power in a transmitter to send out waves strong enough for a receiver to pick up their echoes after they had hit an object and bounced back.

Help came from an unlikely quarter. Philips, the electrical giant based in Holland, had designed a magnetron valve that could generate about 80 watts of power on a shorter wavelength of 13 cm. Using the Philips valve and a frequency amplifier in the receiver, Kühnhold devised a piece of equipment that was able to pick up vessels crossing Kiel harbour at a range of about two miles. This was still nowhere near good enough to meet the demands of the German navy for its gun sighting. Kühnhold had to think again.

Kühnhold consulted several electrical specialist firms, including Telefunken. Turning up unannounced at the office of the company's head of development, Professor Wilhelm T. Runge, Kühnhold tried to sell the possibilities of radar, but much to his annoyance Runge was not interested. All the other firms he approached were doing valuable work for the German navy or air force and had neither the capacity nor the inclination to commit resources to this new field of experimental research. So, along with some radio specialists, Kühnhold decided to set up his own company, Gema.[2] It was set up with an experimental radar outstation at Pelzerhaken in Schleswig-Holstein on the Baltic coast, to the north of Lübeck. This was another exposed and remote coastal spot so beloved of the radar pioneers. Although it was never on quite the same scale, it was the nearest the German engineers had to Orford Ness.

Although progress was slow, on 24 October 1934 tests at Kiel detected a vessel at a range of eight miles and in addition picked up a return signal from a Junkers aircraft that just happened to fly across the beam. This was four months before Watson-Watt carried out his first experiment near Daventry. But in a remarkable prefiguring of Air Marshal Hugh Dowding's offer in February 1935 for the establishment of an experimental radar station in Britain, the German navy were sufficiently impressed with the results of Kühnhold's experiments to award him a grant of approximately £10,000 for the further development of the technology.[3] From now on, Kühnhold's research was concentrated on a frequency of 600 MHz and a wavelength of 50 cm. Moreover, his research was now to continue in absolute secrecy, as in Britain.

Kühnhold realised he could concentrate the radio waves in pulses, just as Watson-Watt discovered, and by experimenting with different types of transmitters he was able to site the transmitting aerials alongside those of the receivers. He requested German industry to improve the quality of its cathode ray oscilloscopes in order to make them easier to read, so as to catch up with progress elsewhere in Europe and in the USA. Development was slow but in September 1935, new tests were at last carried out in front of senior naval officers. The tests were successful in locating the gunnery ship *Bremse* at a distance of about eleven miles with an accuracy in range of roughly a hundred yards. The naval officers saw that they had the makings of a superb tactical gun-aiming device and committed more funds to the research. It was decided for security reasons to disguise the work as *Dezimeter Telegraphie* (Decimetre Radio), or *De-Te* for short, and in the following year a range of further designations appeared, including *Funkmessortungsgerät* (Radio Locating Apparatus), abbreviated to *FmG* or *FuMG*. This was remarkably similar to the term Radio Direction Finding or RDF, invented in Britain to disguise the research work that was taking place there.

The German scientists soon realised the advantages of working at longer wavelengths and when they shifted to a 2 m radio wave they managed to extend the range of their radar. They also started to use parabolic reflectors, large bowl-shaped structures with a diameter five times the wavelength of the radio signal they were sending out. In early 1936 this new system picked up echoes from an aircraft flying over the sea at nearly twenty miles. With further improvements this was soon extended to forty miles. This became the basis of the radar the Kriegsmarine was to use during the war, known as *Seetakt*.

Although the German and British scientists and engineers were working in a roughly parallel direction, there were many differences between the research being carried out in Germany and in Britain. In Britain, radar developed in close liaison with the military and with the senior scientists at the Air Ministry. And Watson-Watt developed a sort of two-way dialogue with serving officers in the RAF. By contrast, Kühnhold's work carried on without regular input from the German navy, although their funding proved vital to its continuation. The navy, and later the German air force and army, laid down the specifications they wanted the radars to adhere to and left the scientists to get on with it.

In Germany in the late 1930s a rivalry also developed between the different civilian companies that became involved. This was typical of the way the Nazi state operated. Different companies with their teams of physicists and engineers worked in isolation and in competition with others. There was little unity of purpose. And it suited the military to have one company trying to outdo another in meeting or surpassing the specifications that had been laid down. It also resulted in the splintering of the German radar establishment, which began to use different forms of the technology, operating on different wavelengths in different ways, for different military clients.

For instance, the Lorenz company, another electronics outfit, produced the Blind Landing System, a set of beams transmitted from the airfield that were used to guide an aircraft in to land during bad weather when visibility was too poor for the pilot to see the landing strip. Lorenz developed a mobile radar using parabolic reflectors that was efficient at twenty miles' range. General Wolfgang Martini, the head of the Luftwaffe's signals division, soon took an interest in their work and out of this association came an anti-aircraft (or flak as the Germans called it) radar that could direct the guns at overflying aircraft with great accuracy. The specifications laid down by the Luftwaffe in 1937 called for the continuous following of a target from a distance of over thirty miles to about six miles. This became known as the *A2-Gerät*, or A2 Apparatus.

Telefunken, the largest German electrical company of the day (which Kühnhold had approached for help in 1934), was also a leading pioneer in all forms of electronic technology. In Berlin in 1936, Telefunken had built a set of giant television cameras to transmit the Olympic Games to halls around the city. Hundreds of thousands who could not get into the main stadia could now watch the action live on giant screens. Although this was a closed circuit and not a broadcast signal, it was the first time an Olympic Games had been shown live on any sort of television.[4] In what was clearly going to be a scientific war, Telefunken would be crucial to the German war machine. And so, soon after Hitler came to power, the Nazis began to extend their influence over the electronics and communications company. Telefunken's chief executive, Emil Mayer, was expelled because of his Jewish origins and a good Nazi named Captain Schwab, who had been a U-boat commander in the Great War, was appointed to replace him. Telefunken was ordered to refocus its business away from customer-related technology and towards original research. And the objectives of this research would, of course, be dictated by the German military.

While Telefunken's head of development, Runge, had been dismissive of Kühnhold's radar ambitions in 1934, a year later he assembled his own apparatus, with a transmitter antenna 1 m square and a simple receiver, in order to seek out the presence of nearby aircraft. He was stunned by the strength of the returning signal he picked up. Almost single-handed he then began Telefunken's long association with radar. Using funds earmarked for other secret projects, Runge went down the route that the other pioneers in Germany and Britain had taken. First he had to make the transmitters more powerful. This he did by directing transmissions using a parabolic reflector, which he nicknamed a Quirl. In the summer of 1936, when Watson-Watt and company at Bawdsey Manor were getting return signals from up to a hundred miles' range, Runge and his team designed their first system, which only had a range of about three miles. It was named *Darmstadt*, and all future systems would be named randomly after German cities.

Step by step, Runge and the Telefunken engineers succeeded in improving all aspects of their radar. After *Darmstadt* came the *Mainz* system and then *Mannheim*, each with a longer range and greater accuracy than the last. Each system used the 'searchlight' approach, focusing its signals on a specific target area, unlike the 'floodlight' approach being developed at Bawdsey. This became the basis of a new anti-aircraft system in which radar guided the guns to fire on their targets. When Kühnhold heard about this research, instead of being pleased at the developments taking place, he accused Telefunken of carrying out unauthorised work on reflecting-wave technology. He was resentful of the heavyweight backing they could now bring to the experimental table. His fury was another sign of the internecine competition between pioneers that the Nazi state encouraged.

Meanwhile Kühnhold's Gema company pursued its work on early warning systems. In November 1938, it trialled a new system that used a large rotating antenna made up of a metal grid 6 m wide by 5 m high. The receiving antenna was placed directly on top of the transmitting antenna. The operators sat in a cabin behind the antenna and the whole apparatus was easy to dismantle, move and reassemble in a new location. It operated on a wavelength of 2.5 m and had a range of 50 miles. There were three cathode ray screens on which the operators could measure the height, bearing and range of approaching aircraft with impressive accuracy. It even had a roller counter, which was like an early form of digital readout.[5] This remarkable piece of technology was named *Freya* after an ancient Nordic goddess associated with beauty, love and fertility. It would soon prove its worth in war.

With war clouds gathering, in early 1939 the Luftwaffe laid down specifications to Telefunken for an alternative anti-aircraft system. It had to be smaller than Kühnhold's Freya and, more importantly, it also had to be mobile. Walter Runge designed the apparatus, which had a 3 m parabolic reflector. This was both transmitter and receiver and so obtained double the performance for half the antenna area. There was an operating cabin behind the reflector and the operators could use handles to rotate the whole device to adjust for height and bearing. In order to make it easier to move, it was designed so the bowl-like reflector could fold in half and the complete system was mounted on four wheels. It operated on yet another wavelength, 53 cm. The designers stuck a pin in the map and named it after the German city of Würzburg. In July 1939 the *Würzburg A* system was shown to the Luftwaffe top brass. They were hugely impressed and ordered a large number of the devices, intending to deploy them along the entire German border to intercept any hostile aircraft that dared to enter the airspace of the Reich.

Telefunken was to become a giant in electronics and communications technology, comparable only to American giants like Bell and GEC. The company went on during the war to develop ever more sophisticated radar systems and to design a system of radio telephones for the Wehrmacht. This network not only covered Germany but was extended to cover all the occupied territories from Narvik in northern Norway to Crete in the Mediterranean. When television research was abandoned because of the war, the whole television team joined the radar researchers and brought in considerable new and valuable expertise, especially in the use of cathode ray tubes. These tubes were used as the basis of all television screens until digital technology came along sixty years later.

So, when war came in September 1939, the Germans had three forms of operational radar. The naval radar known as *Seetakt* was used for gun aiming at sea and operated on a wavelength of around 80 cm. The *Freya* system was in use by the Luftwaffe for air defence at about 125 MHz on a 2 m wavelength and had a range of 50 miles. And there was *Würzburg*, used for directing anti-aircraft guns on a wavelength of 53 cm with a range of about 18 miles, and accurate to within 100 yards. The range and complexity of these radar systems were quite different from the uniform system created in Britain. And while British radar had developed around the use of huge, tall towers, the Germans were using tiny rotating bowl-like reflectors and had produced several pieces of apparatus that were relatively small and mobile. Moreover, all the German radar was superbly engineered, with a stability and precision of performance that far exceeded anything produced in Britain.

Most importantly, these developments had taken place without anyone in Britain knowing of their existence. It was a massive failure of British intelligence gathering. It was all very well for Robert Watson-Watt to climb church towers with his miniature torch-cum-telescope in order to survey the countryside of East Prussia. But the fact that the SIS had no one in scientific intelligence to monitor what was happening in Germany was a blunder of major proportions.

The result of this failure was soon manifest after war was declared. On 18 December 1939, two squadrons of RAF Wellington bombers, a total of twenty-four aircraft, were sent out over Wilhelmshaven, the German naval base on the North Sea. At this point, the war was still known as the Phoney War, since military action in the west had not yet begun. RAF Bomber Command was working under a strict dictum from the War Cabinet not to bomb German property or to risk killing German civilians in case it provoked Hitler into launching retaliatory raids against Britain. So the mission of the Wellingtons was to identify any German naval shipping outside the harbour and to attack it at sea.

As the twin-engined bombers approached the German coast the newly trained radar operators were on the lookout using their Freya radars. They picked up the approach of the slow-moving bombers about fifty miles out to sea. Initially their reports were disbelieved. The German controllers could not fathom why the British would attack on a clear, bright winter's day when visibility was so good. After a short delay, however, a squadron of Messerschmitt 109 fighters was scrambled and directed out to intercept the Wellingtons on their flight path over the coast. Within minutes the fighters had virtually massacred the Wellingtons, who were flying without any fighter escorts of their own. Ten Wellingtons were shot down, while two more were so badly damaged they had to ditch in the sea on the return home. The crews knew that they would be lucky to survive for a quarter of an hour in the freezing winter sea. Only one crew was rescued. The other was never found.

Sixty-six RAF aircrew were lost in this single incident, half of the bombing fleet. The Luftwaffe speculated that it had been some sort of suicide mission. The RAF concluded that the losses had been the consequence of a failure in formation flying.[6] They had no idea that the Luftwaffe had tracked the bombers with their Freya radar sets. Without the RAF realising it, the radar war had begun. Warfare would never be the same again.

4

Airborne

The dazzling new science of radar was not the only new technology developed for military use during the 1930s. The concept behind the parachute had been known about for some time, and its deployment paved the way for the creation of a new type of military unit: airborne forces.

In Greek mythology the winged horse Pegasus had carried his master through the air to attack the fire-breathing monster, the Chimaera. In the late fifteenth century, Leonardo da Vinci had made detailed drawings of a pyramid-shaped parachute. In 1797, a Frenchman jumped from a balloon over Paris with a primitive modern-style parachute. By the late nineteenth century jumping out of a balloon with the assistance of a parachute had become a regular circus or fairground act. There were many showmen and several women who made a living by jumping to the ground in this way, breaking their fall with a silk umbrella or sheet.[1]

During the First World War the military developed two types of parachute. There was the ripcord design opened by the parachutist as he fell, and the type that opened automatically when a static line linked to a rail inside the plane pulled by the weight of the falling pilot opened the parachute. But on the Allied side only observers in kite balloons overlooking enemy lines were allowed to use them as they were particularly vulnerable to being shot down by enemy aircraft making a surprise attack. Although the technology was understood and a supply was available, parachutes were not given out to pilots in the Royal Flying Corps (or, from April 1918, the RAF) because it was thought it would discourage them from fighting and encourage them to bail out and abandon a dogfight instead. As far as the chiefs behind their desks in Whitehall were concerned, a pilot should stick with his aircraft and even if necessary risk a crash landing. Thousands of lives could have been saved if parachutes had been distributed, enabling pilots to bail out of aircraft that had been damaged or were on fire.

In the inter-war years the first nation to realise the possibility of dropping troops equipped with parachutes behind enemy lines was Russia. In the Soviet Union, parachuting and gliding began to develop as a popular hobby in the 1920s and 1930s. This was a modern sport without any bourgeois associations and seemed to fit well with Soviet ideals of building a new society. It was not a big step for the skills involved to be utilised by troops equipped with parachutes or transported by glider as a military force. By the mid 1930s the Soviets had developed the technique of towing several small gliders behind a single, large aircraft in order to get troops to inaccessible areas of the battlefield or to transport them behind enemy lines for a surprise assault. The troops had to be tough, independent minded and able to survive the drop and organise themselves quickly on the ground. The concept of airborne forces was born.

In September 1936 the Soviet Red Army held extensive manoeuvres near Minsk in Belarus and showed off its parachute force to foreign observers from Britain, France and Czechoslovakia. Major General Archibald Wavell was sent by the War Office in London to attend the exercises. Wavell came from a typical military background. His family had come to England from Normandy in the thirteenth century and had produced a long line of generals, including both his father and grandfather. But in many ways Wavell was an unusual soldier in the conservative and tradition-based British Army of the 1930s. He wrote poetry and was something of an academic. A distinguished linguist, he had learnt Urdu and Pashtu on the North West Frontier, and had also learnt Russian before the First World War when the army had sent him to Moscow for a year. It was because of his fluent Russian (a considerable rarity in the higher echelons of the British Army) that the War Office asked him to lead the British delegation to observe the manoeuvres of the Soviet army in 1936.

Wavell watched the exercises carefully as the Red Army put 1200 tanks through their paces. He noted that only three or four broke down and was extremely impressed. The second day's manoeuvres were even more remarkable. About 1500 paratroopers were dropped on to the battlefield in front of the foreign visitors. They were supposed to represent a 'Blue' force that had to occupy a series of bridges over a river and delay the 'Red' force that was about to counter-attack. Wavell was impressed to see that despite the danger of the parachute jump, none of the paratroopers were injured, indeed most were seen fighting ferociously soon after they had landed, many of them moving at the double. But despite this and Wavell's interest in new ideas and in finding ways of increasing the mobility of the army, he concluded in his official report that although it had been a 'most spectacular performance', the 'tactical value' of the paratrooper action was 'doubtful'.[2]

Wavell's conclusion became the official view of the British Army. Although its senior officers recognised that parachutists could be useful as saboteurs behind enemy lines, there were not enough aircraft available either as transports for paratroopers, or to tow gliders. An era of financial restraint did not seem the moment to develop apparently fantastical ideas and build up an entirely new type of military unit. It was easier to stay with the traditional modes of combat. So, the War Office resolved, there was 'little scope for the employment of airborne forces on a scale sufficient to exert any major influence on a campaign or battle'.[3] They took no action to create or train airborne forces, or even to learn how to do such a thing in the future.

In Germany, on the other hand, there was much enthusiasm for this new arm of warfare. As the German military was already beginning to think in terms of aggression, its generals were keen to find new ways of launching surprise attacks that would help to destroy the morale of its enemy in the early, decisive stages of a campaign. The dynamic use of airborne forces also seemed to offer the opportunity of speeding up offensive action, which fitted in with the ideas about *Blitzkrieg*, lightning warfare, that were developing within the German military. Accordingly, training began in top secret to develop forces of both paratroopers and of glider-borne troops. This took place at

a base outside Stendal near Magdeburg and in late 1937 a parachute school was opened within the Luftwaffe. It was to be the
German air force and not the army that provided the first regiment of paratroopers, known as *Fallschirmjäger*.

Training was thorough for what was seen from the start as an
elite unit. The first phase was dedicated to learning the basic
techniques of landing, how to transmit the shock of hitting the
ground into a roll and spread the impact across the body.
Alongside this, recruits had to learn how to handle the parachute harness and how to pack a parachute. German airborne
troops would always jump in parachute rigs they had packed
themselves, psychologically putting the responsibility for
preparing his chute on to the parachutist himself. Next came
training sessions in a captive harness swinging above the
ground and in mastering the process of leaving an aircraft
fuselage.

Then came the air phase of training. An experimental group
tried dropping first with manual chutes and then with automatically opening parachutes that were triggered as the
parachutist left the aircraft. The Luftwaffe decided to use automatic parachutes activated by a static line anchored to a rail or
steel line inside the aircraft. To qualify as a trooper within the
Fallschirmjäger it was necessary to make six jumps, the first of
which was made from an aircraft flying at about 600 feet. The
last was made as part of a squad or 'stick' of paratroopers from
about 400 feet in simulated battle conditions.

But getting the paratrooper on to the battlefield was only the
first stage of the training. The *Fallschirmjäger* had to be trained
in fighting on the ground, in order to take full advantage of the
strengths of this type of assault, that is speed and surprise, and

to minimise the weakness of the troops, that is their lack of heavy weapons. They received extensive training in light infantry techniques, in carrying out demolition under fire, in fast movement behind enemy lines, in the disruption of communications and in causing maximum chaos to the enemy. The *Fallschirmjäger* were only lightly armed, each man usually jumping with nothing but a Luger automatic pistol and a few grenades in his pockets. Rifles and sub-machine guns were dropped in canisters that had to be retrieved and opened before being distributed to the men who had landed.

However, all of this training would have been worthless without the ability of the recently formed Luftwaffe to provide the right sort of aircraft in sufficient numbers to transport the paratroopers to the battlefield. The aircraft chosen was the Junkers Ju 52, a sturdy, reliable workhorse developed in the early 1930s as a civilian airliner and flown on flights around Europe by Luft Hansa. Hitler made the aircraft famous by flying across Germany in a Ju 52 while campaigning for the 1932 elections, and he continued to use it after he became Chancellor.[4] The military version of the Junkers was robust enough to land on rough airfields and to take considerable punishment. Its three engines made it highly reliable and each Junkers could carry eighteen men, or tow two gliders with nine men in each. Hundreds of these transport aircraft were built for the Luftwaffe to transport freight, to drop bombs and to carry paratroopers. General Kurt Student was put in charge of the *Fallschirmjäger* forces and by 1939, four thousand parachutists a year were graduating from training school.

The French and the Poles also both took tentative steps towards developing their own airborne forces after the Russian demonstration. Despite the secrecy, by early 1939 it was known in London that the Germans were developing airborne forces. The Deputy Chiefs of Staff made a request to set up an inter-service training centre to investigate what the Germans were up to and to report back on the feasibility of forming airborne units in Britain. Again, the British military turned down the oppor-tunity. The voices of conservatism prevailed. A group of officers from all three services, tasked with assessing whether it was worthwhile trying to follow the German example, questioned 'whether the present is the time to direct effort to the produc-tion of a weapon which may never be used'.[5] It was six months before the outbreak of the Second World War.

By the late 1930s, the Germans had moved rapidly ahead and during three years of training and development had learnt many lessons about how to organise airborne forces. Hermann Göring, the head of the Luftwaffe, showed a personal interest in the development of the *Fallschirmjäger*. Airborne units were on standby in September 1938 to help 'liberate' the Sudetenland in Czechoslovakia had there been a struggle there. In the event, the British and French handed over the region to Germany without a fight at the diplomatic conference held in Munich. Airborne forces were once more on standby when the Germans invaded Poland in September 1939 to seize vital river crossings but, again, were not called upon in the end.

On the morning of 10 May 1940 the whole world woke up to the remarkable potential of airborne forces. As a curtain raiser to the mighty offensive in the west against Holland, Belgium and France, Hitler unleashed his newly trained airborne forces on a key target in Belgium. Fort Eben-Emael was reputed to be the largest and most heavily defended fortress in the world. On the first morning of the offensive in the west, about six hundred airborne troops assaulted the fort and the nearby bridges over the Albert Canal. One hundred and fifty of them were parachutists and about half of these were engineers who landed on the roof of the fort with heavy explosives. The other 450 men landed by glider inside the fort. The defenders were soon completely overwhelmed by the surprise attack and the ferocity of the airborne assault.

Speed was essential for the German storm-troopers and within ten minutes nine installations had been captured. In a few hours the German engineers had blasted the massive structures with heavy satchels of explosive carried on poles. At noon on the following day the mightiest fort in Europe surrendered and two bridges across the canal were captured intact. No one could ever doubt the effectiveness of airborne troops again.

The loss of a key defensive stronghold on the opening day of the German assault had a massive demoralising effect on the Allied armies. But it was just the beginning of a whole new phase of warfare. The well-trained and highly motivated German army focused its attacks combining fast-moving armour and air support in a series of hammer blows. Within six days a key battle against the French had been won at Sedan and German forces broke through across the Meuse river into northeast France. The French Premier phoned the new British Prime Minister, Winston Churchill, and told him 'We are defeated. We have lost the battle.'[6] Within days the Dutch and the Belgians surrendered. In six weeks France had collapsed and the British Army had withdrawn to Dunkirk, abandoning everything except the weapons each man could carry. In the summer of 1940, Britain itself faced the possibility of invasion. The Cabinet soon wanted to find out if German airborne troops would be used to capture key sites in Britain, like RAF radar stations or control rooms, ports or airfields, or the political and military headquarters from where the nation's fragile defences were commanded.

It was in this context of humiliating defeats in France and the threat of paratrooper drops in southern England that Churchill made one of his most courageous and visionary decisions. On 22 June 1940, the Prime Minister sent an instruction to his chief of staff, General Hastings Ismay, to pass on to the full War Cabinet: 'We ought to have a corps of at least five thousand parachute troops. Advantage must be taken of the summer to train these forces who can nevertheless play their part meanwhile as shock troops in home defence. Pray let me have a note from the War Office on the subject.' No doubt he stamped his instruction with his famous 'Action this Day' sticker.[7]

There was still considerable opposition in the higher echelons of the army to the creation of a new elite force. They had far too much to do in preparing the nation's defences to focus on developing a new arm of warfare. And senior officers believed, quite understandably, that if the best men of every army regiment were siphoned off to an elite unit then the army as a whole would be fatally weakened. But Churchill had fully understood the power and the effect that airborne troops could have. Seeing how the successful attack on the Belgian fort on the opening day of Hitler's invasion of western Europe had so dispirited the Allied forces, he too wanted to start the long process of training a tough, hardened force that could provide the spearhead of future offensive actions and supply men for the daring one-off commando-type raids that he favoured. But at this moment of crisis, with the nation's defences focused on preparations for an imminent invasion, it was a brave and far-sighted decision to create an entirely new military force.

Two days after Churchill wrote his historic note, Major John Rock, a regular soldier in the Royal Engineers stationed in Scotland, was called urgently to the War Office in Whitehall and ordered to take charge immediately of the military side of organising an airborne force. Rock had truly been thrown in at the deep end. He knew nothing of aeroplanes, other than having flown in them as a passenger, and nothing whatsoever about parachutes or parachuting. He did not even know how many men were to be included in the first set of trainees. Utterly baffled by the seemingly impossible task his superiors had set him, he confided in his diary, 'It was impossible to obtain information as to policy or task.'[8] It was lucky that Rock proved to be a resourceful, courageous and determined pioneer. He was immediately sent north and told to report to an airfield near Manchester.

At the same time as Churchill penned his famous memo, the army established a new training centre at the airport at Ringway, just outside Manchester, today's Manchester airport. It was decided to base all parachute training here, but to disguise its purpose, the centre was named the Central Landing School. However, such a strange and confusing name soon became distorted and misunderstood. Rock once received a letter addressed to the 'Central Laundry' and an NCO based at Ringway received a letter addressed to the 'Central Sunday School'.[9]

Ringway had been chosen as the base for paratrooper training because it was well away from the dramas focused on reforming the remains of the British Army in the south of England. It was remote from other military bases, while about five miles south, across flat farming country, lay the estate and country seat of Lord Egerton of Tatton Park, near Knutsford in Cheshire. The noble lord agreed that his estate, consisting of a large area of open parkland, could be used for experimental parachute drops. Tatton Park thus became the first drop zone for the British Army. For the military it was just right, and as private land it was difficult for outsiders to penetrate and to see what strange activities the army was getting up to. It was an ideal location.

When Major Rock arrived at Ringway, still dumbfounded by the bizarre mission he had been asked to fulfil, he was delighted to find Squadron Leader Louis Strange waiting for him. Strange was a First World War fighter ace with a string of impressive medals on his chest. The Air Ministry tasked him with organising the RAF side of the new parachute school. His mission was equally demanding. He had to investigate the technical issues associated with parachute jumping and how best to carry troops by glider. But, like the army, the RAF had absolutely no experience in this type of operation. Although parachutes were by now given to aircrew for use in emergencies, the problem of what aircraft were suitable for soldiers to jump from and what gliders could be built to carry men and their supplies was completely new. Despite the evidence of German advances in this sphere before the war, no work had been done in Britain.

Indeed, the lack of suitable aircraft was to hold up the development of airborne forces for some time to come. In the summer of 1940, the RAF was totally occupied with supplying fighters to defend the skies of southern England in the Battle of Britain, and with providing bombers to bomb Germany and the invasion barges that were beginning to assemble in some of the Channel ports. There was no spare capacity with which to set up a new military force.

As Rock and Strange got to work at Ringway, the memos flew back and forth in London. On 6 August, the Chiefs of Staff told the Prime Minister that five hundred men would be trained as parachute troops but that their training would be held up by the lack of suitable aircraft. The Prime Minister responded bluntly, 'I said five thousand.' The Air Ministry informed the PM that they simply could not find enough large aircraft to carry paratroopers and that they would have to deploy bombers for the task. But there were no bombers to spare and so they could only assign aircraft for training as a secondary role. They would try to obtain Dakota aircraft from America – the military version of the highly successful DC-3 civilian airliner built by the Douglas Corporation in California that had revolutionised civil aviation in the United States before the war. But this, of course, would take time. The Air Ministry suggested it would be better to prioritise the training of glider troops instead, as it might be easier and faster to design and build gliders than wait for suitable powered aircraft to be available.

In September more memos were exchanged trying to define what the role of airborne troops should be. Military strategists still did not envisage that there would be enough paratroopers to provide the vanguard of any major offensive, and in any case, at this point Britain's war effort was totally defensive. So the Air Ministry suggested that airborne forces could provide small raiding forces to land at key positions and then be evacuated by sea or by air. With this in mind, the RAF proposed that the proportion of glider troops to parachutists should be about six to one. The total airborne force proposed was 500 parachutists, with 2700 glider-borne troops and 360 pilots to fly them. This was a considerable reduction from Churchill's demand for a force of 5000 men.

Reluctantly, the Prime Minister agreed to this scaling down of his original plan. But still, the task of having a force of this size trained and ready by spring of 1941 horrified many officials who were struggling to cope with an avalanche of demands on limited supplies. Their frustration was clearly summed up by one senior officer in the RAF who wrote:

> There are very real difficulties in this parachute business. We are trying to do what we have never been able to do hitherto, namely to introduce a completely new arm into the Service at about five minutes' notice, and with totally inadequate resources and personnel. Little, if any, practical experience is possessed in England of any of these problems and it will be necessary to cover in six months what the Germans had covered in six years.[10]

No one asked why nothing had been done in all the years prior to this, when there had been ample warning of what the Germans were up to.

Nevertheless, making the best of an almost impossible job, Squadron Leader Strange and Major Rock got on with their task of establishing the new military force. They were joined by Group Captain 'Stiffy' Harvey, who commanded the training school, and Captain Martin Lindsay, an Arctic explorer. They were given a single parachute and jumping helmet captured from the Germans and a limited supply of RAF silk parachutes. The aircraft selected to carry the parachutists over their target was the Armstrong Whitworth Whitley bomber, a slow moving, two-engined aircraft introduced in 1936 as the RAF's first monoplane bomber. Its two Rolls-Royce Merlin engines were good in themselves and gave the Whitley a great roar as it took off, but they were not powerful enough for the aircraft to maintain height if one of the engines was put out of action. By the beginning of the war the Whitley was largely obsolete and was being replaced in Bomber Command by the Wellington. The problem with using the Whitley for airborne troops was that it had nowhere suitable for the paratroopers to jump from, so a hole was cut in the bottom of the fuselage where there would have been a ventral machine-gun turret. The parachutists would have to squeeze through and drop from this hole. It was very basic, but it would have to do for now.

Further design work was done on a range of gliders. It was decided to build them out of wood so furniture makers could manufacture them, thus avoiding extra pressure on the already strained war factories. A ten-seater, later called the 'Hotspur', was designed to be towed by a relatively small aircraft. A 25-seater, subsequently called the 'Horsa', was also designed and plans for larger gliders were laid down that could carry small vehicles. Again, the problem came back from the designers: what are these troops to be used for? As no one could in all faith answer this question yet, it was decided to build some proto-types to see how they performed and watch how the situation developed.

The one aspect that seemed to offer encouragement was the recruitment of men for the new force. The War Office resolved at the outset that all airborne troops should be volunteers, a policy they maintained throughout the war. In the summer of 1940 all army units were asked to provide volunteers for a 'special service unit'. Very little information was offered to those who came forward except that the work would involve taking part in 'hazardous activities'. The selection committees did not tell those who volunteered that the unit would be a parachute force, but they looked for qualities of physical toughness, mental determination, and enthusiasm for 'having a go' at the enemy. They particularly wanted to recruit men who they thought could act and fight alone if necessary. No one knew if the volunteers who were accepted would have the courage and determination to jump out of an aircraft – and to continue repeatedly to do so.

When the first group of volunteers arrived at Ringway in July 1940, they all wanted to know what sort of hazardous duties they had volunteered for. The men were lined up outside the new training school and Captain Cleasby-Thompson, one of the volunteer officers, carried out a roll call. 'You are in No. 2 Commando,' he told them. The word 'commando' was not in common parlance in the British Army of 1940. There was a pause. Then the officer continued, 'You are all to be trained as parachutists.' Another pause. 'You are privileged to be the first men in the British Army to be asked to jump out of aircraft and reach the ground by the aid of parachutes. You should all feel very proud.'

There was silence. None of the men moved a muscle. It was not clear whether this was due to a sense of resignation or of utter shock and horror. The captain went on, 'I must warn you in the most serious manner that you are not to talk to anyone, either serviceman nor civilian, about the training.' He concluded by saying 'That is all', turned and swiftly marched off.

The stunned men remained where they were for a few seconds. Then one of their number exclaimed, 'That is *all*. Well, it's enough to be going on with, eh pals?'[11]

A few days later the army instructors began to experiment by dropping dummies attached to parachutes from one of the first Whitley bombers provided by the RAF. They noted carefully where the dummies landed and began to formulate ideas about the optimum height and speed at which to jump. After several days of experimentation, the instructors themselves made their first jumps. From each jump they learnt something new. There were two ways to jump. The first method, through the rear of the aircraft, was called a 'pull-off'. The parachutist somehow got himself into position standing with his back towards an opening where the rear gunner's turret had been, facing towards the aircraft's interior. The dispatcher then released the parachutist's ripcord and the force of the parachute's opening yanked the parachutist backwards and out of the aircraft. This must have been a terrifying experience.

The second method, like the German technique, was to attach the parachute to a static line hooked to a steel cord that ran along the ceiling of the aircraft. The weight of a trooper jumping from the aircraft then automatically opened the parachute. First the rigging lines were deployed and then the silk canopy opened to a magnificent 28-foot diameter. As the 'pull-off' sometimes resulted in the parachutist blacking out in mid-air it was quickly decided to adopt the static line method.

This became the standard form of jumping for the rest of the war.

The volunteers watched all the experiments taking place. It was clear to them that while they were on the one hand pioneers, on the other they were no more than guinea pigs. As they were given the first instructions as to how to fall out of a bomber without injuring themselves, one man turned to another and expressed what no doubt they all felt. 'A right lark this is,' he said, 'the blind leading the blind.' It soon became the most repeated phrase among the brave young volunteers.[12]

In order to qualify and to wear the much-prized silver paratrooper wings, the men had to make six jumps. Sliding through the hole cut into the floor of the Whitley was itself a difficult business. The first two men to jump had to sit with their legs dangling through the hole. The order 'Action stations' was the sign to prepare and make last-minute checks that the static line of your parachute was connected to the steel cord running along the ceiling of the aircraft. On the order 'Go' the first man would jump, trying hard to ensure that he did not push himself too far forward in which case he would smack his face into the side of the three-foot-deep tube that marked his exit route. If he leaned back too far, then his parachute would catch on the edge of the hole and again tip him forward with the likelihood of smashing his face into the narrow tube. These variants were nicknamed the 'Whitley kiss', or were known as 'ringing the bell'. After the first two men had gone the rest of the squad had to shuffle forward on their bottoms through the dark and gloomy interior of the fuselage until they were over the hole and could jump. When well trained, all the men in an aircraft, known as a 'stick' of

paratroopers, could get out in about ten seconds. If the aircraft was flying at 100 mph this meant that the ten troopers
would be spread across about five hundred yards of ground
below.

After a little more than a hundred jumps had been made at
Ringway, Driver Evans, who had been in the Motoring Corps,
made a bad exit and got tangled in his rigging, becoming so
twisted that his parachute failed to open. Evans plunged 800
feet to his death in full view of his comrades. It was the first
parachutist fatality. Sadly, it would not be the last. This was not
good for morale. All jumping was cancelled until improvements were made to the packing of the parachute pack. Only
then did jumping resume.

There was still a very long way to go before these first volunteers became anything like an effective military unit. But
their existence was established, even if their fighting role was
still vague. During the tough training that was to follow the
men would be pushed to the limit of their physical and mental
endurance. Many of them would drop out. Others would refuse
to jump. They were told that there was no shame, but they
would be quietly sent back to their units. About 15 per cent of
volunteers refused to jump. Most got as far as the edge of the
hole before refusing. The fear of the unknown, coupled with
fear that the parachute would not open, was too strong. Others
threw themselves out by sheer willpower in a state of near collapse. Even Wing Commander Strange noted that the inside of
the Whitley was 'dark and gloomy with its hole in the middle,
and is bad for the nerves'. With typical RAF understatement he
went on, 'The sight of other men disappearing through the hole
is an unpleasant one and the prospect of scraping one's face on

the side is not encouraging.'[13] By September a little more than three hundred men had qualified. It was going to be a desperately slow process to bring the aircraft, the equipment and the men together into an effective fighting force.

5

Early Warning

When war was declared on 3 September 1939, the radar system around Britain was still very rudimentary. The twenty stations of the Chain Home defensive shield were based along the east coast, where the threat from Germany was thought to be most real. This line of radar stations, from Ventnor on the Isle of Wight to Netherbutton in Orkney, was on air at least. The system was not yet totally reliable. Some of the reading of the radar information was still poor, height finding was not always accurate and very high or very low targets were likely to be missed altogether. But it was good enough to detect massed formations of enemy aircraft as they crossed the Channel or the North Sea.

The commander-in-chief of Fighter Command, Sir Hugh Dowding, who had done much to support the initial development of radar, was therefore sufficiently confident in the Chain Home radar system to rely on it for early warning of enemy attack. Consequently, he was content to do without standing fighter patrols. By conserving the resources of Fighter Command until there was a real threat from enemy bombers, as Colin Dobinson has put it, radar 'began to win the Battle of Britain from the first minutes of the war'.[1]

The main problem was that radar only worked over the sea. Once enemy aircraft crossed into the airspace above the countryside, the air defence system was reliant upon thousands of volunteers in the Observer Corps who would have to track aircraft movements and phone in their identifications. As Winston Churchill had pointed out before the war, this was like passing from 'the 20th century to the early Stone Age'.[2]

Meanwhile, the evacuation of the Bawdsey research team to Dundee University as war was declared had proved nothing short of a disaster. Although Watson-Watt had supposedly set up the move with the boss of his alma mater, when the dozens of research scientists and their equipment arrived in Dundee, nothing had been prepared for them. Valuable days and weeks were wasted getting the teams located, settled in and set up. Morale slumped and research came to a standstill. In October, Rowe's senior officials told him in no uncertain terms that Dundee was an unsuitable site as it was too far from London, too far from RAF Fighter Command and too far from the main contractors commissioned to produce the radar kits. It didn't help that it was also one of the wettest and coldest autumns on record.

As if all this wasn't bad enough, Taffy Bowen and his team had been forced to stop development of the vitally important airborne radar. Based at their godforsaken outpost in a hangar near Perth, they were instructed to act as manufacturers and fitters installing in Blenheim fighters the few sets that were available. Watson-Watt was reluctant to allow commercial contractors to do this. Bowen remembered this as a terrible time and began to feel frustrated and neglected. He later described it as 'the most unpleasant and least productive' period in his life.[3]

There was an obvious need to find a new site within a few hours of Fighter Command headquarters at Bentley Priory in north London and nearer to the major industrial suppliers. This meant the south or the south-west of England. Drawing on the reconnaissance work he had done before the war, Watson-Watt suggested the answer. Rowe went to visit a site on the coast near Swanage in Dorset consisting of an expanse of flat grassland, where there was an opportunity to build a new Chain Home radar station as well as a research centre. There were airfields nearby along with a pretty, picture-postcard Dorset village. Although it was near major urban centres it was still quiet and remote, with only a few farmers as neighbours. Once again, it was an ideal location for a top secret research laboratory. As Rowe wrote, it would remain 'in all probability, a backwater for the duration of the war'.[4] The new site had the quaint Dorset name of Worth Matravers.

It must have seemed an idyllic spot to Rowe, who spent the next few months angling to start building work and to organise the second move in less than a year. Work did not begin until January 1940, but finally the basics were ready and dozens of purpose-built wooden workshops and Nissen huts were completed. The team of 400 packed up their 140 tons of equipment once again, headed south and on 5 May 1940 opened for business. Five days later Hitler unleashed his *Blitzkrieg* attack upon France, Belgium and the Netherlands.

The creation of this new unit, which came to be called the Telecommunications Research Establishment (TRE), could not have come at a worse time. Within weeks of the move, Hitler's forces had charged through northern France, evicting the British Army at Dunkirk, and had occupied the whole of the northern French coastline. By the middle of June, France had fallen and the face of Europe had been transformed. Worth Matravers was no longer a remote backwater but was located directly across the Channel from the Nazi-occupied port of Cherbourg. The neatly laid out research station, situated right on the coast, offered a perfect target for enemy bombers or even commando raiders.

There was discussion of yet another move, but this time Rowe dug his heels in. 'We can do good work here and the site is popular with the staff,' he wrote, 'especially after our experience at Dundee.'[5] He thought that another move to an unsuitable, unprepared site would cause a collapse in morale. The debate went back and forth, and it was some time before the site was given anti-aircraft defences or even machine guns to repel raiders from the sea. It was hardly an encouraging start, but Rowe's will prevailed. The research establishment stayed put.

The original layout of the Chain Home radar shield along the east coast had been intended to protect Britain from an attack coming from Germany. No one had foreseen that France would collapse so rapidly, and the occupation of northern France meant there was a serious lack of radar cover to the west of the Isle of Wight. A whole section of the British coast lay open to enemy attacks. After the opening of Worth Matravers there was another frantic rush to build new stations around the south-west and the Bristol Channel. Peacetime objections by conservationists were quickly set aside and, using emergency wartime powers, the Air Ministry speedily acquired land for new sites. As well as the extension of the main Chain Home system, there was a need for a new smaller type of installation called Chain Low. These were radar stations that would fill in some of the gaps between the main stations and concentrate on spotting low-flying aircraft and vessels on the sea. They had to be built on cliff tops right on the edge of the coast, ideally on headlands where there was no interference from other electrical masts or transmitters. Complete with radar towers and wooden huts to house the equipment and the staff, each site was surrounded by barbed wire and provided with an armed guard. Three of the new Bofors 40mm anti-aircraft guns were allocated to each site, although along with most things at the beginning of the war these weapons were in desperately short supply. Women were found to be particularly good at the detailed, precise work required of a radar operator and many of the new radar stations were staffed by WAAFs (members of the Women's Auxiliary Air Force).

Everything about RAF Fighter Command's defensive armoury for the Battle of Britain in the summer of 1940 was a last-minute affair. The principal fighter aircraft began to appear just before war was declared. The Hawker Hurricane entered service in December 1937 and the first Supermarine Spitfires only went into operational service at RAF Duxford in August 1938. But the mass production of this fast and brilliant aircraft was mired in difficulties that proved too complex for the relatively small Southampton company of Supermarine to resolve. In early 1940, Spitfires were coming off the production line at barely forty aircraft per month.[6] The Air Ministry had ordered another 450 Spitfires but there was no hope of them being delivered for months or even years to come. Meanwhile, the operational command and control system of filtering radar information and instructing pilots where to intercept enemy bombers had only recently been worked out in Fighter Command's operations rooms. And, of course, the Chain Home radar early warning system, with all its faults and problems, had only become operational in the nick of time.

The system now faced its first real test. By the summer of 1940 enough radar stations of sufficient quality existed around Britain to predict the arrival of fleets of enemy bombers. The key issue was one of timing. A raiding fleet of enemy bombers flying at, say, 7000 feet could probably be detected at about 80 miles. It would take about twenty minutes for those bombers to reach the English coast. It took a fighter plane like the Hurricane or the Spitfire between thirteen and fifteen minutes from being scrambled to get to a height above the incoming bombers from which it could sweep down to attack. Radar provided an early warning that gave those crucial minutes to the fighter defenders.

But in the dogfights that followed, victory for the RAF was by no means certain. The RAF fighters were outnumbered roughly two to one by excellent German fighters like the single-engined Messerschmitt 109 and the twin-engined Me-110. The skies of southern England were soon filled with the vapour trails of aircraft in combat, as onlookers on the ground gazed up anxiously and wondered who was winning. If Hitler could command the skies above England then he would be likely to invade.

The RAF enjoyed two strokes of good luck in the Battle of Britain. First, the Germans chose to launch their raids in the long daylight hours of summer, when the Chain Home system worked best. Although the system was still not sufficiently accurate to send RAF fighters to engage with the raiders at night, in daylight the fighters could be scrambled and directed to a point in the skies near enough to the enemy planes to visually identify and intercept them.

Second, the Luftwaffe was not aware how effective the British radar system was in identifying their approach across the sea. On 3 August 1939, a month before war was declared, a large Zeppelin airship, the LZ 130, packed with electrical and radio listening devices, had slowly and majestically flown up the east coast of England, with the objective of monitoring and listening in to the radio waves transmitted by the strange new towers that were being built. But in a disastrous error the Germans tuned in their receiving devices to wavelengths that were too short. The Chain Home system operated at frequencies within the 22–30 MHz range, on a wavelength of about 12 m. The Zeppelin's receivers, tuned in to much shorter wavelengths, failed as a consequence to pick up the pulses of radio waves that were being transmitted from the newly constructed towers. The conclusion passed on to Göring and the other Luftwaffe chiefs was that the British were *not* using radar.

So when the Battle of Britain began, almost a year later, the Luftwaffe did not recognise the importance of the Chain Home radar stations.[7] In one aerial photograph of Bawdsey that came to light at the end of the war, a German photo interpreter had written in marker pencil 'Not a military target.'

In mid August, the battle between the Luftwaffe and the RAF reached its critical phase when the Luftwaffe began to attack British airfields in an attempt to destroy the RAF as a fighting force. On 12 August the Luftwaffe bombed radar stations along the Kent coast, but their defensive revetments restricted the damage and they were soon back in action. Only the station at Ventnor on the Isle of Wight suffered substantial damage and was out of action for ten days. But not realising how important these stations were to the RAF defence of Britain, Göring did not order a repeat attack. The stations carried on with their vital work day after day, predicting when and where the enemy raiders would arrive. Britain's crucial radar 'eyes' were allowed to continue to watch out for the approach of enemy aircraft throughout the air battle that followed. It was an extraordinary blunder by Göring and the Luftwaffe.

Despite the advantage that the radar network gave to the defenders, the RAF began to wilt under the pressure. The pilots and ground crews were on standby from before dawn until dusk, from about 4.30 a.m. to 9 p.m. The strain was immense. In the second half of August the Luftwaffe mounted ever heavier attacks on RAF airfields, destroying planes on the ground as well as in the air. On 18 August, the RAF lost 63 fighters destroyed with a further 62 damaged, the Luftwaffe 69 aircraft with 31 damaged. In the last week of that month the RAF lost 144 Spitfires and Hurricanes; the Luftwaffe lost a similar number of planes, but had larger reserves to draw upon. The attrition was taking its toll and Dowding realised that his supply of skilled pilots was running out. The Battle of

Britain was a prelude to a German invasion. If the battle was lost, it could prove a disaster. Then Hitler announced a change of tactics.

A group of RAF Wellington bombers had hit Berlin. Although the damage was minimal, Hitler was furious that the capital of the Reich had come under attack. He ordered the Luftwaffe to retaliate by bombing London. On the afternoon of Saturday 7 September, the radar stations picked up a huge mass of German bombers and fighters approaching the English coast. It filled a vast airspace of about eight hundred square miles. But to their amazement, the bombers flew on over the airfields they had been attacking, over the green fields of Kent, and over the suburbs of London in order to drop their bombs and incendiaries on the docks and the East End of the city. The docks, the centre of a huge trading empire, were set ablaze. As hundreds of buildings burnt, further waves of bombers arrived and dropped more bombs. Four hundred and forty-eight civilians were killed and 1500 wounded. On the next night further raiders came back to bomb the same targets. Although there were still furious dogfights to be fought between the RAF and Luftwaffe fighters, the RAF had been saved from a loss rate it could endure for not much longer as the Luftwaffe began to attack civilian and industrial targets. The people of London and the other major cities of Britain became the target. The so-called 'Spitfire Summer' ended with plans for invasion of southern England being put on hold.

The triumph of the Battle of Britain was a victory for the men and women of RAF Fighter Command who had fought against a powerful enemy and had refused to give in. But it was also a victory for the men who had developed the radar system and turned it into a powerful agent for the defence of Britain. Radar really did make the difference between victory and defeat for the beleaguered country. For without radar there could have been no victory in the skies over southern England in the summer of 1940.

The Luftwaffe continued its daytime raids sporadically into October 1940, but as autumn advanced a new phase of night bombing began, the offensive known as the Blitz. London was blitzed, with one exception, on seventy-six consecutive nights. The scientists at TRE were still having great difficulty finding a system with the necessary accuracy to guide fighters close enough to bombers at night to be able to locate and intercept them. It proved impossible to convey the detailed information from the linear, time-based displays then in use in the chain radar stations to a control room for a controller to be able to interpret all the data as if in a 3D environment quickly or accurately enough. By the time the information had been interpreted, both the fighter and the bomber had moved on. Moreover, the Airborne Interception system developed by Bowen on a wavelength of about 1.5 m was still basic. It depended on the use of dipole aerials, two aerials along the wing and fuselage of the night fighter in the shape of a T. The navigator had before him a cathode ray tube display, and by comparing the strength of the radar echo of the enemy aircraft on each of the dipoles he could give the pilot instructions to fly left or right, or to adjust his altitude up or down. Such a system was barely operational and by the end of October 1940 only one enemy bomber had been shot down with its use.[8]

During the summer of 1940 a revolution took place in the presentation of information on the radar screen. A new system called the Plan Position Indicator (PPI) was tried out at TRE in which the operator looked at a round, specially treated 'after-glow' screen with a rotating line that picked up objects as blips. The screen represented the surrounding area, with the radar station at the centre, and every rotation of the sweeping beam highlighted the geographical position (the plan position) from the radar station of the objects being followed. PPI is supremely simple in concept and has remained the standard format for displaying radar information ever since.

This was not the only advance made in the summer of 1940. One of the great achievements of Watson-Watt and his team was the close links they established both with the industrial partners who would manufacture the devices they created and with the universities where much original, pure scientific research was taking place. Two physicists, John Randall and Harry Boot, had spent time observing the radar towers in oper-ation at Ventnor before the start of the war and had gone back to their university at Birmingham to try to find a way to reduce the wavelengths at which radar could operate. They set them-selves a target of trying to produce a radar signal of sufficient power at 10 cm wavelength.

It had been known from the beginning that shorter wave-lengths or microwaves would be less vulnerable to jamming, and far more accurate at distance, than radio signals using longer wavelengths. The problem was to develop a transmit-ter that could generate the power to send out sufficiently strong microwaves, and a receiver sensitive enough to pick up the waves when they bounced back. John Randall was in his mid thirties, a tireless researcher who would not take 'no' for an answer. Harry Boot was in his early twenties and was less

conventional, more adventurous and willing to try anything,
but was also obsessed by the challenge the pair had set themselves. Looking at the various devices available they decided
to work on the magnetron.

The magnetron was a vacuum tube inside a magnetic field
that was able to generate small amounts of energy of about 30
or 40 watts to power radio waves. Randall had found a book by
Heinrich Hertz by chance in a second-hand bookshop while on
holiday. Hertz, the great German physicist, had discovered in
the 1880s that electricity could be transmitted by electromagnetic radio waves. Using the principles written up by Hertz
nearly sixty years before, the scientists borrowed a couple of
transformers and used a rectifier Boot built in the workshop.
They began to adapt conventional magnetrons into what was
called a resonant cavity magnetron. The first experiment on 21
February 1940 was a Heath Robinson affair using wax to seal
the joints and a halfpenny coin to plug one end of the magnetron. It was rigged up to a car headlamp. The headlight
glowed brightly and then burnt out, showing that the cavity
magnetron had generated more power than anticipated. Within
a few days Randall and Boot had linked their cavity magnetron
to more powerful neon lights and were generating about
400 watts of energy. They measured the radio waves they were
able to send out on a small antenna and found to their delight
that they were transmitting powerful waves on a wavelength of
9.5 cm, only a few millimetres off their target. It was a remarkable breakthrough. Microwave radar technology had been
born.

Developments now followed rapidly. The crudely assembled
resonant cavity magnetron that Randall and Boot had built was

transferred in great secrecy to the General Electric Company laboratory in Wembley, one of the most advanced electrical labs in Britain. Here, GEC started to manufacture a new series of cavity magnetrons with proper seals and a pulsed power supply. Within weeks they were producing models that could generate 12 to 14 kilowatts (12,000 to 14,000 watts). In mid July the first of these newly manufactured cavity magnetrons arrived at TRE at Worth Matravers. A.P. Rowe allocated it to a team led by Philip Dee, who had worked alongside Rutherford at the Cavendish Laboratory at Cambridge before the war. Dee's team included a brilliant young lecturer and research scientist who had been working on detecting cosmic ray signals at Manchester University, Bernard Lovell. Alongside him was another young luminary, Alan Hodgkin, who before the war had developed sensitive electronic equipment at Cambridge. Both men would later help to shape the face of British post-war science.[9] The team soon eagerly fitted this new toy into an effective radar system and on 12 August, the very day that the Luftwaffe launched its offensive against the RAF's radar stations, the relatively small device, mounted on a swivel, tracked an aircraft flying a few miles away down the coast.

In no time at all, Dee's team were receiving radar echoes from cars, aircraft and from ships at sea. In one bizarre experiment they picked up a strong echo from a colleague riding a bicycle by the cliff edge holding up a small metal sheet – a tiny object that in longer wave radar would have been completely lost amid the interference from cliffs, buildings and other objects on the ground. Lovell wrote in his diary that these results were nothing short of 'amazing'.[10] In a neat metaphor Watson-Watt later wrote that the man on the bike representing this new rush of experimentation at Worth Matravers was driving 'an invisible coach and horses through radar history'.[11] In no time at all the army was beginning to experiment with microwave technology to direct the fire from anti-aircraft guns, and the Royal Navy was adapting microwave radar for ships at sea. This new work put great demands on the scientists at Worth Matravers and marked a high point for British radar research and development.

However, it was clear that the resources available to industry in war-torn Britain were not enough to advance the new era of microwave radar technology as far or as fast as was needed to meet the demands of war. So, in August 1940, Winston Churchill himself authorised Sir Henry Tizard to lead a small delegation of scientists, which became known as the Tizard Mission, to take to Canada and the United States (then still neutral, of course) the latest achievements of British science.[12] It was an extraordinary gesture for a nation at war to share with non-belligerents its latest discoveries and inventions. But it was far from an altruistic act. Churchill was keen to get the United States more closely committed to the war and he thought getting US scientists on board was one way to do this. Moreover, he was aware that if Britain was invaded and defeated that summer he was handing on some of the latest of the nation's inventions to the remaining power base in the free world, where they might be developed further.

So Tizard and his colleagues, including Taffy Bowen, set off for America with a variety of scientific research papers, along with packing cases containing the latest power-driven gun turrets, proximity fuses and a new gun-sight predictor for the Bofors gun. In addition Tizard took a small black box containing the jewel in the crown of British science at that time, an example of the resonant cavity magnetron. When Tizard took the tiny device out of the box and showed it to a gathering of scientists and senior military men in a hotel room in Washington, the Americans were blown away by the implications of the technology. At that point, to generate centimetric radar the Americans had nothing more than a device called a klystron, with a power output of only 10 watts. The cavity magnetron was able to generate power and send out waves several hundred times more powerful than this. The official historian of the American scientific war described the arrival of the cavity magnetron as 'the most valuable cargo ever brought to our shores. It sparked the whole development of microwave radar [in the United States].'[13]

Later that year the Radiation Laboratory (usually known as the Rad Lab) was set up at the Massachusetts Institute of Technology in Boston. It took the cavity magnetron and developed a new generation of microwave radar technology. Within a few years scientists at Rad Lab had developed about 150 different systems for radar early warning, gun direction, bombing and navigation based on this ingenious device. Churchill's trust in sharing the latest British science with the Americans would pay off many times over.

One of the great features of TRE at this time was the freedom of discussion that A.P. Rowe encouraged. Inheriting the concept from Watson-Watt, he took it to new heights. On one or two Sundays every month, a diverse group that might include senior scientific advisers to the government, top military men and scientists from TRE would gather on the Dorset coast. Everyone was encouraged to be totally open and to air the problems they faced or the challenges that were holding up their work. Held on the only day of the week when busy men, carrying the burdens of the war, could find time to gather for this informal sort of exchange, they became known as the 'Sunday Soviets' on the principle that everyone was equal and anything could be discussed.

A lot of myths have grown up around the 'Sunday Soviets'. It is often said that even the most junior scientists working at Worth Matravers were invited to attend. In fact this was rarely the case and Rowe usually only admitted heads of department. Nor were they quite as free ranging as they were later remembered to be. They usually had a structure and a form of agenda. Nevertheless they were remarkable events. Sometimes Professor Frederick Lindemann, Churchill's closest scientific adviser and the man described as possessing 'power greater than any scientist in history', would attend.[14] On most occasions there would be air vice marshals or air marshals in abundance. Other regular attenders included senior civil servants and even government ministers. Goodness knows what the Dorset locals thought about the assembly of all these official cars on a Sunday morning in their once sleepy village.

In a sense the 'Sunday Soviets' represented the best element of a democracy at war in which everyone could speak their mind and senior officers and relatively junior scientists could kick a problem around together until some sort of solution was found. At least one scientist who attended the 'Sunday Soviets' described them as having 'more influence on the outcome of the war than any other single military or civilian activity'.[15]

The TRE scientists at Worth Matravers threw themselves into this new phase of radar development. Instead of the giant

300-foot masts that had characterised the Chain Home system, radar antennae could now be produced that were small enough to fit into aircraft. The challenges of airborne radar that Taffy Bowen had struggled with in the early days could now be met and Airborne Interception apparatus became smaller, easier to operate. In April 1942 a Beaufighter was to achieve the first shooting down of a German bomber at night using on-board centimetric radar. And within a couple of years, a form of centimetric blind bombing radar was designed and built to guide heavy four-engined bombers like the Lancaster and the Halifax to their targets. Similar forms of microwave radar were used to pick up the conning towers of U-boats at sea, leading in 1943 to a turning point in the Battle of the Atlantic.

It was a new lease of life for TRE and they rose quickly to the occasion. All the fundamentals of ground and airborne radar and of what later would be called air traffic control were devised at Worth Matravers and its successor over the next two years. The scientists, engineers and back-up staff who worked in wooden huts spread out across a few miles of Dorset countryside achieved a new peak of creativity and inventiveness and were later described as a 'galaxy of talent'.[16] But located right on the coast, with its tall towers and an array of Nissen huts, TRE was very obvious from the air. How long could this remarkable site be kept secret and secure?

6

The First Raids

While the boffins were making great strides in the science of radar, the military were rethinking their own role in the war. The airborne force of paratroopers created in the face of opposition from most of the senior figures in the War Office was only one of a series of new military and intelligence units created in Britain.

Nearly all of them stemmed from the fertile and inventive mind of Winston Churchill. He knew that for the foreseeable future, Britain's war effort had to be largely defensive. But with most of northern Europe having fallen to the Nazis, there were plenty of Europeans smarting under the humiliation of defeat. If Britain could do something to help them, at least this would provide a beacon of hope. Moreover, Churchill hoped such actions would ignite further acts of resistance within occupied Europe itself. As he famously said of one of these new organisations, the Special Operations Executive, he wanted it to 'set

Europe ablaze'.[1] While preoccupied with the need to resist a prospective invasion of the homeland, British forces could manage only small-scale actions. But Churchill wanted to gain maximum publicity and effect from any mission that could be mounted, to offer hope to the millions of Europeans living under the heel of the Nazi jackboot. And the long stretch of enemy-occupied coastline facing Britain, from the north of Norway to the Spanish border, seemed to offer many rich opportunities for secret missions.

In another of his famous memos Churchill wrote, only a few days after the fall of France, on 18 June 1940, 'There ought to be at least twenty thousand storm troops or "Leopards" drawn from existing units ready to spring at the throats of any small landings or descents.'[2] One of the brightest and most able staff officers working in Whitehall, Lieutenant-Colonel Dudley Clarke, military assistant to the Chief of the Imperial General Staff, the army's top soldier, picked up on this and within weeks, while the first paratroopers were being trained, recruitment for these special units had also begun. The troops were to be called 'commandos', a new term in the British Army but not in warfare. The Boers had called their small units of guerrillas 'commandos' at the beginning of the century. Churchill, who as a young war reporter had been captured by Boer commandos in 1899, had great respect for their unconventional methods. He agreed that this name, suggested by Dudley Clarke, was more suitable than 'Leopards'.

Men were hurriedly selected and all sorts of strange units were thrown together. On average the men were in their mid twenties and they all had several years of military experience. The officers were much younger as a group than officers of similar rank in the regular army. They rarely wore formal uniforms, while the men addressed each other, and sometimes even officers, by their first names – unheard of within the stiffer ranks of the conventional military establishment. There was a lack of red tape so the men could concentrate on training and preparing for action. They were encouraged to be self-reliant and aggressive. Discipline was good and the men were hard, tough and determined.

The first commando raids were carried out within weeks of the formation of the unit. A small-scale attack on the French coast near Boulogne took place in late June, and in mid July about a hundred men led a fruitless raid on Guernsey, which was under German military occupation. The commandos failed to reach their objective, the island's main airfield. These operations were tiny pin-pricks that had little military significance except that they encouraged the Germans to build up their coastal defences, thus tying up men and weapons that could have been deployed on other fronts. Churchill, however, was not impressed, and wrote that it would be unwise to have any more 'silly fiascos' like the 'pin prick raids' perpetrated 'on Boulogne and Guernsey'.[3]

Churchill needed the right man to head these special operations. He would have to be an outsider, as Churchill realised the strength of opposition within the conventional military hierarchy to organising small-scale operations. So the Prime Minister turned to Sir Roger Keyes, an old friend and a hero of his whose daring and ingenuity he had admired for many years. Keyes had been a senior naval officer, but one with a very unorthodox mind. In the First World War he had been one of the few senior figures to support Churchill's naval campaign against the Dardanelles. In 1918 he had led a rare special mission. German U-boats, along with destroyers and torpedo boats, had been using Belgian canals to shelter, repair and refit before emerging into the North Sea to attack Allied shipping. Vice Admiral Keyes planned and led a raid on the port of Zeebrugge with the intention of blocking the route for these enemy vessels to get out to sea. The raid took place on 23 April, St George's Day, and as he set out Keyes sent a Nelson-like message to all his ships: 'St George for England'.

Three elderly British cruisers sailed across the Channel to Zeebrugge, Royal Marines stormed the port defences and the three ships were sunk, blocking the route of the German U-boats out to sea. In a war in which the characteristic form of assault was for tens of thousands of men to get up out of their trenches and walk forward in human waves, the Zeebrugge action was a radically different and risky undertaking. Two hundred men were killed in the assault and the Germans were able to dredge a channel around the sunken blockships within three weeks. But it was a hugely dramatic action which British propaganda hailed as a great victory, and the raiders won eight VCs. The raid was much loved by the press and popular with the British people.

Keyes had remained a friend and informal adviser to Churchill throughout the inter-war years and on retiring from the navy he became an MP in 1934. He was a staunch advocate of naval rearmament and one of Churchill's core supporters in the call for the nation to mobilise for war in the late 1930s. By 1940, aged sixty-seven, he was champing at the bit for action. He was not popular with most military leaders, who regarded him as an adventurer, and he had offended many naval commanders in the late 1930s by describing them as too tame. But he was just the sort of maverick Churchill wanted to bring into the war effort to 'spice things up a bit'. So in July 1940 he was appointed head of Combined Operations, which today would be classed as 'Special Ops'.

Combined Operations was a new concept in British military thinking. Although in the First World War ships had carried infantry to land on beaches, as at Gallipoli, the idea of the three services co-ordinating their activities did not gain much traction. And the concept of combined operations did not flourish between the wars. Although flat-bottomed landing craft, designed by the Japanese, were copied elsewhere around the world, there were only nine landing craft in Britain by 1938.

In the first years of the Second World War, the three armed services tended to jealously guard their own histories and traditions, surveying each other with suspicion, anxious to protect their prerogatives from encroachment. The navy wanted to control amphibious operations as they involved crossing the sea, their domain. The army felt that the navy's role was simply to transport soldiers to the field of battle and so believed they should be in charge. The air force did not like the idea of any other military commander telling them what they had to do. So the creation of a new headquarters that was to bring commanders from the Royal Navy, the 'senior service', the British Army and the youngest branch, the Royal Air Force, together operationally was always going to be a struggle. It would need someone with great diplomatic skill and understanding and a strong sense of authority. Sir Roger Keyes was sadly not that person.

Right from the beginning, Keyes was frustrated by the other

Sir Henry Tizard. Although stern in appearance, he was a popular and much-respected figure.

Robert Watson-Watt. He always remained a bit of an outsider despite being called the 'father of radar'.

Radar has been called 'the invention that changed the world'. These are the Orford Ness pioneers. Arnold Wilkins is second from left; Edward 'Taffy' Bowen is on the far right.

IWM 15183

A Chain Home radar station with a 350 ft transmitting tower. Twenty such stations were completed along the east coast just before war in September 1939.

Getty Images

A WAAF operating a radar in 1940. A green line on the rectangular screen moved up and down when aircraft were identified. The goniometer or 'gonio' on the left helped to measure direction and height.

Getty Images

Bawdsey Manor, a luxurious and well-appointed mansion. It was the home of British radar research and development from 1936 to 1939.

Reginald Victor Jones, aged only twenty-eight at the start of the war. As part of Scientific Intelligence at the Air Ministry, one of his jobs was to find out how the German radar defence system worked.

Claude Wavell at RAF Medmenham. As a photographic interpreter, he measured tiny objects (sometimes less than a millimetre) on aerial photographs to identify different types of aerials, masts and transmitters.

Tony Hill, looking every inch the glamorous Spitfire reconnaissance pilot. He took the photograph of Bruneval.

TONY HILL
famous for his low-level photographs

Tony Hill's famous aerial photograph. A small path ran from the strangely shaped Villa Gosset to the Würzburg, on top of the cliffs at Bruneval.

A Würzburg radar mounted on its portable cabin with Luftwaffe operators behind.

Paratroopers in training at the Central Landing School at Ringway

IWM 22867

Paras learning to land from a descending swing.

IWM 22891

Paras learning to jump through a hole like the hole in the fuselage of a Whitley bomber, but only on to mattresses.

Getty Images

Squadron Leader Louis Strange, the first man to organise the RAF side of parachute jumping. He was a First World War ace, but he had no experience of parachuting.

Army publicity photographs taken during C Company's training on Loch Fyne, February 1942

Men embarking on an Assault Landing Craft (ALC). The naval crew are guiding them up the ramp.

Below: Infantry firing off the side of an ALC. They were to provide the fire to enable the Paras to embark. A Bren gun can be seen in the foreground.

Below left: Lord Louis Mountbatten, the naval hero appointed by Churchill to run Combined Operations; the King's cousin and an inspiring leader.

Below right: Major-General Frederick 'Boy' Browning, the commander of the 1st Airborne Division; a stickler for detail and ambitious for his Paras.

Three of the French underground agents who provided invaluable intelligence about the defences at Bruneval. *Left* – Gilbert Renault, known as Rémy, the shadowy leader of the French underground group. *Centre* – Charles Chauveau known as Charlemagne, the car mechanic from Le Havre. *Right* – Roger Dumont known as Pol, the agent who covered part of the north French coast.

333. ST-JCUIN-BRUNEVAL (Seine-Inf.) — Route de la Mer

Hotel Beau-Minet and the road down to the beach. M. and Mme Vennier who ran the Hotel gave the French agents useful intelligence. At the time of the raid a German platoon was stationed at the hotel.

A pre-war seaside postcard featuring the beach at Bruneval and the imposing villa Stella Maris. Photographs like this helped build up a picture of what the target area was like.

The road running down to the beach at Bruneval. The Germans dug defensive positions on the slope above the road on the left, called 'Beach Fort' by the British.

service chiefs, who saw the whole concept not only as a challenge to their status but also as a nuisance and a sideshow at a time of national emergency. They failed to provide his special unit with the landing craft or the weapons it needed. The commando force soon amounted to about four thousand men and they started a period of rigorous training on Loch Fyne in Scotland. But training without action proved a major frustration. After Keyes complained to Churchill of the obstacles put in his path, the Prime Minister wrote to Anthony Eden, Secretary of War, on 25 August:

> I hear that the whole position of the commandos is being questioned. They have been told 'no more recruiting' and that their future is in the melting pot ... there will certainly be many opportunities for minor operations, all of which will depend on surprise landings of lightly-equipped, nimble forces accustomed to work like packs of hounds instead of being moved around in the ponderous manner which is appropriate to the regular formations ... we must have at least 10,000 of these small 'bands of brothers' who will be capable of lightning action.[4]

But despite his protestations, nothing much changed.

The Special Service Brigade, as the commandos were now called, continued to train and to prepare for missions that were planned but then cancelled. They practised cliff assaults and the use of small boats to get ashore at night in secret. Finally, on 4 March 1941 at the Lofoten Islands off the coast of Norway, two troops each of 250 men carried out the first fully successful commando raid. Its purpose was to attack Norwegian factories that were exporting fish and fish oil to Germany. The raid achieved complete surprise and the commandos captured more than 200 German prisoners and 20,000 tons of enemy shipping, also bringing back more than 300 Norwegian volunteers to join the war effort. Only one commando was wounded, an officer who shot himself in the foot by mistake.

After the success of this mission, it might be thought that Keyes would have had an easier time to argue the case for the commandos. But he was still at loggerheads with most of the Chiefs of Staff and they found it impossible to agree targets and to find the resources he needed. Another raid against Spitzbergen in northern Norway in August once again achieved total surprise and succeeded in freeing more than two thousand Soviet miners stranded there when Hitler invaded Russia. But it was hardly the major operation Keyes longed for and in frustration he resigned in October – or, more probably, Churchill asked him to resign.

To be fair, there was confusion as to how Combined Operations had been set up. Keyes thought he had been asked to report solely to Churchill as Minister of Defence and Prime Minister. The Chiefs of Staff were convinced he reported directly to them. A skilful negotiator might have been able to reconcile the two, but Keyes believed the military chiefs were far too timid in their approach and did not hesitate to tell them so. So it was inevitable that he would not make much progress. In a speech in the Commons he won no further friends by declaring that he had been 'frustrated in every worthwhile offensive action I have tried to undertake'. He summed up his feelings by saying that he fully endorsed 'the Prime Minister's comments on the strength of the negative power which controls the war machine in Whitehall'. It was a heavy salvo against the military establishment fired by an angry, impassioned veteran.

Churchill was determined to see this new type of warfare succeed and picked as successor to Keyes none other than the King's cousin, Lord Louis Mountbatten. Mountbatten's father had been First Sea Lord at the Admiralty in 1914 but had resigned because of his German background. Mountbatten not only had royal blood in his veins but had also enjoyed a distinguished naval career, becoming something of a hero as captain of the destroyer HMS *Kelly*, which had gone down off Crete in May 1941. Tall and striking, Mountbatten had a natural sense of leadership and authority, though only in his early forties.

When Churchill decided to appoint him, Mountbatten was in the USA giving a series of uplifting lectures to groups of naval officers, telling them about the war in the Mediterranean and the role the Royal Navy was playing. Although the USA was still neutral, Mountbatten was a big hit there, meeting all the key naval personnel; he even spent an evening at the White House talking with President Roosevelt. Recalled by Churchill, he was told he was to run Combined Operations headquarters but since he was of too junior a rank to be placed in such a senior command position, his title would simply be 'Adviser'. Mountbatten was amazed to be offered the job, as it involved a substantial promotion to the rank of commodore. The new head of Combined Operations was young, energetic, and lacked neither confidence, drive nor contacts at the highest level. He wrote to a friend, 'I am enthusiastic about this mad job and may even be able to contribute personally towards speeding up the war ... it is all very thrilling and exciting.'[5] He was absolutely determined to make a name for himself as a senior commander and to mount the sort of raids that would really hurt the enemy.

While the creation of the commando force was under way, arguments continued to rage about the efficacy of developing a parachute brigade. Despite the obvious prowess shown by German airborne troops in launching the invasion of northern Europe, many in the senior army ranks were still sceptical. They felt that airborne troops were unlikely to be able to exert any influence upon the war for some time to come and that they would be little more than a nuisance – primarily because of their demand for the allocation of scarce resources. Some in the War Office even doubted that parachutists could ever play a proper role on the battlefield, imagining that they would all be shot as they descended or rounded up before they could organise themselves after landing. Added to this was the rivalry between the RAF and the army as to who should be in charge of the training of airborne troops. And behind everything was a lack of policy agreement as to what role these new troops should play.

At the end of December 1940, the Air Ministry presented a paper to the Chiefs of Staff arguing that, as it was unlikely that many troop-carrying aircraft or gliders would be available for these duties for some time, the provision of airborne troops should be kept to a minimum. The Ministry agreed however that the 'staging and conduct of airborne operations should be a RAF responsibility to meet army requirements'.[6] The War Office responded by insisting that there was a need to get a small airborne force up and ready as quickly as possible and that the RAF should meet the requirements of the army in terms of making sufficient aircraft available. The Air Ministry's answer was that parachute troops should still form only a small proportion of an airborne force, the majority being glider-borne troops so as not to divert the limited number of available bombers from their duties at Bomber Command. The fact was that the Air Ministry had neglected to develop sufficient transport aircraft in the pre-war years. Now airborne forces were being asked to pay the price.

As a form of shuttlecock debate continued back and forth between the ministries, the planners at Combined Operations searched for some sort of mission to try out the first parachute troops that had been trained up, members of the newly designated 11 Special Air Service Battalion. Britain was now involved in the war against Italian forces in North Africa and it was thought that anything that could hamper the Italian war effort would be a useful exercise.

Many supplies for North Africa sailed from the ports of Taranto, Brindisi or Bari, all situated around the 'heel' of Italy. All three ports were fed from the river Sele by a pipeline that crossed the Apennines bringing fresh water to the arid province of Apulia. A weak point in this system was an aqueduct at Tragino. Since this was too far inland to be reached by seaborne commandos and too much of a pinpoint target to be hit by bombers, it was decided to try out the newly trained parachutists. By striking a dramatic blow against the Italian war machine in southern Italy, it was hoped that they would show the world that Britain was developing its own airborne troops with an ability to strike offensively at targets across occupied Europe.

A party of seven officers and thirty-one other ranks started training for the mission in January 1941. Major Trevor Pritchard was put in command. He was tall, 5 ft 10 in, and solidly built. A professional soldier for ten years in the Royal Welch Fusiliers, he had been army heavyweight boxing champion and a top rugby player. He was just the sort of lion of a man the parachute force had been looking for. Captain Gerrard Daly of the Royal Engineers was to be in charge of the demolition party. He was short, 5 ft 5½ in, and another regular soldier from a family of professional soldiers. Serious and quiet, he had picked up a reputation for toughness during the evacuation from Dunkirk. Two of the sergeants in the squad were Percy 'Clem' Clements and Arthur 'Taff' Lawley. Both in their thirties, they had been miners before joining the army. Clements had served in India for ten years, Lawley in Egypt and Palestine. The men they commanded ranged upwards in age from nineteen and had all been among the first to volunteer. They were all enthusiastic about the mission they faced.[7]

Their preparations included practice drops around a mock-up of the aqueduct built in Tatton Park. Tragically, there was a fatal accident during the training when a paratrooper got stuck on the bottom of an ice-covered lake into which he had drifted. An element of farce crept in when strong winds blew some of the men into high trees alongside the drop zone and the local fire brigade had to rescue them.

It was decided to use Whitley bombers for the drop, and so eight aircraft were assembled and flew to Malta with the paratroopers in early February. While two caused a diversion by bombing the airfields around Foggia, the remaining six were to drop the parachutists. After the attack on the aqueduct had taken place, the plan was for the men to march fifty miles to the mouth of the Sele river. There, five nights after they had jumped, a submarine, HMS *Triumph*, would surface to extract them. The plan was codenamed Operation Colossus.

With the paratroopers went two Italians who were to translate on the ground. Trooper Nicol Nastri was short and wiry. He had lived in the East End so long that he had picked up a cockney accent, and was now going into battle using military papers that bore the name of John Tristan to disguise his origins. Fortunato Picchi joined the unit at the last minute. He had been the banqueting manager at the Savoy before the war and was a committed anti-fascist. Both Italians were taking a considerable risk. If captured, they were likely to be shot as traitors.

The Whitleys, loaded with their paratrooper cargo and canisters of explosives, took off from Malta early on the evening of 10 February. Flying over the mountainous terrain of southern Italy at only 500 feet took courage and skill. Five of the Whitleys dropped their men right in the drop zone, within a few hundred yards of the aqueduct. It was an impressive piece of flying. Unfortunately, the other Whitley got lost and dropped its men in the wrong valley, some miles away from the target. This was doubly disastrous, as they included Captain Daly and many of the engineers who were to carry out the demolition, along with many of the canisters of explosives.

Missing this important part of his detachment, Major Pritchard nevertheless assembled his men. The aqueduct was clearly visible in the bright moonlight. With many of their explosives missing and the marker lights on some of the remaining containers not working, it took several hours to find those that had been dropped nearby. Pritchard instructed the senior engineer present, Lieutenant Paterson, to move everything he could to the aqueduct. Paterson was staggered to find that the structure was not made of brick as he had been told, but of reinforced concrete. He gathered about 800 lb of explosives, all he could muster, piled it against one pier and its abutment and at 0030 detonated the charge. The pier fell away and water began to pour into the ravine. They had successfully damaged if not destroyed the target. Now it was time to set off for the coast.

The men split into three parties. They had four and a half days to reach the rendezvous point with the naval submarine. But it was hard going over mostly mountainous terrain, up steep slopes and down across deep ravines. They hid in the daytime and travelled at night. But before long, the *carabinieri* and local militias were in pursuit of each party. On the second day, Pritchard found himself surrounded by a group of women and children who had come out to stare at them. Behind stood a group of soldiers who demanded their surrender. Pritchard took the honourable decision that they could not fight their way out with so many women and children surrounding them and gave the order for the men to put down their weapons. The elite force of British paratroopers had the ignominy of being captured by a tiny group of enemy soldiers and they were marched off in handcuffs.

The other two groups also met with the same fate and were rounded up and taken off to captivity. Captain Daly and the engineers who had been dropped in the wrong valley heard the explosion as the aqueduct was blown and began their march to the coast. They had come within a few miles of the extraction site when they too were surrounded by a group of soldiers and police. They tried to bluff their way out by pretending to be

German airmen who had been shot down and demanded the police provide them with a vehicle. The tactic nearly worked, but when the Italians realised they had no papers they were arrested. All of the paratroopers were eventually taken off into a prisoner of war camp, except for Picchi who was interrogated and then shot. Nastri, with his false English papers and strong cockney accent, successfully convinced his captors that he was as English as the rest of the captives.

None of the men reached the extraction rendezvous. What they didn't know was that even if they had made it, they would not have been rescued. One of the Whitley bombers on the diversionary raid had developed engine trouble and had to ditch in the sea. The pilot sent out a radio message that he was ditching near the mouth of the Sele as this happened to be the nearest point. He had not been told that this was where the extraction was to take place. As the message had been broadcast in an insecure code, the planners at Malta realised that this stretch of coast would be teeming with Italian soldiers for some days to come. Reluctantly, they decided to cancel the orders to HMS *Triumph* to come up in the bay on the night of 15 February to rescue the paratroopers. They judged it was too dangerous for the submarine crew to be in the bay at this time. There was no alternative. The paratroopers behind enemy lines had to be abandoned.

It was certainly not a great first mission for the newly formed parachute force. The aqueduct had been put out of action, but only, as it turned out, for a few weeks. It was quickly repaired and the water supply to Taranto, Bari and Brindisi was restored. Many of the explosives and the leading engineers had gone astray. And worst of all, the entire force had ended up in captivity. If the intention had been to show off the capabilities of the new British airborne force as heroes of a triumphant mission behind enemy lines in the south of Italy, then Operation Colossus was a dismal failure. At least, however, the planners at Combined Operations were left with plenty of lessons to ponder about the use of airborne troops. And it left the men in the new force with a grim legacy to reflect on as the parachute unit's baptism of fire.

Despite the failure of this first mission, the parachute force continued to grow. On 26 April Churchill himself visited Ringway to watch a demonstration. He was disappointed in that he only saw forty men jump. Although he didn't show his disappointment to the men, on his return to London the PM asked urgently for the latest proposals for increasing the parachute and glider force beyond the early target of five hundred men.

The following month the Germans launched their airborne assault on Crete using 500 Junkers Ju 52 transport aircraft, 80 gliders and 16,000 airborne troops, both parachutists and glider borne. It was the greatest airborne invasion launched by the Germans during the war. The paratroopers were to seize key targets such as airfields and ports and hold them until supplies and reinforcements arrived. The Allied troops on Crete, many of whom were New Zealanders, fought back ferociously. But after eleven days of bitter fighting, Crete fell to the Germans and the remains of the defending force were evacuated from the south of the island. The assault was yet another German victory, although at a high cost. One in four German paratroopers involved was killed in the battle. The Germans concluded that airborne troops would not be used again. Hitler told General

Student, 'Crete proved that the days of parachute troops are over. The parachute arm is one that relies entirely on surprise ... the surprise factor has exhausted itself.'[8] For the rest of the war, German airborne forces were used instead as ground infantry, mostly on the Russian front.

Ironically, Churchill drew the opposite conclusion from the German success on Crete and lamented that he had not pushed for more progress in the development of British airborne forces. He wrote, 'I feel myself greatly to blame for allowing myself to be overborne by the resistances which were offered ... We ought to have 5,000 parachutists and an Airborne Division on the German model ... A whole year has been lost, and I now invite the Chiefs of Staff to make proposals for trying, so far as is possible, to repair the misfortune.'[9]

The Chiefs of Staff were finally stung into action. They agreed to build up the paratrooper force to Churchill's original request of five thousand over a twelve-month period, by May 1942. There would be one brigade based in the UK and one in the Middle East. Finally, the RAF agreed to provide up to ten squadrons of transport aircraft, although they pointed out that this would reduce the capacity of Bomber Command to expand its own effort as much as had been intended. In addition an order was placed for four hundred Hotspur gliders in order to develop a Glider Brigade of about the same size, although it was not expected that the gliders themselves would be available until the following year. All this required a scaling up of the work at the Landing School at Ringway, which was now to take a hundred men at a time to pass through a training course lasting three weeks.

In July, Squadron Leader Maurice Newnham took over the

Ringway school and, realising that the whole process of jumping from aircraft had to be made less frightening, he began to revolutionise the process of parachute training. Newnham insisted on the use of balloons from which men were to make their first jumps. These were safer and much easier to jump from. Not only did they lack the din of being inside an aircraft and the disturbing sight of men dropping one by one in front of you, but also there was no aircraft slipstream to cope with.

To run the training he brought in RAF instructors, whose mission was to be far more matter-of-fact about the idea of jumping from aircraft. It was to be regarded as a normal military procedure. The RAF instructors introduced the use of the para-roll on hitting the ground to spread the impact of the landing. Both safer and less gymnastic than the forward and backward roll taught by the army instructors, it was also closer to the German technique developed at Stendal before the war. The RAF was to train men in the use of parachutes and in jumping and the army was to concentrate on everything from the point at which the paratrooper landed on the ground. It was a sensible division of labour that lasted for decades to come.

In September, the 1st Parachute Brigade was formed under the command of Brigadier Richard Gale. He proved to be a far-sighted commander who could at last spend time to develop the tactics of parachute forces. A new burst of recruitment was instigated and again the call went out for volunteers.

Among the many to respond was Captain John Frost. A solid, stocky man who sported a stubby, dark moustache, he came from an army family and had been born in India. He was a tough, no-nonsense Englishman who after officer training at Sandhurst was commissioned with a Scottish Rifles regiment, the Cameronians. On service at home and in Palestine he learnt to be an experienced professional soldier. Just before the war, Frost was transferred to command a rifle company of Arab and Kurdish tribesmen in an imperial force called the Iraq Levies, based eighty miles from Baghdad. Returning to his old regiment, the Cameronians, in late 1940, he was posted to guard a stretch of the Suffolk coast. This turned out to be rather a cushy billet, with plenty of leisure time for him to pursue his hobbies of hunting and game shooting. Yearning for a bit more action he responded to the call for volunteers, although he felt very uncertain about the prospect of jumping from aircraft. After a brief interview and medical examination he was ordered to report for duty at Hardwick near Chesterfield, the new base of the 1st Parachute Brigade.

The camp was still under construction when Frost arrived. Ugly brick huts were provided as living quarters, and Frost was disappointed to find he was to be adjutant to a new battalion that had not yet been formed. As adjutant, Frost was in charge of the day-to-day administration of the battalion, which involved checking the new volunteers. He was shocked by the quality of the new recruits. Many were misfits of one sort or another and some even had criminal records. It was clear that many had been 'volunteered' by their commanding officers simply to get rid of them. Many such men were sent back to their previous units within days.

Another volunteer who arrived at Hardwick at this time was Lieutenant John Timothy. Having grown up in Tunbridge Wells in Kent, where he been a keen rugby player and cricketer at school, he had joined Marks and Spencer just before the war as a management trainee. On the day after war was declared he had eagerly queued with hundreds of others outside a recruiting office, only to be turned away as there were too many volunteers. In early 1940 he badgered the recruiting sergeant so much that he was eventually allowed to join up, although because there was a six-month waiting list for his preferred service, the Royal Navy, he decided to join the army instead. At first he went into the Grenadier Guards and later was commissioned into the Royal West Kent Regiment.

Because nothing much was going on, he too put his name forward when the call went out for volunteers for the paratroopers. When asked why he had volunteered he replied, 'Well, as the war wasn't coming to me, I thought I'd better go and meet it.'[10] He was selected and told to report to Chesterfield station, where the soldier who met him had himself only arrived the day before. On the following day, Timothy led the reception committee that welcomed the next batch of recruits. Everything in the Parachute Brigade was new and everyone was learning together.

Slowly, a form of order and organisation settled on the business of forging a new fighting force. The men did endless hours of work in the gym to get them up to a high standard of fitness. As the first novices departed for the training school at Ringway, more men arrived to take their places. And when they returned a few weeks later proudly wearing the shiny white wings with a parachute in the middle, they spoke of the excitement of parachuting and infected the rest of the unit with their enthusiasm.

Everyone realised how fit you had to be to survive the knocks of a parachute jump, but John Frost worried that, with so much paperwork to handle, he was unable to keep up with the level of physical fitness required. When his turn came to transfer to Ringway for parachute training he had a fit of nerves. Writing later, he remembered ascending for his first jump in a crazily swinging basket to a balloon 600 feet above Tatton Park with the battalion's commanding officer: 'We smiled at each other the learner parachutist's smile, which has no joy or humour in it. We fiddled anxiously with our harness and occasionally threw a quick agonized glance at the ground below, but in the main we stared upwards, praying hard.'[11]

When it came to the jump, the first sensation Frost remembered was the breath drawing from his lungs, until he heard a crackling sound from above and the sudden pull on his harness told him that his parachute had opened successfully. The rest of the descent was 'heavenly'. After a very gentle landing, Frost decided to make his second compulsory jump from the balloon straight away. Cocky and confident, he chatted away to his fellow jumpers as he ascended to 600 feet once again. As he leapt out of the balloon for a second time he remembered hearing someone call out, 'Keep your legs together,' but he found himself caught in a slight wind and he landed with all the weight of his body on his left leg, causing his knee to be savagely wrenched. After a few seconds he got up and managed to hobble away. But the next day he had a huge swelling in his left knee and he was taken to hospital in Manchester. Frost was convinced that this was an ignominious end to his parachuting career. But after an operation on his knee he began to make a gradual recovery and, amused to find that nearly all the other officers in the ward around him were injured parachutists, determined to get fully fit before completing his parachute course.

Private Tom Hill was one of the early members of Frost's

new battalion. A friend of his had seen the notice calling for volunteers and said he had put his name down. Hill said, 'Oh, if you're going, I'll apply as well.' His friend replied, 'Don't worry, I've put your name down too.' He was happy to have been 'volunteered' and looked forward to some action. Having been selected, he remembered the fitness training, which included constant runs carrying a full pack – seven miles in an hour one day, then twelve miles in two hours a week later. He was told that landing after a normal parachute jump was like jumping from a twelve-foot wall, so you had to keep your feet together and brace yourself well. When he ascended to the balloon for his first jump he felt his stomach knot up as he swung from the basket, looking down the hole to the ground 600 feet below, a terrible feeling. But he went ahead with the jump anyway. The second time he remembered as being even worse. It took several jumps before he began to get less tense and relax. But he never really enjoyed the jumping.[12]

Macleod Forsyth used the training at Hardwick to get really fit. One of nine children of a Scottish miner who had joined the army in 1933 to try to find a better life than mining, he had gone into the Argyll and Sutherland Highlanders but thought the training of the pre-war British Army was very amateurish – more like the Boy Scouts than a professional army. And he had little time for the officers, who he thought 'didn't have a clue' about how to lead a group of men. He spent much of the early part of the war on guard duty in Orkney, so when in 1941 the call went out for volunteers for special duties, Forsyth decided he 'wanted a bit of action'. Having applied, he was one of three men from his famous Scottish regiment to be selected at this time for the Parachute Brigade.

As a paratrooper he then realised 'what training really was'. After general fitness training, the men practised their landing by falling out of the back of army trucks travelling at 25 mph. They had to roll on the ground and then get quickly back on their feet. When it came to jumping, Forsyth like everyone else was terrified at first but was elated at having completed his first jump. He later remembered that 'in those days, damn few had ever jumped and you thought "My God, I've done it" and felt so good.' Anyone who refused to jump in training was allowed to leave – after qualifying as a paratrooper you were no longer allowed to refuse to jump, as that would be classed as 'cowardice in the face of the enemy'. But Forsyth only recalled one lad who refused and was returned to his unit.

Forsyth remembered the hard physical work, day after day, and 'being on the gallop from when you got up to when you went to bed'. He was so hungry that he was delighted at the Ringway canteen to discover you could go back for seconds. One evening he ate three dinners. Finally, on qualifying as a paratrooper, Forsyth remembered the immense pride of having his wings sown on and the feeling that 'we were the best.'[13]

One final but vital administrative change was needed before the hundreds of men training at Hardwick and on the course at Ringway could be classed as a military body fully prepared for action. At the end of October 1941, the commander-in-chief of Home Forces, General Sir Alan Brooke, decided to create an Airborne Division to consist of both the Parachute Brigades and the soon to be formed Air-Landing or Glider Brigade. This new headquarters would co-ordinate the expansion of the airborne forces. The man appointed to command this new division would become one of the most legendary figures in the story of British airborne troops.

Major-General Frederick Browning, universally known since joining the army as 'Boy' Browning because of his youthful looks, was another highly unusual figure. He was an old Etonian and a graduate of the Royal Military Academy at Sandhurst. In the First World War he had fought in the Grenadier Guards, winning a Distinguished Service Medal for gallantry at the Battle of Cambrai in 1917. After the war he turned to athletics and winter sports and competed in the British bobsleigh team in the 1928 Winter Olympics at St Moritz in Switzerland. In 1931 he read the novel *The Loving Spirit* by Daphne du Maurier and was so captivated by the author's descriptions of the Cornish coast that he took his own boat to Cornwall to explore the area. The following year he met du Maurier and after a whirlwind romance married her. He was commanding the 24 Guards Brigade, one of the elite units within the British Army, guarding London from an attack from the south, when he was appointed to head this new airborne fighting force. Unlike many senior army commanders he had already shown an interest in the use of airborne forces by working out in his spare time how to equip and man an airborne unit and how to deploy it in offensive actions.[14]

Browning was ambitious and determined to make a success of his newly formed division. The only precedent for organising a new type of fighting unit within the British Army was the establishment of the brand new Tank Corps in the First World War, but Browning was a good organiser and he immediately set himself to develop tactics for the use of airborne troops. He selected a new headquarters at Syrencote House near Netheravon on the edge of Salisbury Plain.

Realising the importance of building up a strong *esprit de corps* within the airborne unit, he encouraged this by introducing new variations of clothing for the men who would jump from aircraft or land in gliders behind enemy lines. The old British Army helmet that had been in use since the First World War was no good for parachute forces, as the lip sticking out at the base of the helmet could be dangerous when jumping. A new helmet, made of canvas with rubber padding, was designed that fitted the head more tightly. It became standard paratrooper headgear until the late 1950s. A number of smocks were issued to be worn over conventional battledress. Copied from the German *Fallschirmjäger*, these were designed to prevent the paratrooper's uniform from getting entangled in the parachute harness. The paratroopers were issued with new lightweight trousers, easier to jump in than the heavy serge trousers worn by the rest of the British Army. All this helped to make the airborne soldiers stand out from other army units and to create a sense of pride in being in the division. Browning was a stickler for discipline and for smart dress. He wanted everyone not only to feel they were the best within the army but also to feel pride in the achievements of their fellow paratroopers. His men were going to be a special type of fighting force and he had great ambitions for them.

So, despite all its early problems, the Airborne now at last had a clear organisation, a proper structure and a dynamic commander. And the new airborne troops soon began to establish their own spirit, their own values and an immense pride in being among the toughest and bravest men in the British Army.

All that was needed was a badge and an emblem. Browning decided to look back to ancient Greek mythology and the story of Bellerophon, who had ridden the flying horse Pegasus to attack the fire-eaters. The airborne troops adopted the Pegasus image as an emblem and wore it as a flash on their shoulders.

But there were still doubts about what the unit could achieve. Its first mission against the aqueduct in southern Italy had been a humiliating failure. What the new force urgently needed to prove its worth was a new mission and a triumphant success.

7

Scientific Intelligence

Late on a wintry afternoon in November 1939, a young scientist in Air Ministry Intelligence by the name of Reginald Victor Jones was working in his office when a colleague, Frederick Winterbotham, came in and dumped a small parcel on his desk. 'Here's a present for you,' said Winterbotham. Jones asked where the parcel had come from and Winterbotham, who was a senior figure in the Secret Intelligence Service (also known as MI6), told him that it had come from the naval attaché in Oslo. Norway was still neutral at the time.

Apparently, the attaché had received a personal note telling him that if the British wanted to know about secret scientific and technical developments taking place inside Germany, the BBC should be asked to make a particular change in the opening words of their German-language evening news broadcast. The attaché passed the message back to London and the BBC made the change, giving a sign to the mysterious figure that there was interest in hearing what he had to say. Within a couple of days a parcel had been left on the window ledge of the British embassy in Oslo. Jones opened the package now on his desk and found seven pages of typed text, along with a small sealed box. Fearing that there might be some sort of bomb or booby trap enclosed, Jones slowly and carefully opened the box. Inside was a sealed glass tube, rather like an electronic valve.[1]

When the letter was translated, Jones was amazed by what he read. It contained a list of various scientific research projects that were under way in Germany. As well as a description of work going on at an aviation research establishment at Rechlin, the German equivalent to Farnborough, which the British knew about already, it referred to strange-sounding rocket research taking place at a site on the Baltic coast known as Peenemünde, of which the British knew nothing. It included details of two new types of torpedoes that were being developed by the Kriegsmarine, one guided by radio and one with a magnetic fuse. And it reported that the twin-engined Junkers Ju 88 was to be used by the Luftwaffe as a dive bomber alongside the Stuka.

Astonishingly, it also revealed that RAF bombers on a raid on Wilhelmshaven in September had been picked up at a range of 75 miles by a radar station with an output of 20 kilowatts. Although it didn't give the wavelength of the radar signal, the letter suggested that this could be worked out and the radar should be jammed. More revealingly still, the letter claimed that there was another radar station using paraboloid aerials operating on a wavelength of about 53 cm. There was further information about a set of radio beams called *Y-Gerät* that were in some way to aid aircraft navigation. The letter was signed simply 'A German scientist who wishes you well'.

When British scientists examined the strange glass tube they found it to be a form of proximity fuse for anti-aircraft shells, designed to trigger an explosion when close to a metal object. The British, too, were developing such a device but this one was more sophisticated than anything being worked on in Britain. It took some time for the young British scientist to absorb all this information. But to Jones it seemed that Christmas had come early that year.

However, the reaction of his colleagues was quite different. The letter became known as the Oslo Report and it was circulated within military intelligence. Senior intelligence officers quickly decided that the report was a hoax, intended to divert British Intelligence into useless byways to waste time. The Deputy Director of Intelligence at the Admiralty, John Buckingham, was convinced that the whole document was a 'plant', because no single scientist could possibly have known about the range of work that was going on across Germany. When Jones argued that the report confirmed German research that was already known about, Buckingham replied that this was standard practice. By informing the other side of something they already knew, the intention was to convince the victim that the rest of the information, which was false, was in fact true. Buckingham said it was only because Jones was an innocent in intelligence that he would fall for such a trick.

Other scientists agreed. Since Robert Watson-Watt's spying holiday in East Prussia, it had been accepted in British scientific circles that the Germans did not have radar. The descriptions in the Oslo Report were assumed to be wrong, to leave a false trail for the British to pursue. It was decided to ignore the report and copies of it were destroyed so as not to mislead future intelligence officers. Amazed at this conclusion, Jones decided to keep his copy, mystified only by who could have written the document.[2]

Dr Reginald Victor Jones was just twenty-eight years old when the Oslo Report was dumped on his desk. But he was mature and experienced beyond his years. He was a scientist through and through, certain that there was a scientific explanation for everything and that it was the duty of research scientists like himself to find it. But despite his serious aspirations, he had a wicked sense of humour and delighted in setting up practical jokes to trick his friends. His speciality was in telephone hoaxes. He would call a colleague and pretend to be a telephone engineer who had to fix a fault on their line, asking him to take up various improbable poses like standing on one leg and waving the receiver in the air, or putting the receiver in a bucket of water while waving his free arm. All the while other friends would be in hiding, watching the hapless victim. Jones tricked some of the finest brains in Oxford into performing this form of foolery in front of their colleagues.

Brought up in south London, Jones had taken a First at Oxford in physics in 1932. He did his Ph.D. research at the Clarendon Laboratory where Professor Frederick Lindemann, the director of the laboratory and Churchill's close friend and adviser, picked him out. But, Lindemann was sceptical about radio detection finding and believed that the future lay with the use of infra-red rays, so Jones's research was concentrated in this field for some time. Jones visited Bawdsey Manor and could see the advantages of radar, but continued to believe that infra-red could be used to detect approaching aircraft at close range when radar was less effective.

Although still only a junior researcher, Jones was caught up in the rivalry between Lindemann, on the one hand, and Sir Henry Tizard and Robert Watson-Watt, on the other. His academic research was brought to a close and Watson-Watt arranged for him to be recruited as a civil servant in the Air Ministry. Jones was reluctant to leave Oxford and felt he had become 'a pawn in a distinctly unpleasant game'.[3] In fact, it was the best thing that could have happened to him as well as to British wartime science, for it brought Jones into the top secret world of the intelligence community.

There had never been a scientist in Air Ministry Intelligence before, and over the next few years Jones gained a fast-track grounding in the military application of science. He worked with most of the leading figures in pre-war military science and did stints for both the navy and the RAF. When war came, Jones completed his crash course with a placement to Bletchley Park. Here, the mysteries of the German Enigma machine were explained to him and he spent some time with the brilliant young Cambridge mathematician, Alan Turing, who was already starting to devise ways of breaking the seemingly impenetrable codes that the Germans were using. Two months after the declaration of war, in November 1939, Jones was sent back from Bletchley Park to 54 Broadway, near Victoria, the headquarters of the SIS, and it was here that late one afternoon Winterbotham passed on to him the parcel containing the Oslo Report.

The task Jones had been given was to obtain early warning of any new weapons or systems the enemy might be developing for use against Britain or British forces. He was staggered at how little real scientific intelligence had been gathered before the war; in particular the lack of knowledge about the Germans' development of radar. He was convinced that the Germans were using radar, a belief confirmed by the Oslo Report, but he could get no one to believe him. So, despite the warning in the report about the use of radar to pick up bombers heading for Wilhelmshaven, another raid went ahead in December, resulting in the dreadful losses described earlier.

Jones's wide-ranging experience in the run-up to war gave him the confidence to say what he thought and to stick his neck above the scientific parapet when be believed he was right. The first real occasion for this came in June 1940. Before the Battle of Britain had begun, Jones thought he had picked up indications that the Germans were using a system of beams to guide bombers to their targets. The beams could work by day or night and in all weathers. He had been given details of various intercepted messages referring to a system described as *Knickebein* which, puzzlingly, translated as 'crooked leg'. It appeared to be linked to a radio transmitting station at Cleves. Jones reported his fears to Professor Lindemann, who by this time was running a special unit in Downing Street to advise Churchill, recently appointed Prime Minister. Lindemann was sceptical as he believed short wave beams could not travel far as they could not follow the curvature of the earth. Jones had to find more evidence for his theory.

Jones got one of his colleagues, Squadron Leader Denys Felkin, who ran an interrogation centre for captured Luftwaffe PoWs, to ask them about the Knickebein system. But they would say nothing. Then, talking among themselves, one pilot was overheard saying to another that no matter how hard the British looked, they would never find the system. This comment was secretly recorded and passed on to Jones. It gave him the clue that maybe Knickebein was not some additional piece of kit but existed within the radio equipment already in use in German bombers. Technicians examined a Heinkel III bomber that had come down in Scotland and found it contained a blind landing system developed by the Lorenz company that was intended to help aircraft line up with the runway in bad weather conditions. However, it appeared that the receiver was far more sensitive than it needed to be for such a purpose. Jones believed he had found the device the Germans were using to guide the bombers to their targets. He went back to Lindemann, who was now persuaded to take the idea seriously.

Lindemann passed this information on to Churchill, who immediately recognised the importance of such a discovery and was keen to explore the problem further. Fearing that it would get bogged down in endless bureaucratic delays, Churchill called several senior figures to an urgent meeting. Present were the Minister for Air, Sir Archibald Sinclair, the Minister for Aircraft Production, Lord Beaverbrook, both Lindemann and Tizard, Watson-Watt and several senior RAF figures, including the Chief of the Air Staff and Sir Hugh Dowding, the head of Fighter Command. The meeting was called for 21 June in the Cabinet Room. Arriving at work that morning, Jones received a summons to attend the meeting with the Prime Minister but as a renowned practical joker he thought this was his friends getting their own back and did nothing. When he realised it was no joke he rushed to Downing Street, but arrived half an hour after the meeting had started. It was his first meeting with the PM, and this was not a good start.

When Jones entered the Cabinet Room, he found Churchill, Lindemann and Beaverbrook seated on one side of a long table, with Tizard, Watson-Watt and the RAF folk down the other side. Jones detected a tense atmosphere in the room, almost a sense of confrontation. So he decided to sit across one end of the table in a sort of no-man's-land between the two sides. He realised in the next few minutes of conversation that no one had grasped the situation accurately, so when Churchill turned to ask him a point of detail, Jones said, 'Would it be a help, sir, if I told the story right from the start?'

Churchill was rather taken aback but replied, 'Well, yes it would.'

The twenty-eight-year-old, confident that he alone understood the whole picture, then spoke for about twenty minutes in front of the nation's top political leaders and the top brass of the RAF, a long time to hold the attention of such senior men in the midst of a grave national crisis. Coolly recounting his suspicions, he explained how he had raised his concerns and deduced that the beam reading system was part of the Lorenz blind landing mechanism. Churchill later wrote, 'For twenty minutes or more he spoke in quiet tones, unrolling his chain of circumstantial evidence, the like of which for its convincing fascination was never surpassed by the tales of Sherlock Holmes.'[4]

When Jones fell silent, Churchill asked him what could be done. The young man replied that first an RAF aircraft must fly with the captured equipment and see if it could navigate along the beams. Then, attempts must be made to put in a false crossbeam to get the German bombers to drop their bombs miles off target. Another option was to consider jamming the beams. There was a general air of incredulity among the RAF chiefs, who raised various objections. Churchill flew into a rage and banged the table angrily, exclaiming, 'All I get from the Air Ministry is files, files, files.' The young scientist had at least offered him a programme of action. Churchill demanded that counter-measures be explored as a priority and the meeting broke up. What was later called the Battle of the Beams now began.[5]

Jones had been correct in his belief about the use of the beams and once their operation had been fully understood it was possible for the scientists at TRE to work out ways to jam them and to throw the German bombers off course. The first round in the Battle of the Beams had gone to Jones and the British radio scientists. But as the Blitz began in earnest, the Germans soon realised their secret had been uncovered. They started to use a far more complex system of five very high frequency short wave radio beams that when intersected by another beam provided key Pathfinder aircraft with an accurate siting to within a hundred yards of a target. The second round belonged to the German scientists. British radio operators could pick up the existence of the beams but were unable to work out where they were pointing.

On the night of 14 November, a big raid was predicted, but its target remained unknown. That night the Luftwaffe carried out their biggest raid outside London on the city of Coventry: 554 men and women were killed and more than twenty factories around the city, along with hundreds of homes, were destroyed.

Eventually, during the winter of 1940–1, the boffins at TRE

found a way of reading the beams and warning where the raiders were heading. But even before a victory had been called in this round, the Germans began to use the new device called the *Y-Gerät*, or Y-Apparatus, using a sophisticated form of radar to guide their bombers to the target. This too was hacked into and distorted and it is thought that the bombing of Dublin in neutral Ireland in May 1941 was a consequence of twisting the radar beams that were guiding the German bombers. Interestingly, for Jones, an early form of the Y-Gerät had been described in the Oslo Report. He was glad he had kept his copy.

The Battle of the Beams made it absolutely clear not only that the Germans had radar but that they were capable of using it in inventive and ingenious ways. But there were still some doubters in the intelligence community. So while still struggling with the beams, the next round in Jones's secret war began in July 1940 when his team began to pick up radio signals that suggested at least two German radar stations were in operation, one on the westernmost tip of the Cherbourg peninsula near Auderville and a second further west on the Brittany coast near Lannion. During the autumn and winter of 1940–1, Derek Garrard from TRE, who had been assigned to work for Jones, went down to the south coast with his own receiver to listen in to various frequencies. At one point, setting up his strange receivers in a forbidden area, he was arrested as a spy, though Jones soon got him released. Garrard not only picked up the transmissions but was even able to find fairly precise bearings which confirmed where they were coming from.

Jones found it difficult to make sense of all the different systems that appeared to be in operation for the Wehrmacht, the Kriegsmarine and the Luftwaffe. He was struggling with the fact that German radar had been developed by several different companies using different wavelengths. But he realised that the generic term in use was DT (*Dezimeter Telegraphie*). The Kriegsmarine seemed to be using one system to target coastal guns against British shipping in the Channel on a wavelength of 80 cm. Another system was in use to provide early warning against the arrival of British aircraft over occupied France. Intercepted signals suggested that the principal form of this radar was named Freya. Jones initially calculated that it had a range of about 90 miles. Jones realised that with the fall of France, the Germans had simply moved the Freya radar stations that had guarded their western border, *en masse*, to the Channel coast.

It greatly helped that before proper telephone landlines were laid to connect all these stations, they broadcast to each other and to their controllers on open radio frequencies. They adopted a very basic code and it was soon possible to break this and read the communications. Jones was able to further deduce that the Germans had no integrated system for aircraft early warning such as that created for RAF Fighter Command in Britain. Instead, they had simply 'grafted the new development on to a well established system [of the Observer Corps]'.[6] But it was still impossible to calculate how the Freya stations operated.

Abandoning its previous policy of complete secrecy, the government decided in June 1941, following leaks in Canada, to reveal the existence of its radar programme. On 18 June, the Deputy Prime Minister, Clement Attlee, made a short speech in the House of Commons admitting the existence of a new science of 'radiolocation' that was in use to detect the approach of enemy aircraft. Not much was said as to how it operated, but Attlee made clear that it had been in development for many years. The announcement was linked to a call for volunteers from around the Empire to come forward to train as operators. The press picked this up and on 29 June, the *Sunday Times* ran a recruiting ad for the WAAF: 'Radiolocation – one of the best kept secrets of the war. It helped to win the Battle of Britain and it's going to win many more battles for the Royal Air Force.' Quoting a supposed WAAF operator, the ad continued, 'I can't tell you just what I'm doing [but] ... The Radiolocator sends out electric waves that patrol the air. The waves radio messages back to me.' The ad clearly admitted that 'Radiolocation is a brand new science ... it may well be the "discovery of the century".' The work was presented as being exacting and exciting, with enormous possibilities after the war when 'trained operators will be invaluable'.[7]

It was a curious decision to come clean about the new science at the heart of Britain's air defence. But the British public now knew about this new-fangled activity and that its operation was in the hands of WAAFs, who had shown great courage when under fire in radar installations the previous summer. And the new word 'radiolocation' had entered the English language.

During the summer of 1941, the War Cabinet resolved to commit Bomber Command to a policy of night bombing, both in occupied Europe and in Germany itself. Air Vice Marshal Charles Medhurst, assistant to the Chief of Air Staff in charge of intelligence and Jones's boss, asked him to compile a picture of the German night defences that the RAF bombers would encounter. The control of these defences was likely to depend very largely on radar, just as Britain's defence had done during the Battle of Britain and the Blitz. Jones would have to find out how the whole complex German defensive radar shield fitted together.

On 22 November a vital breakthrough came when Jones saw two aerial photos that recorded a couple of strange, circular objects near the coast at Auderville. Photo interpreters had measured the two unknown sites as being about twenty feet in diameter. Moreover, the hawk-eyed interpreters had spotted that in the gap of a few seconds between the exposure of the two photographs, the shadow of the objects had moved fractionally. Using magnifying equipment, they measured a broadening of the shadows of about one-tenth of a millimetre between the two pictures. From such tiny measurements, major conclusions were drawn. The photo interpreters suggested that the aerials might be rotating and were therefore unlike any other radio towers that had yet been detected. Jones realised that this might be the first sighting of a Freya radar station and asked for further low-level photography of the site.

The taking of aerial photographs was still a young science. The RAF had only begun to use Spitfires, the fastest aircraft available, for the task a matter of months before. The principle of aerial photography in wartime was for a reconnaissance aircraft to fly fast and high at about 30,000 feet over enemy territory and for the pilot to turn on his cameras when he was above the target area. All the guns and the armour plating were taken out of the photo recon Spitfires to make room for the cameras and lenses, and to lighten the aircraft in order to give it extra speed and height. They flew above the range of the anti-aircraft batteries, but if an interceptor came up in pursuit, the recon pilot had to turn on full throttle and head for home. He could not stop to fight as he had no guns. It took particular bravery to be a reconnaissance pilot, flying for hours on end over enemy territory in order to get his photos and then having to make his way home again with nothing but his speed and his daring to get away from any fighters sent up to intercept.[8]

Occasionally photographs taken from such a great height were not suitable, as they were at too small a scale, and it was necessary for a pilot to fly a low-level sortie at maybe just 100 feet in order to get a detailed close-up picture of an object on the ground. These sorties were enormously dangerous, as they brought the aircraft within range of the anti-aircraft guns and any enemy fighters that happened to be in the area. In RAF parlance these sorties were known as 'dicing' missions – short for 'dicing with death'. Aware of the risks, Jones now asked with suitable diffidence for a low-level 'dicing' sortie to be made over the circular objects near Auderville.

The first such mission was a failure as the aircraft flew at nearly 350 mph past the radar emplacements on the ground. Pilots were always told they could never have two goes at a 'dicing' mission as if you went back a second time, the enemy's gunners would be waiting for you. The pilot of the first sortie thought the object he had been asked to photograph itself looked like an anti-aircraft gun emplacement and reported with some irritation that he had been sent on a crazy suicide mission. But Jones was sure of himself and requested a second low-level sortie. It was on this mission, on 22 February 1941, that Flying Officer William Manifould took a magnificent oblique photograph from about 200 feet that clearly showed the two radar aerials and three rectangular support buildings nearby.

Realising from these shots what the photographic signature

of a Freya radar station looked like, the photo interpreters managed to identify more and more of the stations that made up the German radar chain along the Channel coast. Meanwhile, the specialists at TRE were able to measure the wavelength of the radar signals, the intensity of the pulse transmissions and the method by which the detections were reported from the isolated stations.

In the summer of 1941 investigation of the sites went a stage further. Pilots made test flights from the south coast of England, TRE tuned in its listening devices and was able to follow the whole process as the Freya operators went on to alert, found the RAF aircraft on each occasion and monitored it in their reports. The accuracy of the German range and bearing identification could be carefully plotted. From these it seemed that the Freya radar was not good at measuring the height of approaching aircraft.

Using this information, by the autumn of 1941 Jones was able to report to the Air Ministry chiefs in great detail about the Freya system. Each station, he said, consisted of two sets of antennae, one acting as standby or reserve for the other. A rotating aerial was mounted on a turntable, as was the operator's cabin, complete with transmitting and receiving equipment. The aerial antenna was both transmitter and receiver and operated, Jones calculated, on a waveband of 2.3–2.5 m. Freya could operate at various ranges, from a distance of about ninety miles to as close as about a mile and a half. The reports picked up from the stations suggested an accuracy of about half a mile. The equipment was capable of 360-degree rotation, but once an enemy aircraft was sighted the Freya usually only rotated within the few degrees needed to keep it in sight. Jones was even able to report that the equipment was made by AEG in Berlin and the operators probably used cathode ray tubes on which to base their plots.

From aerial photographs it was possible to calculate that each station was manned by an officer and about thirty men, usually from the Luftwaffe but sometimes with Wehrmacht and Kriegsmarine personnel present. In 1941, the organisation of the system came under control of a new Luftwaffe unit called *Luftgau Nachrichten-Regiment 12* (the 12th Signals Regiment of Luftwaffe Regional Administration). Jones estimated that there were as many as 150 Freya stations in operation.[9]

Jones also realised that the Germans used a grid system made up of rectangles measuring about 1 km east–west and 0.75 km north–south in which to plot the approach and passing of Allied aircraft. This approximately matched the accuracy of the Freya network. However, in late 1941 bomber crews began sending back reports of a significant increase in interception by enemy fighters at night. The Germans seemed to be using something far more accurate than could be expected from the Freya network. In addition, the enemy fighters always seemed to be at exactly the right height to intercept the Allied bombers – and Freya was not good at detecting height. For some time the boffins at TRE had been picking up signals which appeared to come from a completely different German radar system, operating on a much shorter wavelength of 53 cm.

Jones realised that, once again, this had been predicted in the Oslo Report. According to the report's author this system used paraboloid or bowl-like reflectors. Jones calculated that they would probably have to be about ten feet in diameter. This would mean that the whole installation was probably half the size of a Freya antenna.

The word that came up a few times in intercepted messages was of another system called 'Würzburg'. But what did this mean? How did the so-called Würzburg link into the Freya radar chain? Was it some newer and far more accurate radar system? If so, would this disrupt and potentially lead to the cancellation of the bombing offensive against Germany? Moreover, would it ever be possible to find anything as small as one of these new radar installations along the coast of occupied Europe? This was the next challenge the British scientists faced.

8

Photo Intelligence

R.V. Jones had built up a strong working relationship with some of the interpreters whose job was to analyse aerial photographs. In April 1941, the entire photo intelligence community had finally moved from the primitive conditions of their first headquarters in Wembley, where the roof of the building leaked and many of them had to work beneath umbrellas to keep dry when it rained. A new organisation called the Central Interpretation Unit was opened in a grand country house that had been requisitioned on the banks of the Thames between Marlow and Henley. A splendid mock-Tudor building with tall chimneys and magnificent gardens with views along the Thames valley, its name was Danesfield House.

The photo interpreters could barely believe their luck. From the trials and tribulations of trying to work in a busy suburb of London during the Blitz, they now found themselves laying out their photos and equipment in the grand wood-panelled halls of a turn-of-the-century mansion. The exterior of the house was swathed in wisteria, whose delicate scent drifted inside during the summer months. Danesfield even had central heating, which was extremely rare at the time. And instead of commuting through the bombed streets of London, the photo interpreters were now billeted in luxurious houses in the countryside of the Chilterns. One photo interpreter stayed in the lodgings of a wealthy businessman where a butler who had formerly worked for a duke woke him every morning with a cup of tea. The new establishment, called by the RAF, like all air force stations, after the local village, was named RAF Medmenham.[1]

The RAF was in the process of inventing nothing less than an entirely new science: that of photo interpretation. The analysis of aerial photographs was broken down into a number of stages. First Phase was carried out at the airfield. As soon as the reconnaissance aircraft landed, ground crew collected the film from the aircraft's cameras and rushed it to be processed and printed. A photo interpreter was on hand to examine the photos and to provide an immediate analysis of urgent tactical questions. Was that ship still in the harbour? Had that squadron of German fighters deployed at the airfield? Were those Panzer tanks still sheltering in the same place? Had a bombing raid succeeded in hitting the target? This intelligence was passed on within three hours of the aircraft touching down.

Then the aerial photos were taken to Medmenham, where Second Phase photo interpreters put together a more considered daily intelligence briefing. Interpreters worked in shifts around the clock to produce this report. Second Phase usually involved some form of numbering or measuring of the details on the photos. By counting the aircraft lined up on an airfield the interpreters could see if a new squadron had deployed to that particular base. By measuring the dimensions of a group of buildings they could calculate the storage capacity for coal, fuel or munitions. By measuring the width of a bridge in front of an intended advance they could predict whether it was strong enough to support Allied tanks.

Finally, the photos were passed on to Third Phase, in which a range of experts divided into sections would examine the photos in yet more detail. The aircraft specialists could spot not only if the numbers of aircraft on an airfield had changed but if a new mark or design of German aircraft had been photographed. The shipping experts could see if a new keel had been laid in a shipyard, and if so could predict what vessel was under construction and when it would be completed. The industrial experts could examine a factory and calculate exactly what it produced and what its annual output would be. In their damage assessment reports after a bombing raid the photo interpreters could calculate precisely how much damage had been done and how long it would take for the factory to be back in production. They could even recommend, if necessary, the optimum time to bomb the factory again, when maximum effort had been put in to rebuilding it but before it was back at full production.

The RAF recruited an extraordinary mix of academics, boffins and mavericks to work at Medmenham. Not only did they need individuals with particular expertise, they also needed problem solvers who could deduce what the enemy were up to simply by looking at a set of photos. Archaeologists were especially good at this as they were used to making deductions from fragmentary evidence. So the entire Archaeology Department at Cambridge University was recruited, from the senior professor to the most junior research fellow. Geologists, physicists, mathematicians and other scholars joined them and Medmenham soon acquired an intensely academic atmosphere. One young graduate nervously arriving for his first day was astonished to find that the first person he met on arrival was his old college botany tutor. But musicians, artists, cartoonists and showbusiness people also found their way to Medmenham. An Oxford professor would give a talk one evening, while the next night West End entertainers would lay on a show or a musical concert. The photo interpreters formed a sort of elite within the RAF.

Women were found to be particularly good at the detailed, painstaking work of photo interpretation and were recruited as WAAF officers to do exactly the same job as the men. The RAF even put women in charge of some of the teams. The formidable Constance Babington Smith, known as 'Babs', had been a journalist on *The Aeroplane* magazine before the war and at Medmenham led the Aircraft Section. Later in the war she was to discover the first V-bombs at their research establishment at Peenemünde and the first Messerschmitt jets before they were rolled out for combat. Uniquely in the British war effort, female officers doing equal work with men were in command of male officers.[2]

And the only weapons the photo interpreters used were slide rules, magnifying glasses and pairs of optical glasses that enabled them to work in 3D – or, as they called it at the time, Stereo. By this means they could measure objects like small radio transmitting aerials or radar towers with remarkable accuracy.

As the war progressed the RAF photo interpreters were able to extract ever more accurate tactical and strategic intelligence from aerial photos. While the codebreakers at Bletchley Park produced startling revelations by cracking the German Enigma communications, an immense amount of day-to-day information about enemy activities came out of the work of the photo interpreters at Medmenham. An American general, Lee Chennault, later claimed that 80 per cent of all intelligence in the war had come from photo intelligence.[3]

Claude Wavell was a brilliant mathematician who before the war had been working on a commercial project using aerial photographs to map Rio de Janeiro and other parts of South America. At the outbreak of war, one of the leading figures in photo interpretation got in touch and asked him to come back to Britain to join the RAF team. He hesitated at first, but after hearing of the evacuation at Dunkirk his patriotic spirit got the better of him and he cabled his friend saying 'If you still want me, I'll come.' He received a telegram back almost immediately that read 'Come at once.'

So Wavell joined the small group learning photo interpretation for the purposes of military intelligence. He soon began to specialise in the identification of aerials, towers and transmitters, and was put in charge of the team known as G Section. It was on this work that he first met and got to know R.V. Jones. It was Wavell who spotted the first Knickebein transmitters at Cleves that helped to guide the German bombers in the summer of 1940. And, a few months later, it was Wavell who first drew Jones's attention to the tiny circular installations with what appeared to be rotating antennae near Auderville.

By the end of 1941, Wavell and his team had found a total

of fifty Freya sites along the enemy-occupied coast from western France to northern Norway. However, the task of studying thousands of square miles of occupied Europe to find the smaller Würzburg German radar stations, probably only ten feet in diameter, was going to be like looking for a needle in a haystack. However, Jones guessed that the Germans might well site the Würzburgs near to the Freyas so as not to have to build and defend additional radar sites. So he and his assistant Charles Frank asked Wavell to send them the aerial photos of all existing Freya installations. They started searching these one by one. It was Frank who made the first dramatic sighting.

On top of the cliffs not far from Cap d'Antifer, about twelve miles north-east of the French port of Le Havre, was a radar encampment with two Freyas. Frank noticed that a track appeared to run for a few hundred yards from them to a large and rather flamboyantly designed villa further along the cliff top that was presumably the headquarters for the radar station. However, he spotted that the track did not run right up to the villa but seemed to end in a loop a short distance from the house. Why would the track stop short of the villa? Near the loop there was a tiny blurred speck, so indistinct that Frank asked for repeated photographic cover of the site to check that it was not just a speck of dust on the photographic negative. But there definitely appeared to be something there. On a hunch that this just might be what they were looking for, Jones put in a request for a low-level sortie to take a closer look and photograph the site. Mindful of the fuss he had caused the last time he had requested such a 'dicing mission', Jones made it clear that this was only to be done when conditions were entirely favourable. Then he telephoned Wavell at Medmenham to tell him of his suspicions.

Most reconnaissance sorties were flown out of RAF Benson, a station centrally located in Berkshire and only a few miles from the Central Interpretation Unit at Medmenham. The pilots used occasionally to pop over to Medmenham to chat with the interpreters in order to get a sense of how their photographs were being used. It so happened that a couple of days after Jones had put in his request, two Spitfire recon pilots were at Medmenham chatting with Claude Wavell before going out for a few beers. One of these pilots, Flight Lieutenant Tony Hill, was every schoolboy's idea of a hero. With his combed-back hair and a silk scarf under his flying suit, he presented a glamorous figure. He had a laid-back, devil-may-care attitude but was utterly determined to persevere with a task until it was complete. And he never ducked tough assignments. It was as though he thrived on the risk.

Wavell showed Hill the photograph that Jones and Frank suspected might include the new type of German radar and explained how important it was to find this final piece of the jigsaw. Jokingly, he said to Hill and his friend, 'You pilots annoy me! You go over this place time and time again but you never turn on your cameras.' Hill stared hard at the photograph. He asked if the tiny speck really could be the device that completed the story of German radar and Wavell assured him that this could be it. Fascinated by the thought of a new challenge, Hill offered to photograph the site the next day.[4]

Sure enough, the following day, Hill took his Spitfire and flew over the site. Taking low-level, oblique angled photographs on a 'dicing' sortie was not easy, as the oblique camera on a Spitfire was mounted below the aircraft, pointing out to the left. So the pilot, flying maybe as low as 50 feet and as fast as 300 mph, had to line himself up just to the right of the object and the tendency was for a pilot to turn on his camera after he had shot by, thus missing the target. On the day that Hill flew over the site his cameras failed, but he still got a good look at the object on the ground. He called Wavell that evening and told him that the apparatus was about ten feet in diameter and looked like 'an electric bowl fire' of a type that was then fairly common. From now on the photo interpreters referred to the object as 'the bowl fire'.

Hill's flight had been entirely unofficial, and he prepared to fly over the site again on the following day. As he was about to leave, he was told that another three aircraft from a different squadron had been formally allocated the task of photographing the site. Not wanting to leave a task unfinished, Hill taxied over to the three aircraft and told their pilots that this particular target was his and if he found any of them within twenty miles of the location he would shoot them down. He did not explain how he could have done this without guns, but the other pilots left him to it and Hill had the place to himself.

This time his reaction speed was just right and everything worked perfectly. The shot he took, one of the most famous aerial photographs of the war, showed the seaside villa with its unusual high-pointed roofs. And right in the middle of the picture, a short distance in front of the house down a path, was the squat bowl-like structure with a low wall around it, almost on the edge of the cliffs facing out to sea. Hill's low-level oblique captured the radar installation in perfect detail. The date was

5 December 1941. The name of the nearest village to this mysterious site was Bruneval.

Jones studied the photograph when it came through and realised this was different from anything else he had seen before. Claude Wavell and his team measured the installation and confirmed that it was indeed about ten feet in diameter and was situated in a shallow pit. Attached to the device itself was a small control cabin about five feet high, and the whole apparatus was capable of rotating. Because of its paraboloid shape, the bowl could tilt upwards as well as rotate horizontally. With the information about the radio waves that Jones had already picked up, he knew that the new German radar operated on a wavelength of 53 cm, with a pulse rate of about 3750 per second. Jones calculated that it must have a range of about twenty-five miles, and further deduced that it could be used to measure with some accuracy the height of approaching aircraft. Thus it would complement the Freya system, which was accurate in detecting range and bearing but not height. Through a brilliant combination of Jones's scientific investigation, Charles Frank's alertness, the observations of Claude Wavell and his team at Medmenham, and the precision flying of Tony Hill, the British intelligence establishment had found what must be a Würzburg, the missing link in the German defensive radar network.

Once the intelligence officers knew what they were looking for, they were able to brief the Resistance groups that were now starting to spring up across Europe. They told the Resistance agents what to search for and asked them to report back any relevant findings. So, following this first identification of a Würzburg, things began to move quickly. The Belgian

Resistance reported the existence of a similar sounding apparatus just north of a German night fighter base at St Trond,
thirty-five miles east of Brussels. Jones again asked for aerial
photographs to be taken and when these came through he
realised that this was an even larger bowl-like structure.
Moreover, there were two large radar bowls and three searchlights situated around this site. Then another large site was
spotted at Domburg on an island in the Scheldt estuary. Once
again, Jones let Tony Hill know of this and he went out and
took two more perfect low-level photographs, giving a full face
and a side view of the equipment. Again there were two radar
installations but this time there were no searchlights. Jones
called these new structures 'Giant Würzburgs'.

A debate began within the scientific intelligence community as to how these devices worked. Was the second Giant
Würzburg merely a back-up to the first? Or did the two
machines work in tandem in some way? Jones speculated that
one machine was there to track an Allied bomber, while the
other followed the intercepting German fighter and directed
it precisely to the bomber. If this was the case, the Würzburg
must operate on an extraordinary level of accuracy for the two
machines to line up together. Jones realised that this required a
level of precision engineering and manufacturing that was way
beyond anything British scientists had designed so far.

Others disagreed, saying it was not possible that two
machines could be linked. British bomber crews were increasingly reporting terrifyingly accurate anti-aircraft fire when
they approached the western borders of Germany and said
this was directed at them by searchlights. Could the Giant
Würzburgs be some form of gun-laying system that controlled

both searchlights and anti-aircraft fire? The discussions and the disagreements continued. But it was clear that there were many unanswered questions about the Würzburg, how it operated and what its real function was.

Jones noticed that although the Würzburg photographed so brilliantly at Bruneval was on the top of a 300-foot cliff, there was a descent through the cliffs nearby to the beach below. It occurred to him that a raiding party might be able to land on the beach, climb the cliffs and capture the equipment. If they were able to bring it back to England it might be possible to examine it and answer many of the questions that were bothering the scientific community. Moreover, once they understood how the device worked it might be possible to devise ways to jam it or distort it as had been done with other systems, like the navigational beams used by the Germans to guide bombers to their targets. But Jones realised that to send a raiding party would be a highly dangerous exercise and put many lives at risk. So he hesitated to put a proposal forward.

A few days later, in mid December 1941, Jones was talking with W.B. Lewis, deputy superintendent of TRE and A.P. Rowe's assistant. He too had seen the intriguing photographs of the installation at Bruneval and his team had joined the debate as to how the Würzburg worked. The idea of a raid came up and Lewis immediately said that if Jones proposed it, TRE would support the idea.[5] Both men knew that Churchill strongly favoured such missions, relatively small-scale actions designed to create maximum disturbance for the enemy.

Jones was a member of the Air Staff, effectively the governing body of the Air Ministry, and so he raised it here. With TRE's active backing, the idea of a raid to capture the radar equipment was taken up. The Air Staff passed on a request to Combined Operations headquarters, where it landed on the desk of its ambitious new commander, Lord Louis Mountbatten, who was eagerly looking for opportunities to show off the skills of his newly trained forces. He realised what a great coup and a tremendous boost to morale a successful raid would be, not only at home but also in showing the Allies and the rest of the world that British forces could hit back at the enemy. All the pieces were falling into place.

9

Combined Operations

As he surveyed his new command at Combined Operations headquarters in late December 1941, Admiral Louis Mountbatten was more conscious than most that the war was going disastrously for the Allies. Britain had received a boost when, on 7 December, two days after Tony Hill had taken the spectacular oblique photograph at Bruneval, America joined the war following the Japanese attack on the US Navy's Pacific Fleet at Pearl Harbor. When Churchill heard the news late that evening on the radio at Chequers, he was elated. For eighteen months he had tried to persuade the United States to commit to the war effort. He spoke on the transatlantic telephone to President Roosevelt, who told him, 'We're all in the same boat now.' With America in the war, Churchill was sure that victory would follow ... eventually. He went to bed that night and 'slept the sleep of the saved and thankful'.[1]

But in the days and weeks following the entry of the United

States into the war, the situation became dire indeed. Only four hours after the air strike at Pearl Harbor, the Japanese army in China launched its assault upon the British colony of Hong Kong. On that same day Japanese troops began landing in Thailand and Malaya. Admiral Sir Tom Philips sailed from Singapore with two Royal Navy battleships, HMS *Prince of Wales* and HMS *Repulse*, to challenge the Japanese invasion fleet in the Gulf of Siam. But, sailing without air cover, they were spotted, and both ships were attacked and sunk by the Japanese air force. With the American fleet heavily mauled at Pearl Harbor and the last two Allied capital ships in the area now gone, Japan was supreme in the Pacific. If there had been any doubt beforehand, this victory for Japanese air power showed that the era of the battleship was finally over.

Japanese forces swept south into the Malayan peninsula and launched an invasion of the Philippines. On 24 December, US Marines on Wake Island surrendered to a Japanese invasion force. The following day, after a brief siege, the British garrison at Hong Kong surrendered. It had been a dreadful month of disaster and humiliation in the Pacific.

On the Russian front, the Soviets had lost more men and resources in the first six months after Hitler's invasion in June 1941 than any army had ever lost in history. Well over a million men had been taken captive. But the winter frosts and thick snow slowed the German advance and the Soviets succeeded in stopping the German army within just twenty-five miles of the capital, Moscow. Fresh winter troops from Siberia launched a counter-attack against the German forces, who were not prepared for winter fighting in the bitter cold. But the good news from Moscow was balanced by the horrors facing the men and women of the second city of Leningrad, under siege from the German army whose Panzers surrounded the city. Under constant artillery bombardment and cut off from supplies, the civilians began a bitter ordeal of endurance and starvation. On Christmas Day alone, more than four thousand Leningrad residents died of starvation. Their suffering was to continue for another two years.

In the Mediterranean, Italian divers disabled two British battleships, HMS *Valiant* and HMS *Queen Elizabeth*, in Alexandria harbour. The Royal Navy had four battleships put out of action in ten days. Adding in the American losses at Pearl Harbor, the Allies had lost an incredible total of twelve battleships in two weeks. In North Africa, Hitler had sent his favourite general, Erwin Rommel, with a Panzer corps to assist his retreating Italian allies. A see-saw war then developed, and after Rommel's early victories, the Eighth Army under General Auchinleck turned the tide. As Rommel retreated, British forces advanced once again into Libya, captured Benghazi and pushed on towards Tripoli. But the British advance ran out of steam and on 21 January Rommel launched a counter-attack. Within a little more than a week he had recaptured Benghazi and pushed further east until he was stopped on the Gazala Line, not far from Tobruk and the Egyptian border.

As a trading, maritime nation Britain depended upon supplies arriving by sea, especially ammunition, vehicles and war material coming by convoy from North America across the Atlantic. But U-boats roamed the choppy Atlantic waters and caused carnage when they spotted a convoy in mid-ocean. Churchill called it the 'Battle of the Atlantic', and knew that winning this conflict was essential for Britain's survival. But here too, the war was going badly. The U-boats had a field day after America's entry into the war. Ranging up and down the eastern seaboard of the United States they sank unprotected vessels along the coast with impunity. The U-boat crews enjoyed the easiest hunting of the war and spoke of it as the 'happy times'.

Moreover, before Pearl Harbor, the Royal Navy had been making progress in hunting down the U-boats by intercepting German Enigma messages. Every time a U-boat reported back giving its precise location, the coded message was picked up and deciphered at Bletchley Park. But in early 1942, the Kriegsmarine, growing suspicious, added a fourth rotor blade to their Enigma machine. This meant that the code permutations were increased by a factor of twenty-six. The code-breakers at Bletchley Park were left completely in the dark. It took nearly a year to recover from the blow and to compute a new system for breaking the codes. In the meantime, the U-boats were sinking nearly a hundred ships each month. Not only were thousands of merchant seamen tragically losing their lives, but hundreds of thousands of tons of much-needed rations and war supplies were ending up at the bottom of the sea. Britain faced ultimate defeat if the country were starved of the necessities of fuel and foodstuffs and of the supplies needed for keeping up the war effort.

It was in the context of the grim ongoing news of these disasters at sea and retreats on all fronts that Lord Mountbatten began to reorganise Combined Operations. He inherited from Sir Roger Keyes an office on loan from Scotland Yard in Richmond Terrace off Whitehall with a tiny staff, including typists and messengers, of only twenty-three people. But Churchill had great ambitions for the new command. He wanted it not only to plan small raids along the coast of occupied Europe, but also to begin planning for the full-scale invasion of Europe that would inevitably come, now the Americans were in the war, in a year or two. With his characteristic bulldog spirit, Churchill told Mountbatten, 'I want you to turn the south coast of England from a bastion of defence into a springboard of attack.'[2]

Within six months, Combined Operations' staff had grown to over four hundred. The generations-old jealousies between the three services that had held up the development of a true combined spirit under the prickly Keyes were soon dispersed under Mountbatten. Genuinely committed to finding new ways of carrying offensive operations into Europe, he found himself surrounded by men who were not only a lot older but who had decades more military experience. About this strange new world he wrote that he was often 'taking the Chair at meetings at which I always seem to be the youngest person in the room'.[3]

Mountbatten reorganised the headquarters staff, splitting it into two. The first section, Administration, was to be largely run by naval officers. The second, Operations, was itself split into Planning, Intelligence, Training and Communications. It was charged with finding targets for small-scale raids, co-ordinating the intelligence work of several different agencies, finding the right equipment and training units in the new techniques needed. Most of this was done in Scotland.

There was some overlap between the work of Combined Operations and that of the Special Operations Executive, which Churchill had created to liaise with European underground movements to carry out acts of sabotage and create havoc in occupied territories. This had caused friction under Keyes. Mountbatten met with Hugh Dalton, the head of SOE, and they agreed to work together rather than to squabble. All raids of under thirty men were to be carried out by SOE, larger incursions by Combined Operations.[4]

Mountbatten started a recruitment drive, but only wanted officers who had a genuine commitment to working with the other services. He toured the Royal Navy's officer cadet schools and encouraged the next generation of naval officers to put down 'Combined Ops' on their preference forms for where to be allocated on graduation. By contrast, Mountbatten was heavily criticised in private for bringing in some of his old cronies to support him. The man he recruited to head the Intelligence section, the Marquis of Casa Maury, was a rich, glamorous racing driver who had been part of Mountbatten's 'set' before the war. But he also brought in many brilliant minds who applied new thinking to the challenges ahead. They included scientists such as the maverick boffin Geoffrey Pyke, whose vivid imagination was to come up with some of the most remarkable ideas of the war. One of these was for a giant, impregnable aircraft carrier to be constructed out of reinforced ice in the middle of the Atlantic. Pyke constantly railed against the Whitehall and military machine, which seemed to believe 'nothing should ever be done for the first time'.

Mountbatten then recruited as scientific advisers physicist J.D. Bernal and Professor Solly Zuckerman, who had carried out important research on the impact of bombing. Zuckerman's first task was to estimate the number of nights in a month that would be ideal for small raids on the French coast. He scrutinised the meteorological records to find the number of nights at which wind speeds were less than Force 5, and combined this with a study of when the moon was full and the tides were right. He came back to Mountbatten to report proudly, 'it turns out that there will never be a night suitable for a small raid.'[5] Despite this useless conclusion, Zuckerman went on to carry out invaluable work for Combined Operations, including a later study that established to everyone's surprise that most injuries to soldiers taking part in raids came not from rifle or machine-gun fire but from mortar shells. Zuckerman went on to a distinguished career and in the 1960s became Chief Scientific Adviser to the British government.

By the end of 1941, the headquarters at Richmond Terrace had become a lively place where all sorts of remarkable and adventurous ideas were debated and pursued. Mountbatten called it 'The only lunatic asylum in the world run by its own inmates.'[6]

The initial thinking was that Combined Operations should attempt to mount commando raids on a rather bigger scale than the tiny pinpricks launched along the French coast so far. On the night of 23 November 1941, just four weeks after Mountbatten had taken over command, one of the old types of raid took place when a group of eighty-eight officers and men from 9 Commando landed at Houlgate, near Deauville, on the French coast. The raid was on a small scale but the radios failed and the operation showed that the commando forces had not yet learnt how to keep communications open between the men on land and the ships out at sea. This would prove to be a continuing problem in the months ahead.

A far bigger commando raid, and one much more in line with Mountbatten's ambitions for his forces, took place at the end of December on the western coast of Norway. The country was a vital link in Germany's supply chain of Swedish iron ore, which was carried via the port of Narvik onto shipping that took it south to Germany. Mountbatten's objective was to get the Germans to strengthen their forces in Norway as a way of reducing the pressure on Russia. On the morning of 27 December, a commando force of 51 officers and 525 men supported by a small flotilla of cruisers landed at the port of Vaagsö. An air raid by RAF Hampden bombers was timed to divert the Germans from the raid. German shipping gathered in the fjords around Vaagsö before making the dash south into the Baltic. The commando raid achieved complete surprise, overwhelmed the small German garrison, captured many PoWs and blew up much of the port's infrastructure. The raiders departed just a few hours after they had arrived.

Although there were losses among the raiding party, the mission was a total success in that it encouraged the Germans to substantially reinforce the Norwegian coast. Knowing how important it was to maintain the supply of iron ore for his war machine, Hitler announced that the Kriegsmarine must defend the long coastline of Norway as a matter of priority, and early in 1942 three extra divisions of ground troops were sent to reinforce the garrison. Hitler declared that 'Norway is the zone of destiny in this war' and continued to send troops to guard his supply routes that could instead have been playing a role on the Russian front or in North Africa. By 1944, the garrison in Norway was to stand at 372,000 men. The Vaagsö raid helped to distract German forces from other fronts and to divert them into spending months and years defending thousands of miles of ice and fjords. And it had been the first

genuinely combined operation organised by Mountbatten's
new and growing staff.

In the days following the Vaagsö raid, Mountbatten set up a
team to search for objectives in France. His planning staff
included two key players. Captain John Hughes-Hallett of the
Royal Navy was a distinguished sailor who had fought in the
Norwegian campaign and was at this point Mountbatten's chief
of staff. He was keen to encourage raids on the French coast to
probe the strengths and weaknesses of the enemy's defences.
David Luce was a young commander from a naval family and
would rise to be First Sea Lord in the 1960s. In late December
these members of Mountbatten's staff started to consider
whether to commit soldiers for a combined forces raid on the
Würzburg radar installation at Bruneval.

In addition to achieving the specific object of capturing vital
radar equipment for the scientists to examine, Mountbatten
knew that a successful raid would act as a great fillip to the
nation. So, from the first assessment of the concept of the
Bruneval raid, the value of a successful raid in boosting morale
was part of everyone's thinking. But there were several questions for the planners to answer before a full-scale plan could be
put forward. Was a sea landing possible? Not only was the
coast at Bruneval well defended with minefields, machine-gun
posts and gun emplacements, but once ashore a raiding party
would have to advance up the steep ascent in the valley
between the cliffs. If the enemy defenders were unable to repel
the commandos on the beaches, then they would certainly be
waiting for them as they advanced up the cliff. Even if the landing was successful, the Germans would be fully warned and
likely to rigorously defend the radar installation on the cliff top.

Mountbatten's staff quickly decided that the best way to maintain the key elements of speed and surprise was not to use commandos to land on the beaches but to employ the other new force available to Combined Operations. Mountbatten decided he would use airborne troops for the first time. Paratroopers would drop about half a mile inland and would advance to the coast in order to launch the attack on the radar battery. But even if this were successful, there were further challenges to consider. How should the fragile equipment itself be captured? And then, most importantly, how could they transport it, along with the raiding party, back to Britain?

On 8 January 1942, Mountbatten summoned General Browning, the new commander of the 1st Airborne Division, to Combined Operations headquarters to ask if he thought his men could carry out the raid. Mountbatten also approached Group Captain Sir Nigel Norman, the man at the RAF charged with co-operation with the Airborne, to ask if he could organise transportation of the paratroopers to the French coast.

Browning was immediately impressed with the plan and with Mountbatten's enthusiasm for it.[7] He was keen to carry out such a mission and to make amends for the miserable baptism of fire twelve months earlier when all the men in the raid on the Italian aqueduct had been captured. But there were real problems for him in mounting a raid of the scale needed with his troops in their current state. Trained men were thin on the ground. To mount an effective operation, Browning realised that he would need to find troops of roughly a company in strength, that is about 120 men. Moreover, realistically, he had to face the prospect of losing the entire force if the raid went wrong or the men were captured *en masse*, as in southern Italy.

This would be tough to take for a unit that was only slowly coming up to strength.

Within the recently formed Parachute Brigade, the 1st Battalion was nearing the completion of its training. It was led by a tough, forceful commander, Lieutenant Colonel Down, whose nickname was 'Dracula'. But Browning felt he wanted to keep the unit intact in case there was a sudden call for an operation of battalion strength. Browning and the brigade commander, Richard Gale, decided that although the 2nd Battalion was only partially trained, it was better to select a company from this unit. If it was lost in its entirety it could be replaced and the battalion could carry on with its training and later come together as a complete unit.

So Browning and Gale settled on the 2nd Battalion. Looking across the range of companies on offer, they quickly decided to select C Company – known in the battalion as 'Jock Company', since it was made up mostly of Scottish troops. These were hard men originally from some of the toughest regiments in the British Army. There was only one problem. Major John Frost, who until the end of the previous year had been adjutant to the battalion, had recently been appointed the new commander of C Company, but he was still recovering from the knee operation following his disastrous second parachute jump. He had not made sufficient jumps to qualify as a paratrooper and wear his wings. But his predecessor, Philip Teichman, was a good soldier too. Browning knew that whoever was in command would do a good job and so he decided to put up C Company for this very special new mission.

On 21 January, the same day that Rommel launched his counter-attack in Libya, the three Chiefs of Staff discussed

Mountbatten's plan in Downing Street. This was the highest
group within the British military, a sort of battle headquarters
at the apex of Britain's war effort. At this time of the war the
Chiefs of Staff usually met daily in the morning and consisted
of the heads of the three military services, Admiral Sir Dudley
Pound, Air Chief Marshal Sir Charles Portal and General Sir
Alan Brooke, the newly appointed Chief of the Imperial
General Staff (CIGS). Churchill as Prime Minister and Minister
of Defence had the right to attend meetings but rarely did so.
He was represented by his military chief of staff, General Sir
Hastings Ismay, who would report back to him after every
meeting.[8] Other military and intelligence chiefs would attend as
and when necessary.

The Chiefs of Staff meeting on 21 January had a variety of
major issues to weigh up, including the response to the dramatic Japanese advance down the Malayan peninsula, the
defence of Burma, which was key to defending India from
Japanese assault, and whether or not to order the sinking of
Italian merchant ships carrying supplies to the enemy forces
in North Africa. At this meeting, Mountbatten presented the
case for the paratrooper raid at Bruneval, explaining that it had
been suggested by Air Ministry scientific intelligence and was
intended to provide long-term help to the RAF by obtaining
details of a new German radar. He pointed out that Churchill
was in favour of this type of raid.

Portal, the RAF chief, supported the raid as expected, on the
grounds that the RAF wanted to reduce their losses from
radar-directed anti-aircraft fire and night fighters. Pound, the
head of the Royal Navy, was unenthusiastic. Against the avalanche of calamities that faced Britain, it seemed like a drop in

the proverbial ocean. The CIGS, Brooke, sat on the fence and tried to assess objectively the possibilities of success.

It was unusual for a group at this high level to discuss the objectives of a military unit of barely 120 men. But so important were such small missions at this stage of the war that Britain's top military chiefs devoted some time to assessing the risks and the possible advantages of a raid at Bruneval, even when they had so many other weighty strategic matters to consider. They realised the propaganda value of a successful paratrooper mission and, with Mountbatten arguing persuasively for the raid, gave formal approval two days later on 23 January.[9]

As the bitterly cold winter month of January 1942 turned into the even harsher month of February, so the war situation became even worse. On 12 February, the Germans jammed British naval radar installations in the area around Dover and so effectively blinded the eyes of the Royal Navy along the south coast. Then, two German battle cruisers that had been sheltering and refitting in Brest harbour, the *Scharnhorst* and *Gneisenau*, along with the cruiser *Prinz Eugen*, slipped out of their moorings and made a dash up the English Channel in broad daylight. They succeeded in sailing the length of the Channel, evaded the batteries at Dover and reached the safety of the German ports in the North Sea. All three German ships were badly damaged during their journey, but as far as most Britons were concerned what became known as the 'Channel Dash' was a shocking humiliation. Where was the Royal Navy? Where was the RAF? Why did the big guns at Dover not engage with the German capital ships? The press were up in arms. Even the *Daily Mail*, usually so loyal, published a leader criticising the Prime Minister.

Only three days after this humiliation came one of the greatest disasters of the war. In early January, Japanese troops had
broken through the defences of the Slim river on the Malayan
peninsula and poured further south. After the fall of the
capital Kuala Lumpur, the demoralised, disorganised British,
Indian and Australian defenders had retreated to the fortress of
Singapore that was believed in Britain to be impregnable. The
British had spent huge funds on building up the defences of
Singapore in the inter-war years and the heavy guns placed
there had become a symbol of British power in Asia. But the
defences had been designed exclusively to prevent an attack
from the sea. Now, the Japanese advanced down the Malayan
peninsula and attacked from the undefended landward
side. The fortress of Singapore surrendered to Japanese land
forces after barely a fight. More than sixty thousand British and
Australian troops became captives of the Imperial Japanese
Army and began a three-year nightmare in Japanese prisoner-
of-war and labour camps where half of them would die. News
of the defeat went out like ripples across Asia, where it was
seen that British power and authority had been challenged yet
again by the Japanese Blitzkrieg, and had failed. Churchill felt
the surrender was not just a defeat but a disgrace and described
it to Conservative Party colleagues as 'the greatest disaster to
British arms which our history records'.[10]

Even though there were further defeats to come, the second
half of February 1942 was possibly the lowest point in the war.
After Rommel's advances in North Africa, a dramatic increase
in shipping losses in the North Atlantic, the humiliation of the
'Channel Dash' and the surrender of Singapore, Churchill was
under pressure to reshuffle his government and agreed to

refocus the War Cabinet. He was exhausted by the strain. His daughter, Mary, had lunch with him on 27 February in Downing Street and wrote in her diary, 'Papa is at a very low ebb . . . He is not too well physically . . . and he is worn down by the continuous crushing pressure of events.'[11] The nation and the Prime Minister desperately needed a success to promote British arms and restore confidence.

10

Underground Intelligence

The proposed raid on Bruneval was codenamed 'Operation Biting' and the first great need in its detailed planning was to find out details of the German troops deployed along this stretch of coast. It was also essential to discover the locations of minefields and other defensive measures like machine-gun emplacements that might be hidden from aerial photography. This involved human intelligence (known in the business as HUMINT), which entailed getting someone on the ground to take a detailed look at the various locations.

It was not going to be easy. The Channel coast of northern France was well defended and heavily garrisoned, and parts were closed military zones. The coast was crawling with enemy soldiers and visitors were most definitely not welcome. But there were friends in France, members of the French Resistance, who demonstrated extraordinary bravery and had built up networks to report back on enemy activities in the occupied territories. Most of these organisations were controlled out of London by the Bureau de Contre-Espionage, de Renseignement et d'Action (BCRA), commanded by a French Intelligence chief known as 'Passy'. His real name was Major André Dewarin. He worked for General Charles de Gaulle, the self-appointed leader of Free French troops, based at offices in Carlton Gardens in central London.

One of the biggest underground networks in northern France was called La Confrérie de Notre Dame (the Brotherhood of Notre Dame), a network that believed itself to be a brother-hood aided by God. Its leader was a Frenchman named Gilbert Renault who was an extraordinary individual, as one needed to be to survive and operate as an underground intelligence officer in occupied France. His father was a professor of philoso-phy and he was brought up in an intensely Catholic family. Before the war Renault had worked in the French cinema indus-try and in finance and had travelled extensively to London, and even more frequently to Spain.

Aged thirty-six when war was declared, he was frustrated when on volunteering for military service he was turned down because of the size of his family. He had four young children including a baby, Manuel, of just a few months. He lived in Vannes near the Brittany coast and was there when the Germans invaded in May 1940. A month later, with the com-plete collapse of the French army imminent and German forces speeding across northern France, Renault decided to take the bold and rather romantic step of trying to get to England to join a volunteer army to fight on abroad. His wife, Edith, had only just become pregnant again, but Renault decided it was his duty to France to somehow continue the struggle.

With the Germans only a few miles away, he explained to Edith, 'We don't have the right to let ourselves be taken. The war must go on. If we give in, if Germany becomes mistress of Europe, life won't be worth living.' If, on the other hand, she told him he must stay, he said, then he would remain. 'No, go!' she said tearfully.[1]

He and his younger brother escaped on a trawler and a Norwegian cargo ship, finally reaching Falmouth only to hear that their Great War hero, General Pétain, had asked for an armistice. France had surrendered. Renault was shattered by the humiliating news.

In London, Renault and his brother, Claude, volunteered for General de Gaulle's nascent Free French forces. Claude eventually joined up. Frustrated by endless delays, Renault managed to convince the authorities that he could do better work by setting up an intelligence network in Madrid through which he could smuggle messages in and out of France. British SIS officials were asked by the French to give him instructions on how to operate as a secret agent. They proved to be very rudimentary: a talk on how to code messages into five-letter sets lasted only ten minutes. Renault was left bemused by the lesson, but was a great lover of codes and soon worked out the practice of coding he was to adopt. He briefly met General de Gaulle on the staircase of his headquarters and explained that he was about to lead a secret mission to France. The tall Frenchman, now commanding the Free French army in exile, turned to him, shook him by the hand and said, 'Au revoir, Raymond. I rely on you.'[2]

The following day Renault flew out to Portugal on an Imperial Airways flying boat. From Lisbon he made his way to

Madrid and began to formulate his network, on the pretence
that he was a French film producer setting up a film about
Christopher Columbus. Despite an amateurish start, somehow
Renault picked up the necessary techniques to begin to create
a communications network and started to send dispatches back
to London. In November 1940, he managed to return undercover to his beloved France. He entered the non-occupied
zone run from Vichy which at this stage of the war made up
most of the south-eastern half of France. But he quickly made
contacts and crossed into the German-occupied zone in the
north-western half of the country. There he met old friends
and family contacts, and on the basis of introductions to what
he was told were honourable patriots who wanted to 'do something to help', he began to recruit agents to report on German
activities in occupied France. He looked for people working at
key locations like docks, ports and railway stations, and inside
requisitioned factories.

The recruitment of many volunteers only took a few minutes.
'You understand what you are taking on?' Renault would ask
the stranger.

'I do, monsieur,' would be the reply.

'You realise that it is dangerous work and what the consequences could be for you and your family if you are caught?' he
would ask.

'I do, monsieur,' was the second reply. If Renault was convinced of their integrity, they were in.

Renault relied upon personal recommendations, as there was
nothing else to go on. He took relatively few precautions in the
early stages and even the extended families of the recruits
would know what was going on. Renault himself wore a rather

flashy suit, bought in London, that made him stand out from the crowd, quite unlike most undercover agents who preferred to look completely anonymous.

Renault gave every new agent a nickname, and these were the only names by which agents knew one another, so no one knew anyone else's real name. 'Hilarion' was someone who made Renault laugh, 'Lhermite' was the quiet one, 'Pedro' the one who looked like a Spaniard, 'Pol' the one called Roger who liked champagne. Renault himself acquired several names, but the one he became best known by was 'Rémy'.

Rémy's instructions were to obtain information about German activities in the French Atlantic ports, from Bordeaux in the south-west right up to Brest in Brittany. The intelligence chiefs in London wanted to know where U-boat pens were being built and how they were being constructed, as well as where some of the big German warships took refuge between outings into the Atlantic. Local dock employees began to acquire valuable information. In April 1941, Rémy's agents were first to spot the *Scharnhorst* and *Gneisenau* in Brest harbour. But the process of getting information across the border to Madrid and from there to London was cumbersome and slow, taking at least two weeks.

So, in May, British Intelligence sent Rémy a radio transmitter to speed up messaging. But this brought new risks, as the Germans could detect the sending of radio signals and in time track down their source. The first radio operator, Bernard Anquetil, was caught while in the process of sending a message. He was taken away and tortured by the Gestapo. Suddenly, Rémy's network became far more aware of the risks it was taking. It had to be assumed that Anquetil had named names under torture and the whole network was closed down. But like many French underground agents, the radio operator did not talk, and the network survived.

In August, the Gestapo infiltrated and broke another underground intelligence network covering the northern coast. Rémy himself was arrested briefly, but remarkably managed to talk himself out of trouble and get away. Once his network had recovered, Rémy was asked by the BCRA in London to take on a new northern operation and more patriots were recruited to make up the losses. New, smaller radio transmitters were dropped in by parachute and before long Rémy was managing a vast supply of intelligence dispatches to London, providing increasingly important information about what was happening along the French coast. A radio operator known only as 'Bob' was sent from Britain to help in the process of sending messages. It was at this moment, with his underground network still growing, that on 24 January 1942, while he was staying in a rented flat in Paris, Rémy received a detailed message from London requesting some new and precise information.

Like most of the coded messages sent to the French underground from London, there were two halves to the communication, neither of which would mean much without sight of the other. Rémy himself decoded the messages. They asked for details of the defences along the stretch of coast northeast of Le Havre, in the area around the villages of Bruneval and Theuville. The message asked for five specific pieces of information. First, how many machine guns were there defending the road heading inland from the coast? Second, what other defences were there in the area? Third, what was the number and state of preparedness of the defenders? Fourth, where were they billeted? And, finally, there was a request for information on the existence and positioning of barbed wire and minefields along this stretch of coast. It was made clear that Rémy was not to undertake a mission to Bruneval himself and that he should tell the agent who was to carry out the local search that several other coastal locations were being investigated in the same way, so that in the event of the agent being captured and tortured not too much emphasis would be put on this single underground reconnaissance.

On decoding the message, Rémy immediately called up one of the leaders of his northern section, the man he had named Pol, whose real name was Roger Dumont. Pol came over to Rémy's flat that evening. The two men discussed the message and what it could mean. They studied the local Michelin map of the area. Dumont knew there were well-guarded German radio installations just to the north of the spot they were being asked to reconnoitre. But it didn't sound to them as if the British were planning a bombing mission, so they concluded they must be thinking of organising some sort of coastal raid and needed ground intelligence about what they would be up against.

Rémy instructed Pol to carry out the investigation as discreetly as possible. If the area was well defended it was not going to be easy to uncover the details the British were asking for. Rémy asked Pol how long he needed. 'Ask them to give me a fortnight,' replied Pol. As Rémy bade him goodbye, he said, 'Watch yourself now, my dear fellow.'

Pol sought the local services of another underground agent he knew only by the nickname of Charlemagne. The agent's

real name was Charles Chauveau and he knew this stretch of
coast well. A garage proprietor and mechanic in Le Havre, he
was one of the few Frenchmen who had a permit to drive anywhere in the Département of Seine-Inférieure, which covered
the coastal area around Bruneval.[3] He was allowed access in
order to visit and repair cars that had broken down. After a few
days, Pol met up with Charlemagne and travelled to Le Havre.
They stayed overnight in a hotel Charlemagne knew where no
questions would be asked and no identity cards were needed.
But it was bitterly cold, the room was damp and Pol sat up fully
dressed all night, shivering.

The next morning the two men headed off along the coast
road in Charlemagne's French Simca car, its permit to travel
clearly on display in the windscreen. Charlemagne had
obtained chains for two of his tyres, as he had been warned that
the steep roads in the Bruneval area were covered with up to
two feet of snow lying on compacted ice.

Pol and Charlemagne kept to the side roads, driving cautiously through this heavily garrisoned stretch of coast not
wanting to attract attention. Before too long they entered
Bruneval village from the east, and one of the first houses they
came to was the Hotel Beau-Minet. This was a well-known
establishment that had opened in 1914 in a nineteenth-century
chateau that used to belong to the local count. Located in a
quiet, tranquil and fairly remote valley, in the 1920s and 1930s
the hotel was often used on weekday nights by couples who
wanted to get away for a discreet romantic break. Questions
were never asked about whether the couple were married or
not. At weekends the Beau-Minet became a seaside hotel used
by local families. The fifteen rooms were well appointed and,

rarely for its time, the hotel had central heating, meaning it could stay open for most of the year.[4]

Charlemagne knew the couple who ran the hotel, Paul Vennier and his Swiss wife, and believed they would be willing to tell Pol what they knew. He was right. The couple were happy to explain that sixty Luftwaffe men were stationed in a big square of farm buildings called Le Presbytère, just to the north on the cliffs. This was the spot near Theuville where the Germans had built the radio transmitters that Pol already knew of. It was obviously a closely guarded fortification, and the fact that it was manned by the Luftwaffe meant that it must have something to do with aircraft communications.

But when Pol asked about the other building on the cliff tops, the Venniers admitted that they knew nothing about what had happened to the large villa up there since the Germans had occupied the area, nor did they know who was based there. A strange structure, clad in flint, with tall, steep roofs, the Villa Gosset had been built in the 1930s by a renowned surgeon, Professor Antonin Gosset, as a summer retreat by the sea. It was a well-known local landmark but, of course, the Venniers explained, it was now a military area and no civilian had been allowed up there for some time. They spoke about taking food and supplies up to Le Presbytère, but no one had been to the lone villa or the radio station nearby. They confirmed there was a guard post in another old seaside villa down by the beach named Stella Maris. Here there were about ten men who kept guard and manned the machine-gun positions. The Venniers thought they were not manned all the time but that the gunners could take up their positions quickly, within a few minutes.

They told their visitors that the Bruneval garrison consisted of an infantry platoon of thirty men under an enthusiastic and energetic sergeant. They were quartered in the hotel itself, which was now closed to all other visitors. The Venniers said they thought the troops were of a high calibre and were kept on their toes as the whole stretch of coast swarmed with German units that were regularly coming and going, some of them armoured.

The Venniers were taking a great risk in passing on this information about German military activity. If caught, they might face execution or, at best, transportation to a concentration camp. They would never have talked like this to strangers, but because Charlemagne was well known to them, they trusted him. They asked no questions as to why they were being quizzed. Far better, they realised, not to know.[5]

At the end of the conversation, Pol turned to Charlemagne. 'Right,' he said, 'let's go and have a look at the sea.'

'Oh, that's impossible,' Monsieur Vennier responded. 'The beach is mined.'

'Well, let's go and have a look anyway,' Pol insisted, and the two men headed off down the road towards the coast. They walked down through a sort of gorge cut between steep sloping cliffs on either side. Before the war this had obviously been a beautiful, peaceful spot. After a few hundred yards they came to a large barbed wire entanglement blocking the road. To the right, climbing the steep cliff side, was a path heading in the direction of the mysterious radio units on the cliff tops. Next to the barbed wire was the old seaside villa called Stella Maris. It was large and had clearly once been quite grand, but was now looking rather neglected and its paint was peeling off. Alongside it were large signs daubed with the message *Achtung*

Minen! A tall German sentry emerged from the villa to see what the two visitors were up to.

Charlemagne spoke good German and in a cheerful, jokey manner engaged the sentry in conversation. 'Good morning,' he said. 'I'm just taking a stroll with my cousin here. He's from Paris, you know, and feels he must see the sea before he goes home – shut up in a dark office all day long, you see. You know how they get, desperate!' By now the sentry was smiling and Charlemagne knew his friendly banter was making progress. 'Lucky you're here,' he went on, 'without you we wouldn't have dared to go any further. We see there are mines. Just imagine that!'

'*Ja, Tellerminen,*' came the response.

'I wonder if I dare suggest such a thing, but would you accompany us down to the shingle for a second. It would give my cousin so much innocent pleasure, I assure you.'

The Frenchman's sheer bravado paid off. The German sentry, clearly bored to death by his endless shifts in this godforsaken spot, replied '*Jawohl.*' He came forward and pulled aside an opening in the barbed wire. The two Frenchmen walked through, looking jolly and acting as though totally innocent. The German pulled the barbed wire across behind them and made them follow him as he walked across the top of the beach. They were amazed at how relaxed he seemed to be in walking through a supposed minefield.

Soon they were on a short stretch of beach underneath the cliffs. The beach was steep and consisted of large round pebbles. They had timed their visit for low tide and they could see no evidence of any underwater obstacles to prevent landing craft from coming ashore. While Charlemagne chatted away merrily to the German sentry and offered him a cigarette, Pol stood there, apparently daydreaming and enjoying the sea breeze. He turned right around and, still smiling with pretend delight at being by the sea, he looked up. He saw two machine-gun positions. One was just above the villa on the southern side of the gap in the cliffs. The other was on the northern side, much higher up the cliff. He could see the tip of a machine gun protruding from the lower position and could appreciate it was sighted to have an all-round field of fire across the beach. He even saw a German soldier up there, looking bored stiff, wearing a forage cap rather than a steel helmet, and a heavy greatcoat to try to keep out the icy wind. He could see no other barbed wire emplacements.

Thanking the German for his kindness, Charlemagne and his supposedly sea-loving cousin returned with the guard across the minefield and said goodbye. The two agents had only been there a few minutes, but their recce had been a stunning success and they had gathered immensely valuable intelligence. Not only had they located and identified the exact position of two machine-gun nests and established that there was no evidence of underwater beach obstacles, but they were convinced from the lack of caution shown by the sentry that the beach was in fact *not* mined. The menacing signs were there simply as a deterrent to keep any visitors with prying eyes well away. If the Germans did intend to mine the beach, no one had got around to it yet. This piece of intelligence by itself was priceless.

The two men returned up the gorge to the hotel. There they spent thirty minutes talking with local car owners, all of whom were having problems with getting spare parts. Replacing tyres was a particular problem, most of them being taken by the occupying forces. As a garage owner, Charlemagne's knowledge and contacts were much sought after. The conversation also provided a good cover for their visit.

On leaving it was nearly lunchtime, so Charlemagne took his 'cousin' a few miles inland to the local market town of Gonneville-la-Mallet. Here they stopped at the Restaurant des Vieux Plats, which Charlemagne knew well. It was a typical black market restaurant of the kind that had sprung up all across occupied France. The restaurant had the equivalent of two Michelin stars, and offered excellent local food at exorbitant prices. A few wealthy Frenchmen would visit such places, but they were more often frequented by senior German officers.

While finishing an excellent lunch with coffee and calvados, Pol called for the visitors' book. When they were alone he quickly copied the names of all the German officers who had visited the restaurant and signed the book. He knew that back in London their regiments could be traced from the German army lists. It would be a helpful guide as to which units were stationed along this stretch of coast.

Pol returned to Paris with a mass of detailed information which, written out and put into code, made up a message of several pages. He met up again with Rémy, who was shocked at how long the message was. It would be dangerous for a radio operator to send such a long message, as it would give the Germans plenty of time in which to track down the signal and locate where it was coming from. Rémy divided the message into two and tried hard to shorten both halves, but he realised there were some real gems of intelligence here. He was delighted with the work of his friend and colleague.

When the radio operator known as Bob came to collect

the message, Rémy warned him to be careful. It was now 9 February and Bob transmitted both messages to London that evening. By pure nerve and a dose of good luck, the two French underground agents had obtained invaluable intelligence from right under the noses of the German defenders at Bruneval. The information they had picked up would immediately be factored into the planning for the upcoming raid.

11

Training

In the third week of January, the company commanders of the 2nd Battalion of the Parachute Brigade were called together and informed that C Company was to go for special training immediately at Tilshead on Salisbury Plain. Nothing more was explained about what lay ahead. Major John Frost had still not completed his jumps after his knee injury and so was not qualified as a paratrooper. Instead, its previous commander, Philip Teichman, was told to lead the company. Suspecting that there might be action ahead and determined not to miss out, Frost protested that *he* should lead C Company. He was told that if he could complete his parachute training within a week then he could go as company commander. Otherwise, Teichman would resume command. Frost had to complete his six jumps as fast as possible.

At nine o'clock the following morning, Frost was waiting at the hangar at Ringway airport with his parachute loaded up and ready to go. The RAF had allocated only six Whitley bombers for training and they were now taxiing around the runway preparing to take the next stick of trainees on board. Frost was hoping to get in two jumps that morning. Then a mist began to drift across the airfield. In no time at all it had become a thick fog, and all flying was suspended. Frost waited with his parachute rolled up in his bag all day long, but there was not even a brief break in the fog for the Whitleys to get airborne and fly over to Tatton Park, where as usual the jumps were to take place.

On the following morning, thick fog still enclosed the airfield. With growing frustration, Frost swung, twisted and rolled through the various gym pieces that had been set up on the ground for paratroopers to train on. He watched the women of the WAAF folding and packing parachutes. In the British forces, WAAFs, not the parachutists themselves, packed the parachute bags. A sign on the wall reminded each WAAF that a man's life depended upon her packing the parachute correctly. Frost mused that very few of the fatalities that now occurred were due to bad packing; usually they were the consequence of some freak accident. But each packer had to sign for the parachute bag she had packed, and Frost imagined that a poor WAAF would come in for a lot of grief if a jump did go wrong in one of her parachutes.

Late in the afternoon the fog began to clear. Frost got himself a place in the first plane out and ten minutes after take-off had made a safe landing at Tatton Park. He persuaded a driver to take him quickly back to Ringway and talked his way on to the last plane that afternoon. He managed to complete a second jump, but as it was getting dark he nearly landed in a tree in the middle of the park. Jumping out of aircraft was still something that Frost, like most of the other men, found counter-intuitive. But he screwed up his courage, even though each jump took a lot out of him, emotionally as well as physically.

Including the two he had made in December, he took his fifth jump the following afternoon. And on the following day, in near perfect, clear January weather, he made his sixth. He had qualified at last. A WAAF assistant sewed the wings on to the right shoulder of his jacket – the insignia was worn here so as not to mix up paratroopers with the RAF, who wore their wings on their left breast, above the heart. Frost was relieved to leave Ringway and proud to walk out with his silver wings on his shoulder. He celebrated with the colonel that night over drinks in Chesterfield. But he was rather deflated when a friend told him that being a paratrooper was the surest way of becoming a prisoner that had ever been invented.[1]

Proudly wearing his wings, Frost now had to get back to his company to take command of the new and mysterious mission. He rushed down to Tilshead to replace Teichman. Teichman was angry and couldn't hide his disappointment at the speed with which Frost had qualified, but told him that as far as he had gathered, the whole exercise had the purpose of nothing more than training the company to put on a show for the War Cabinet. Only if the demonstration went well would something possibly follow. Teichman then made his way back to Hardwick to continue bringing B Company up to spec.

Frost was not encouraged by what he found at Tilshead. A new Glider Pilot Regiment had been formed and C Company were to share barracks with them. Salisbury Plain in late January was pretty desolate. There was mud everywhere, not only out in the field but inside the accommodation as well. Tilshead itself was a tiny village and the new camp outside it was an ugly, dirty dump.

His men arrived on 24 January dishevelled and exhausted after a long, arduous journey from Yorkshire. They had been delayed for several days by snow. Everyone looked wretched and felt miserable when, a day later, General Browning came over from the headquarters of the Airborne Division to inspect the company. Frost knew that Browning was a stickler for detail and believed that paratroopers should always look smart and behave well. He feared his men would not come up to muster and would be sent back to base.

Browning spent a long time on the inspection, talking to many of the paratroopers. At the end he turned to Frost and said, 'I think you've got a good lot of men here but I have never seen such a dirty company in all my life.'[2] But, instead of the rebuke he expected, a group of staff officers descended on Frost and for the first time ever began drawing up a long list of everything the company needed, in terms of new uniforms, warm clothing and equipment. In addition, the company was to be provided with enough transport to make them completely mobile, and enough ammunition to last for several days of training. Despite their demeanour, the men had obviously convinced Browning they had what it took.

On the following morning, Major Peter Bromley-Martin, a bright and cheerful staff officer with a bushy moustache, came over to see Frost and explained that a site had been found about twenty miles away at Alton Priors, near Devizes, that was similar to the site of their demonstration for the War Cabinet. The men were to practise dropping behind enemy lines and capturing an enemy headquarters. Then they were to drop down steep hills to a canal, terrain that resembled sea cliffs, which was where the real show would be laid on for the top brass, probably in the Dover area. Bromley-Martin explained that the company would be broken into four units, each of which would be dropped at intervals and would have a separate task for which it would be differently armed.

Frost took an instant dislike to the plan, and probably to the armchair staff officer who explained it. He insisted that he knew better. Everything in the British Army went in threes: a battalion was made up of three companies, a company was made up of three platoons and a headquarters section, and this should be the basis on which it operated in the field. He had experience of action and knew this was the way to function. The row rolled on into the afternoon when Frost followed Bromley-Martin back to Airborne headquarters and asked to see the general, only to be told that he was away. Another officer vehemently defended the four-unit plan. Frost argued with equal determination that he knew best and that if the demonstration was to look good it had to be done his way.

On the following day Bromley-Martin returned to Tilshead and took Frost aside. Swearing him to utter secrecy, he proceeded to explain that the story of the demonstration was a cover and that his company had been selected for a top secret mission behind enemy lines in occupied France. The men were to land with a group of Royal Engineers, capture some new kind of enemy apparatus, dismantle it and escape down steep cliffs to the coast, from where the Royal Navy would evacuate them. The plan had been devised to achieve this specific object. It was finally explained to Frost that if he had any further objections to the plan, then he would be replaced and someone else would be found who approved of it. At this point, still aghast at what he had been told and with a swell of excitement at the task ahead, Frost forgot all his objections and agreed that the plan sounded very strong – as long as the drops went well.

In fact, detailed operational orders for Operation Biting were still being drawn up in late January. The information from the French underground about the precise strengths and locations of the German defences had not yet come in. But planning was well under way. It had been decided that the mission would require technical support and that this would come primarily from the Royal Engineers section of the Airborne Division. They would jump with the rest of the paratroopers, but would not be expected to fight to capture the enemy installation unless absolutely necessary. Their responsibility would be the dismantling of the apparatus on the top of the cliff, and the paratroopers would then escort them down the steep gully to the beach, carrying everything that had been taken with them. This was why an unusual division of the company into four parties had been planned.

Headquarters needed to know that Frost would go along with this, and indeed with any changes that might come up in the planning of the raid over the next few weeks. Hence the decision to confide in him the true purpose of the training. Leadership of the operation would be vital. But divisional HQ had to be certain not only that he was the right commander but also that he would not breach their trust and let the men know what their mission really was. If there was any breakdown in security and the enemy knew of the arrival of the paratroopers, it would spell disaster for the raid.

Frost now enthusiastically set about organising a training schedule for his men. He kept to his word and did not reveal the true purpose of the training, despite tricky questions from his officers and senior NCOs. Company Sergeant-Major Gerry Alexander Strachan was a bull of a man who had been in the Black Watch, a tough Highland regiment, before transferring to the Parachute Brigade. He knew exactly how a company should be organised but was puzzled by the quantity of ammunition, usually in such short supply, that now started to arrive. Frost maintained that nothing was being spared for the demonstration. However, several men, like Sergeant Macleod Forsyth, immediately began to suspect that with all this ammunition being provided there was a combat mission in the offing.[3] Frost explained that the demonstration was to be a combined operation. The RAF would fly the men over to the drop zones and the Royal Navy would extract them from the beaches.

The company was split into four parties. An officer and nine sappers from the Royal Engineers arrived and started to train with the men. They had no more information about the real purpose of their training than anyone else. Reinforcements arrived from B Company to make up the numbers to the 120 men required. As they were transported around southern England in the bitter winter weather they would arrive back at their Tilshead base at all times of the day or night. The second-in-command, Captain John Ross, an unflappable, calm-talking Scotsman from Dundee, had to ensure that food was available for everyone at whatever time they got back. Despite the challenges, Frost was pleased to see that the company now started to settle down and to get on with its rigorous training regime.

The men were equipped with a brand new weapon in the

British Army, the Sten gun. This was a simple, easy-to-fire, light sub-machine gun with a side loading magazine that gave the weapon its distinctive look. Two British gun designers at the Royal Small Arms Factory at Enfield had designed the weapon to act as a homegrown version of the American Thompson sub-machine gun, the 'Tommy gun'.[4] The Sten, not unlike the Soviet AK-47 Kalashnikov in a later era, could be mass produced easily and cheaply and was the weapon SOE gave out for guerrilla, resistance and partisan operations. Manufactured in great numbers to equip the ever-growing British Army, it was an effective weapon at short range and could be fired at a sufficient rate to ensure that the enemy would keep his head down.

Its biggest fault was that the chamber had a tendency to clog up, resulting in stoppages.[5] The men of C Company soon discovered this horrible weakness and struggled to find ways to compensate. They now had to learn how to use the weapon in order to minimise the risk of blockages and to work together to lay down the firepower needed to be effective. Bruneval would be the baptism of fire for the Sten gun. Many questions would be asked of its combat use after the raid was over.

Along with the Sten came a new radio communications system called the 38, which was intended to keep the company commander in constant touch with his officers. Lighter than the standard British Army radio in use at the time, it was carried in a backpack, along with batteries. The 38 also seemed to be temperamental and, like the new weapon, required a lot of practice to use efficiently.

As this was a combined operation, it was not only the paratroopers who in January started to prepare for the raid. The air chiefs had to select a squadron to transport the Paras to their drop zones. Group Captain Sir Nigel Norman was put in command of the RAF operation. Norman was the most experienced officer in the RAF for this role. Before the war he had worked in civil aviation and his firm had helped in the design and layout of airfields at Gatwick, Birmingham and Manchester. From 1940, he had commanded the Central Landing Establishment at Ringway for some time. He had wanted to go on the first paratrooper mission to Italy but had been told he was not able to do so. In mid January 1942 he had begun to form a new wing to operate as an Army Co-operation Command to provide transport for airborne operations.

After months of delays due to lack of aircraft, the Air Ministry finally began the process of preparing specialised squadrons to drop paratroopers. But, like Browning when he was asked to select the men to carry out the raid, Norman now had to confront the problem that he did not yet have a single squadron trained, ready and available to support Operation Biting. So he selected 51 Squadron from Bomber Command and ordered it to withdraw its twelve Whitley aircraft from bombing duties and to begin training for this new mission. Each aircraft would carry ten men.

A hardened bomber unit, 51 Squadron had been flying night sorties over Germany and occupied Europe for nearly eighteen months. Its commander, Wing Commander Percy Charles Pickard, was a well-known and rather glamorous figure within the RAF. He had played a leading part in a dramatised documentary called *Target for Tonight* made by the Crown Film Unit in the summer of 1941, piloting his Wellington bomber, 'F' for Freddie, on an imaginary sortie over the Ruhr. The film had been widely shown in cinemas across Britain and had gone down especially well in the United States, where it won an honorary Academy Award. But Wing Commander Pickard was not just a film star in the eyes of his colleagues, he was a brave pilot who had already been awarded the Distinguished Flying Cross (DFC) and the Distinguished Service Order (DSO). He was one of the most experienced bomber pilots in the RAF. One of his pilots, Flying Officer Geoffrey Osborn, remembered him as a tall man and a magnificent leader who was widely liked, as he was known for looking after the crews he commanded. Dogs were not allowed on RAF stations but somehow an exception was made for Pickard, whose collie followed him everywhere around the base.[6] Pickard and his crews now cut holes in the fuselages of their Whitley bombers and began training in the science of getting men in pitch dark right over their precise drop zone and then dropping them out of the base of their aircraft.

On 7 February, Frost and some of his officers travelled to Thruxton airfield, where Pickard and his crews from 51 Squadron were starting their training. Frost was mightily impressed with the brash, confident attitude of the boys in RAF blue. Everyone recognised Pickard as the pilot who had starred in *Target for Tonight* and his coolness struck them all. RAF lingo at this point was all about understatement, about playing down the risks ahead and of assuming a casual, nonchalant attitude. All of this went down very well with the army officers and Frost concluded, 'We were left in no doubt as to their efficiency and we felt that if anybody was going to put us down in the right place, they were the people to do it.'[7]

The other component in the combined operation was the Royal Navy. Admiral Sir William 'Bubbles' James, the commander-in-chief at Portsmouth, was put in overall command of the operation. His rather unusual nickname came from the fact that he had sat as a four-year-old for his grandfather, the celebrated pre-Raphaelite artist John Millais, for a well-known Victorian painting showing a boy blowing bubbles with a pipe and a bowl of soap. The painting was later acquired by Pears Soap and used in a renowned advert for their product.[8] Living down this childhood association, Admiral James had gone on to lead a distinguished career in the Royal Navy. In 1916 he had joined the codebreakers in Room 40 of the Admiralty and had later become Deputy Director of Naval Intelligence.

Reporting to Admiral James was Commander Frederick Norton Cook of the Royal Australian Navy, who was appointed Naval Force Commander for the operation. Cook had joined the RAN at the age of thirteen and had spent his life at sea. In October 1939, he had been on board HMS *Royal Oak* when, at anchor in Orkney, it was hit by four torpedoes from a U-boat whose brave commander had dared to penetrate the holiest of holies of the Royal Navy, the anchorage at Scapa Flow. The *Royal Oak* went down in minutes with the loss of 810 men. In May 1940 he had been on HMS *Curlew* when it had been sunk off the Norwegian coast. Undeterred, Cook went on to establish and run the commando training base at the mouth of the Hamble in Southampton Water and he took part in some of the small-scale commando raids on the French coast during 1941. He named his training base HMS *Tormentor*.

In mid-January 1942 he was called to a meeting at the offices of Combined Operations in London where he met Captain John Hughes-Hallett and Commander David Luce. Hughes-Hallett immediately launched into a detailed outline of the plans for an airborne operation to raid the French coast. Cook listened with growing puzzlement as to what any of this had to do with him. Then Luce interrupted his colleague and said, 'Sir, shouldn't we tell Cook that he is to be the naval commander of this operation?' Cook realised that he had to pay serious attention to what was being said and the plans for the Bruneval raid were laid out before him. The planners told him that the first need was for complete secrecy. They explained that a conversation overheard in a pub could be reported back to Berlin in fifteen minutes, after which the entire stretch of French coast would be reinforced and on the alert for the raiders.[9]

On 9 February, Frost and C Company left their barracks on Salisbury Plain. Told they were going north by train, they had to remove all their wings and other insignia for the journey for security reasons, to prevent anyone from spotting that a parachute unit was heading north for training. Their new destination was Inveraray in north-west Scotland, on the northern bank of the long, thin sea loch known as Loch Fyne.

Inveraray was an old Scottish garrison town and the base from where much commando training and preparations for special operations took place. From there the Paras boarded the naval vessel HMS *Prinz Albert*, the parent ship of the flotilla of landing craft that were to take part in the raid and their base while in Scotland. A large and roomy vessel of about three thousand tons, the former Belgian passenger ship had been requisitioned by the Royal Navy after Belgium's fall in the summer of 1940. The function of the *Prinz Albert* was to carry landing craft to their point of embarkation. They were then lowered over the sides using davits. In addition to its crew of about 200 sailors, it could carry up to 250 soldiers who would normally climb down the side of the ship into the landing craft when they had arrived at their destination. Two and a half years later, the *Prinz Albert* was to play an important role off Omaha beach on D-Day.

After the desolation of Salisbury Plain, conditions on the *Prinz Albert* were rather good. The cabins and wardrooms on the naval vessel were far superior to the army barracks in Wiltshire and Frost and the officers were able to eat as much as they needed and to enjoy their spare time in the lounge given over to them as guests of the Royal Navy. The bar even served drinks at duty-free prices, and both officers and men took up the offer of cheap booze with relish.

A group of infantrymen were also sent north to train for the mission and assigned to the *Prinz Albert*. Their role would be to provide covering fire from the landing craft that were to go into the beaches to extract the Paras. John Brooker was in the Royal Fusiliers and found life on board a naval ship very strange. He had to sleep in a hammock and received a tot of rum each day in true Royal Navy tradition.[10] Sergeant Eric Gould of the South Wales Borderers also found himself training on the *Prinz Albert*, which became his home for a full seven weeks. He was delighted with what he called the 'luxury' conditions and later remembered, 'We were looked after marvellously as far as food was concerned. By comparison to army food, navy food was far superior.'[11]

On 12 February, soon after their arrival, the paratroopers were ordered to leave the ship, go ashore and make themselves scarce. So they deployed into the snow-covered hills above the loch. The captain of the *Prinz Albert*, Henry Peate, had been told that none other than Lord Louis Mountbatten was going to make a visit and he naturally assumed that the purpose was to inspect his ship and the flotilla of landing craft under his command. In fact, Mountbatten was visiting as commander of Combined Operations, in order to see the men who were going to take part in the raid. When he arrived on board the *Prinz Albert* he was astonished to find that none of the paratroopers were present. The embarrassed captain immediately gave orders to recall the Paras and the ship's sirens were frantically hooted. Thinking the ship was in trouble, Frost and his men rushed to the shore, where they were quickly transported back to the command vessel.

Mountbatten called all the men together, the paratroopers and the crew of the *Prinz Albert* alike. An inspiring speaker with a natural sense of command, he made a short but stirring speech which gave a great boost to everyone present. Mountbatten made it clear that they were working on a special mission. As far as Lieutenant John Timothy was concerned, he 'blew the gaff' that they were all now preparing for an actual mission and not a demonstration for the Prime Minister.[12] But he did not give away any details of what that mission was. The sailors were however told for the first time that their guests were parachutists. Few of them had ever met a parachutist before and the speech did a lot to impress the naval men with the calibre of the soldiers they were hosting. From then on they took a lot more interest in the Paras and in the task they were performing.

The purpose of this stage of the training programme was to practise linking up with the navy in order to be taken off beaches along Loch Fyne by landing craft at night. The idea was that the same sailors who operated the naval vessels here would man them during the operation in France. Most of the Paras had never before seen the new mark of vessel, called an Assault Landing Craft (ALC). It was forty feet long and ten feet wide, with a flat bottom and a draft of only about two feet. It could carry thirty-five soldiers and had a crew of four. In the bows there were doors, and beyond them two ramps that dropped down to allow the men to disembark.

Frost and his men were alarmed by the fact that on several practice night-time evacuations, the sailors commanding the ALCs were unable to find the beach where the paratroopers were waiting. Embarking at night was clearly not going to be as simple as they had imagined. Frost agreed with the flotilla commander to synchronise their radio communication throughout each planned evacuation. This seemed to improve the co-ordination between the Paras and the sailors. But Frost and his men were still troubled by the number of practice runs that went hopelessly wrong. Frost did not relish the thought of being abandoned on the coast of France after their raid because the navy could not find the right beach – although at this point he could not share this fear with his men, most of whom still thought they were preparing for a demonstration to senior politicians.

After a few more days practising night rendezvous along Loch Fyne, still without much success, the *Prinz Albert* headed south out of the loch. The parachutists were dropped off at Gourock from where they took the train back to Salisbury. It was now mid February, and the company next had to organise a practice jump outside divisional headquarters at Syrencote House. This was the first drop 51 Squadron had carried out and it took some time to organise the packing up of men and equipment at Thruxton airfield. The jump did not finally take place until late in the afternoon. The ground was rock hard but apart from a few bruises and strains there were no serious casualties. General Browning seemed pleased with the display.

The final stage of training for the raid took place along the south Dorset coast on army exercise grounds around Lulworth Cove, where the cliffs were similar to those the men would find on the other side of the Channel. The naval staff had mysteriously changed the system of radio communication that Frost had set up with the flotilla commander in Scotland. This did not help co-ordination between the navy and the army. They had four practice attempts at linking up with the landing craft, which had now sailed south from Scotland. Not one resulted in a successful evacuation.

Bad weather played its part in this dismal performance. On one run the landing craft successfully beached on the shore and the men clambered in, but the tide was going out and the landing craft could not get free to move off the beach. The men got out and pushed and shoved the landing craft, getting soaked in the freezing sea. But no amount of manhandling would free the landing craft, which were left like beached whales lying on the shingle as the tide went out.

Almost every day the paratroopers drove south from Tilshead to the coast, carried out another failed attempt and then drove back again in the dark, often soaking wet, freezing cold and miserable, to their camp on Salisbury Plain. As if all this was not exhausting and dispiriting enough, the last evening practice proved to be the most chaotic of all. The weather was too bad to allow the men to jump by parachute. So near to the actual raid it was thought too dangerous; if some of the trained men became casualties they would have to be removed from active operations. So their trucks dropped them on a flat stretch of land not far from the sea. The Whitley bombers of 51 Squadron were scheduled to drop the containers of weapons and supplies, and a specially designed folding trolley to carry away the German apparatus, over their positions. After attacking an imaginary objective near the cliffs, the raiding party were then to form up on the beach and call in the landing craft by radio and with the use of a radio beacon. Then they would depart from the beach.

However, everything that could go wrong did. The Whitleys dropped the containers in the wrong place. The landing craft went to the wrong beach. And to cap it all, the paratroopers found themselves caught up in a minefield that had been laid along part of the beach against German invaders, several miles from where they were supposed to be. They were lucky to get out without any casualties.

The dates for the raid itself had been set well in advance. The planners had chosen nights when the moon was nearly full to provide maximum light and when the tides were rising, ideal for a pre-dawn evacuation from the beaches. The first of these dates was fast approaching, but Commander Cook insisted that there should be one further attempt to evacuate the Para company successfully as all previous attempts had failed. Again, the exercise was delayed due to bad weather and was finally scheduled for Sunday 22 February – only two nights before the first possible opportunity for the raid itself.

This time the exercise took place in the Solent, not far from HMS *Tormentor* on Southampton Water. That night the weather was at last perfectly clear. The communications worked and the paratroopers linked up with the landing craft. But due to an error in their calculations, the navy had got the tides wrong and the landing craft had to beach about sixty yards out. There was nothing for it. Frost ordered his men to wade out into the sea to the vessels. They decided that as this was only an exercise they should not risk ruining their weapons with sea water, so they left them on the beach. They waded out into the dark, forbidding and frozen sea until the water was three feet deep, but they still had not reached the landing craft. As they went further out the sea got even deeper and began to lap over their thighs. Some of the men almost froze with cold and cramp. And when they reached the landing craft, the vessels were once again caught on the tide and would not budge. The men had to wade back ashore and the exercise was abandoned.

This, the last possible practice run before the raid itself, had been a fiasco like the others. Frost, and no doubt several of his men, worried that they had not had a single successful dress rehearsal for the raid. He worried even more about being stranded on the French coast and taken prisoner by the enemy.

At the heart of Operation Biting was the need to dismantle and carefully remove the key parts of the radar installation in order to take them away for examination back in Britain. To do this, the raiding party would need specialist skills beyond what could be expected of regular paratroopers. Finding the right men for this part of the operation would therefore be essential for its success.

12

Volunteers for Danger

Since the original idea for the raid on the Würzburg radar installation at Bruneval had come from Air Ministry scientist R.V. Jones, his assistant, Derek Garrard, volunteered to go on the operation in order to provide the technical advice that would be needed in dismantling the radar to bring it back. And once Garrard had volunteered, Jones felt he had no choice but to volunteer himself. He was still young, aged thirty, and could be trained to join the mission. But he was somewhat relieved when Air Chief Marshal Portal vetoed his involvement, not on the grounds that he could not be spared, but on the basis that if he was captured, as all those dropped in the first Para operation a year before had been, he was a security risk. He knew far too much about Britain's war science and under torture might reveal a great deal of immense value to the enemy.

Portal furthermore forbade anyone on Jones's staff to take part in the operation. So the planners had to find someone else who understood the working of radar systems but was less knowledgeable about the latest developments in British science.

RAF Flight Sergeant Charles Cox was stationed at the Chain Low radar station on the remote, rugged coast of north Devon at Hartland Point. Hartland is a tiny, picture-postcard Devonshire village on the edge of a wild stretch of coast where strips of granite head out into the sea like lines of ploughed fields. For centuries it had been one of the most out-of-the-way spots in England. Emphasising its remoteness, the old sign as you entered the village read 'Welcome to Hartland – Farthest from Railways', and it was indeed the furthest point from the network of railway lines that at the time linked almost every part of England. For centuries Hartland had been best known for its tradition of 'wrecking', whereby sets of smugglers moved lights on the shore inland to lure passing vessels in storms onto the rocks. Groups of locals would then go down to the wrecks and help themselves to the proceeds.

Cox was not a local but had grown up near Wisbech in the Fenlands of East Anglia. His father was a postman and his mother an actress. Before the war he had been a cinema projectionist and a radio ham, never happier than when tinkering with valves and bits of radio equipment. He had joined the RAF in 1940 and his interests naturally took him towards the technical side of aviation and into the brand new and fast developing world of radar. He was enjoying his stint at the recently constructed Chain Low station at Hartland. Something of a cushy number, it was a quiet spot without many distractions and gave him plenty of time to learn about the technology he was operating. As an experienced radar operator and mechanic, he was a highly valued member of his team and was known as someone who could repair the equipment when it went wrong or was damaged by the winds that tore across the north Devon coastline. He had acquired a reputation as one of the best radar mechanics in the RAF. Although in the air force, he had never flown in an aircraft, nor had he ever been to sea. And he had never travelled abroad.

At the end of January 1942, Cox was surprised when his commanding officer gave him a railway voucher for the train from Bideford to London and told him to report to the Air Ministry immediately. When he arrived at Air headquarters on 1 February he reported to Air Commodore Victor Tait, at which point a rather surreal conversation took place.[1] Tait said to the young flight sergeant that he was pleased he had volunteered for 'a dangerous job'.

Cox, puzzled, said that this was the first he had heard about it and that he had not volunteered for anything. 'There must be some mistake,' replied the equally puzzled Tait. 'I asked for volunteers from the comparatively few with exactly your qualifications.' There was a pause. Then Tait continued, 'But now you're here, Sergeant, will you volunteer?'

'Exactly what would I be letting myself in for, sir?' asked Cox.

'I'm not at liberty to tell you,' replied the air commodore. 'However, I can tell you that although the job is dangerous it offers a reasonable chance of survival. It's of great importance to the Royal Air Force. And if you're half the chap I think you are, you'll jump at it.'

Cox did not take long to decide. His wife had given birth only a few weeks before. He had no wish to risk his life and leave his wife and baby without a husband and a father. But he was a patriot and devoted to the RAF. Although the task sounded daunting, he felt he could do with a challenge. After only the briefest hesitation he replied, 'I volunteer, sir.'

Delighted, Tait then told him that he would be required to help in the capture of a radiolocation post in enemy territory. Before Cox had time to reconsider, he was ordered to proceed to the travel office where he was given another railway voucher, this time to Manchester, and a chit with instructions to report at once to Ringway aerodrome.

As Cox's adventure continued, he probably felt as if he were in some kind of dream. He later described arriving at Ringway and not really knowing what was going on. It was unlike any airfield he had visited before. He noticed that busloads of soldiers kept arriving and flying off in old bomber aircraft, but not coming back. He noted that they all had 'queer pots of helmets on' that he had never seen before. They looked rather like the Boys' Brigade, he thought. He wondered what the letters CLS on the main gate stood for. Eventually someone explained to him that this was a parachute training school, and that he and another RAF flight sergeant by the name of Smith had 'volunteered' for a mission to parachute into occupied France in order to bring back some German radar apparatus. Both men had to make their statutory six jumps before they could qualify to join the mission. So the two RAF technicians began an intensive course of parachute training. Cox made two jumps from a balloon at a height of 500 feet in the space of an hour on his first training day. The young father found the whole experience 'rather nerve-racking'.

There then followed four days of bad weather during which all jumping was cancelled. After this, Cox made his first 'singles jump' from a Whitley at about 800 feet. A 'singles jump' involved the Whitley circling the airfield and dropping trainees one at a time when it passed a given point on the circuit. Flight Sergeant Smith, who had already torn a muscle in his leg in the balloon drops, now 'fell ill' and withdrew from the operation. Cox never saw him again and realised that without a reserve it was now down to him to continue with the training and qualify as a parachutist in order for the mission to succeed. He began to feel the pressure.

Cox made two more jumps, this time jumping in twos. But he still had to complete his sixth jump to qualify and as the operation was going to take place at night, he was told he would have to make a night jump, even though this was not part of the usual training programme. The night jump would be from a balloon again.

Up he went with his flight instructor in the balloon to 500 feet. 'It was a sort of eerie experience for everything was dark and quiet,' he wrote in his report. He felt much more scared than during a daylight jump, remembering that 'The hole in the bottom of the basket seemed suddenly to me to look like a bottomless pit.' With great courage, and with the instructions drummed into him that he must keep his legs and feet pressed closely together, he jumped into the darkness. He could see nothing until what looked like a line of trees suddenly appeared out of the black below him and he panicked that he was going to crash right into them. In fact they were further away than he thought and he missed them and made a perfect rolling landing. As he gathered up his chute, and with his adrenalin still pumping, he felt better than he had ever felt in his life before.

With six successful jumps behind him, on 15 February Cox was sent down to Tilshead to join C Company who were part way through their training for the mission. Frost and Ross welcomed him and put him on another intensive training programme, this time consisting of heavy physical exercises, including route marches with full kit and cross-country runs, a combat course that featured weapons training and knife fighting, the scaling of barbed wire (which entailed one paratrooper lying across the wire while others ran over him) and night patrols. For the first time, Cox got to know the paratroopers he was training with. They struck him as a tough bunch who had a positive 'Come what may, I'm OK' attitude. He began to enjoy their company and to admire them for their aggressive fighting skills. He particularly liked his fellow sergeants in C Company, and was able to join them in their own mess. He only had one problem. With their thick Scottish accents, he could barely understand half of what they said to him!

Soon after Cox arrived at Tilshead, Sergeant-Major Strachan introduced him to the small group of Royal Engineers who had been seconded to join the mission. The Royal Engineers were in many ways the most modern and forward-looking section of the British Army. They had a long history of providing support for every type of military operation and their motto was *Ubique* – 'Everywhere'.

From the beginning, the Engineers, or sappers as they were called, had been closely associated with new forms of technology often adopted only very reluctantly by a deeply conservative army high command. In the eighteenth century, they had carried out an extensive mapping operation in

Scotland and Ireland and had laid the foundations for the Ordnance Survey. In the Crimean War they had been the first to use telegraphy in military communications. In the latter decades of the nineteenth century they had pioneered the use of balloons for aerial reconnaissance in the army. In the early twentieth century they had experimented with different types of aircraft after the advent of powered flight, giving birth in 1912 to the Royal Flying Corps. They had been involved with developing tank warfare in the First World War. And in the inter-war years they were the only branch of the British Army committed to exploring new technologies and how they might relate to developments on the battlefield. For Operation Biting, a group of Royal Engineers who were part of the Airborne Division Air Troop were assigned to provide technical support. Ten sappers joined C Company under the command of twenty-four-year-old Lieutenant Dennis Vernon.

Vernon was a Londoner by birth but had spent most of his life in Cambridge, first at the Leys School and then at Emmanuel College where he read economics. He was a bright young officer with an interest in new ideas and new technology, and a lively enquiring mind. He and Cox immediately got on well together. Vernon admired Cox for his knowledge of technical equipment. And Cox respected Vernon for his ability to pick up the essentials of radar and pass it on in a meaningful way to his men. The unit purloined a mobile radar that was in use by local anti-aircraft gunners and brought it to Tilshead. Cox was asked to explain to the engineers the principles of radar and how it worked. The improvised lecture went well and the men, who had barely heard of radar before, were drawn into what seemed like the fantasy world of detection by radio beams.

Vernon then organised a course for the men on recognising electrical equipment and how to take it apart without electrocuting yourself.

A more senior radar expert then arrived. Like many scientists in the war, Brigadier Basil Schonland, a South African expert on lightning, had built up an expertise in an entirely new field, in his case radar. His task was to show the engineers how to dismantle a mobile radar set, and the men practised taking it apart and putting it back together over and over again in order to familiarise themselves with it. The planners had to reckon with the possibility that Cox and Vernon might be disabled or killed during the operation and the remaining engineers therefore had to be capable of operating successfully without them. In addition, a further back-up plan was required.

On 20 February, both Cox and Vernon were summoned to the Air Ministry. There, Cox reported back to Air Commodore Tait that he was very impressed with Vernon and that he thought that together they would be able to dismantle the German apparatus for transport back to London. But first of all, before taking it apart, they had to photograph the entire unit. Vernon was asked if he was familiar with the Leica 35mm camera. Fortunately, he was. He was asked if he had taken photographs using a flash attachment with the camera. Fortunately, he had. Vernon was issued with a Leica, given a few rolls of 35mm film and told to practise using the flash at night. On the raid itself, there would be no time to change rolls of film, so he was told to load the camera with a single roll. He would have only the thirty-six exposures on that roll to photograph the Würzburg in its entirety.

While Cox was at the Air Ministry, R.V. Jones asked to see

him for a private conversation. Jones had realised that as the sole RAF man on the mission, Cox would stand out in his blue uniform, if captured, and would attract special attention from German interrogators. So Jones asked the War Office to dress Cox in an army uniform and to give him military papers with an army registration number. The War Office adamantly refused to do this, claiming they could not break official rules and make a man from another service a temporary member of the British Army. Concerned about this, Jones felt it was his duty to meet Cox and warn him that although he had tried to get him out of his RAF uniform, he should be aware of the risks he faced if he were captured.[2]

'Yes, I've been thinking about that, sir,' Cox responded. He had come up with his own cover story. He would explain to an interrogator that he was in fact the dispatcher from the Whitley bomber aiding the paratroopers in their jump, and in a moment of confusion he had jumped by mistake with the soldiers.

Jones had to admit to Cox that although it was a clever ruse, he doubted if the Germans would 'wear that one'. Cox, sadly, agreed that this was probably the case. Jones felt a sense of responsibility to the young RAF radar mechanic who was risking his life to carry out the mission that Jones had instigated. 'Don't be worried too much about physical torture,' he explained, 'because I don't think they are using it.' He continued, 'What you have to be tremendously careful about is being thrown into solitary confinement in a cold damp cell, with nothing but bread and water for a few days. Then a new German officer will come and protest about the way you are being treated. He will take you out of your cell and will explain that he will try to make amends for your bad treatment. He will give you cigarettes, a decent meal, a warm fire and something to drink. After a while you will feel such a glow and so grateful to this very decent officer that when he starts asking you questions you will hardly be able to resist telling him everything he wants to know.'

Cox listened in silence to what he was being told. Jones summed it up by saying 'So, for God's sake, Cox, be on your guard against any German officer who is kind to you.'

After the short lecture Cox stood to attention and said, 'I can stand a lot of kindness, sir.' Then he saluted the scientist and departed. Jones was left in his office reflecting on the impressive courage of the man who had volunteered for this dangerous mission. He hoped desperately that Cox would come back from it safely to see his wife and baby again.

While they were at the Air Ministry, Cox and Vernon were also given advice on how to evade capture if the raid went badly. The officials told them about the existence of the French underground networks, which were already well practised in smuggling shot-down airmen out of France. They explained that many local villagers or farmers might risk their lives by offering to hide the men. The pair were told to memorise two addresses in France and one in Switzerland, and were given a password to use if they could reach these addresses. Finally they were given maps of France printed on fine silk along with miniature compasses hidden in collar studs. Cox came away from the briefing feeling that everything had been planned down to the last detail and he was lucky to be part of such an important and special mission.[3]

As a final back-up in case everything else went wrong, it was decided to send a scientist from TRE, Donald Preist, on the final stage of the mission. Preist had been at Bawdsey from the early days of radar development and was one of the pioneering engineers who had developed the Chain Home Low system. As one of the TRE specialists in radar he knew about the interest in the Würzburg. In mid February the Air Ministry telephoned him out of the blue and asked him to go across to the headquarters of the Airborne Division at Syrencote House.[4]

Confused as to why he should be asked to visit a parachute unit, Preist drove across to Airborne headquarters and was welcomed by the genial Major Bromley-Martin, who announced he had arrived just in time for lunch. Preist was sat next to General Browning, whom he had never heard of before, but he quickly became aware that Browning was widely respected by everyone else present. After lunch Bromley-Martin showed Preist the aerial photograph of the parabolic dish on the cliff top at Bruneval. He explained that a paratrooper raid was being planned to seize the equipment. 'Would you like to come along?' asked the affable major.

'I certainly would,' replied Preist. 'When do we start?'

'Come back in a couple of days and we'll train you in parachute jumping,' said the major. Preist returned to TRE feeling hugely excited, thinking this was 'going to be a great adventure – heady stuff'.

However, the staff of Combined Operations soon realised that Preist, like Jones and Garrard, knew far too much to be risked on the raid. They therefore decided that Preist would go over with Cook's naval force and approach the beach at Bruneval in one of the landing craft that would evacuate the paratroopers in the early hours of the morning. He was to wait offshore until word was received that C Company had control of the whole area.

A couple of days after his heady visit to Airborne head-quarters, Major Bromley-Martin called up Preist and explained the change of plan. 'Sorry to disappoint you, old boy,' he began. 'Somebody pointed out that you are a radar expert loaded with information, most of it secret. If you fell into enemy hands it could be a bit awkward, possibly very unpleasant for you.' So the jolly major explained the new plan to send Preist in with the naval landing craft instead. Only if the cliff top was completely secure was he to go ashore and investigate the German radar installation.

'Disappointing,' said Preist. 'But I see your point. I'll be glad to go with the navy.' He was told to report to Combined Operations headquarters in London where the full plan for Operation Biting and his role in it would be explained to him.

There was one final piece of the jigsaw for the planners at Combined Operations to put in place. They realised that when the paratroopers reached their objective, they would be likely to capture some of the German guards or even some of the radar operators. With speed of the utmost importance, it might be of great value to discover from these captives where the German defenders were based and how many the raiding party was likely to encounter. As neither Frost nor any of the other officers, nor any of the men, spoke German, they needed a fluent German speaker on the raid.

On the day before C Company left Tilshead to head north to Loch Fyne, Sergeant-Major Strachan introduced to Major Frost a new addition to the raiding party. A small, smart man with brown hair and blue eyes, dressed in the uniform of the Pioneer

Corps, he was introduced as Private Newman. Frost was immediately suspicious. Why was he being asked to take along a private from the Pioneer Corps on this high-level operation? He soon realised that it was because Newman spoke perfect German. He interviewed the new addition at some length and realised he had all sorts of admirable qualities, he was tough and determined to do his bit. But soon Frost became even more suspicious. Not only did Private Newman speak German but he *was* German.

Frost was gravely worried. The German army seemed invincible, in Russia and in North Africa, as they had been in Poland, France and the rest of northern Europe. All the talk at this stage in the war was of the German genius for planting fifth columnists in Britain to spy on what was going on. Frost said that they had all been taught to 'fear the enemy's Intelligence'. He was commanding a small-scale, top secret mission in which a thousand things could go wrong. And now he was being asked to take along a German in his party. 'I could not help think,' concluded Frost later, 'that the enemy probably knew all about us and what we were training for.' Was it possible that this determined young man was a German spy who had successfully been implanted in the British Army? 'There was a distinctly eerie feeling to having a Hun on the strength.'[5]

The man introduced to Major Frost as Private Newman was actually Peter Nagel, a German Jew, who had quite a history behind him. He had been born in 1916 in Berlin, the son of a wealthy German-Jewish textile manufacturer who had married a Catholic, a marriage that caused some scandal in smart Berlin society at the time. Although Nagel had gone to a Protestant school, his Jewish origins had been recognised and in an expression of the anti-Semitism that was characteristic of the times, the young Nagel was repeatedly told by his teachers and his fellow students, 'People like you are not wanted in Germany.'[6]

When the Nazis came to power, Nagel decided he must try to leave Germany and he concocted an elaborate plan to fool the Nazis and to get himself, his family and much of the family wealth out of Germany and into England. Here, his father planned to settle in Leicester, a centre of the woollen trade. Nagel lived in Paris for a year before settling in England. He was fluent in both French and English and he began to work in the family clothing business, now split between Leicester and Soho in London.

In March 1940, Nagel joined the British Army, giving his religion as 'Church of England'. Nagel was officially listed as a 'friendly alien', and along with about eight thousand German and Austrian refugees was allowed to serve in the Army Pioneer Corps. Many of these refugees went on to serve in SOE or in special forces of one sort or another, and they were jokingly known as 'His Majesty's Most Loyal Enemy Aliens'. In 1941, Nagel trained with SOE and became skilled with explosives and in using Morse code, before going on to train with the commandos. He was regarded as a good, enthusiastic soldier and an educated, intelligent man.

In February 1942, the staff of Combined Operations headquarters selected Nagel to join C Company on the Bruneval raid. He was given the papers and the army number of a Private Newman, an actual soldier who had deserted in the late 1930s. If he was captured and the Germans checked the army lists, they would find the real Private Newman and hopefully be convinced that this was who Nagel was. As a German Jew in the British Army, Nagel would face instant execution at best if captured. A man had to have a special form of bravery to put himself forward for a mission that involved this level of risk.

In C Company, only Frost, his second-in-command, Ross, and Sergeant-Major Strachan had any inkling that Private Newman was not who he claimed to be. Frost still had his fears about the raid being infiltrated; even though Newman came across well, he was unhappy about having an unknown, untried soldier on a mission of this complexity. He feared that if things went wrong Newman would become a liability. When Frost met Admiral Lord Mountbatten on the *Prinz Albert* during the commander's visit to Loch Fyne, he asked for a private word. Knowing that Newman had been sent to him on direct orders from Combined Operations, Frost shared his fears with Mountbatten and requested Newman's removal.

Mountbatten asked for the young man to be brought in. In his impeccable German, he subjected Newman to a 'tremendous barrage of questions'. Despite being interrogated by a senior naval officer and someone as formidable as the King's cousin, Nagel held his own and answered every point that was put to him. The man left and Mountbatten turned to Frost. He told him he was deeply impressed with the German and that Frost would find him invaluable as an interpreter on the raid.[7]

The matter was closed. Private Newman was in the squad. Including Flight Sergeant Cox, Lieutenant Vernon and the ten Royal Engineers, and Private Newman, there were exactly the required number of 120 men now training for the Bruneval raid.

13

The Plan

Thanks to the invaluable intelligence picked up on the ground by the French underground, alongside the mass of detailed information gleaned from aerial photography, and with the men going through the last stages of their training, the final details of the plan for Operation Biting were coming together.

The essence of the operation was speed and surprise. The force of 120 men would not be able to hold out for long against a determined counter-attack mounted by German reinforcements. There were plenty of German troops along this stretch of coast within a few miles who could be rallied to defend the installations at Bruneval, while the British paratroopers only had light machine guns, rifles and pistols. The new short-range Sten gun was their principal automatic weapon, backed up with a few Bren guns. But not everyone had taken to the Sten gun. Major Frost himself later described it as 'bloody awful ... a most inaccurate and unreliable weapon'.[1]

The Paras would be no match for enemy troops supported by armoured vehicles, let alone tanks, or against mortar attack from enemy positions. They had to get in, overwhelm the local guards, capture the equipment, photograph it, dismantle it and remove the key sections to the beach, and evacuate by landing craft before the Germans had time to realise what was happening. Any delay would be fatal.

The purpose of the night raid was quite different from previous commando raids where the objective had been to cause as much mayhem, damage and disruption as possible. The main objective of Operation Biting was to capture and remove the vital radar technology and escape with it. The foremost secondary objective was to capture any technicians who were known to operate the Würzburg radar and to bring them back to Britain. The Paras were not to waste time in capturing and transporting away other prisoners. Their operational orders were crystal clear: 'No prisoners will be taken other than officers and technical personnel.'[2]

The location of the Würzburg radar station had determined how the raid would be carried out. It was sited on a flat plateau about 200 to 300 yards square, on top of a cliff. The plateau was 370 feet above the sea and there was a steep gully running down to the small beach, nestling between the high cliffs. The pebble beach was only about 300 yards long. Inland from the radar installation, the ground sloped more gently but was cut by a series of steep-sided valleys, many of which were wooded. This was the landscape that the planners in Combined Operations had studied so carefully from pre-war maps and aerial photos before coming up with their plan for the raid.

Operation Biting was scheduled for the night of Tuesday

24 February, when tide conditions and moonlight would be ideal. If the weather prevented the raid that night then there were two further consecutive nights in which conditions would be suitable, if not ideal. It was only a brief window of opportunity and everything had to come together on those nights. The final version of the operational plan was littered with code names for different groups and places in the raid.[3] At the centre of the operation, the Würzburg equipment itself was code-named *Henry*. The code names for the raiding parties were the names of leading admirals from naval history, as a tribute to the senior service that would play the vital role of getting the men back to safety after the raid.

The numbers of men involved in the raid were tiny. The first group of forty, with the code name *Nelson*, were to jump from their four Whitleys to a drop zone about a half a mile east, a short way up the inland road to Bruneval, at exactly 0015 hours. This group had a major role to play in the raid. Their overall objective was to secure the beach for the withdrawal of the main body of the raiding party, along with the radar equipment and any prisoners.

Nelson was commanded by Second Lieutenant Euan Charteris. Only twenty years of age and the youngest officer taking part in the raid, he was accordingly known to the other officers as 'Junior'. He led a party of twenty men who were to capture and hold the beach, take out the guard post and the two machine-gun positions to the north and south of the road that had been spotted by Charlemagne and Pol on their recce of the site.

The remaining members of *Nelson*, under the command of Captain John Ross, were to act as a rearguard and to hold the road from the beach towards the village of Bruneval. Aerial photographs had identified the recent construction of pillboxes along the southern side of this road, built to prevent invaders and invasion vehicles moving inland if they had successfully landed on the beaches. These installations were collectively known as *Beach Fort*. But the pillboxes would be an equal threat to the paratroopers who were moving in the other direction, towards the beach. Ross's party included two sappers, equipped with anti-tank mines that were to be set to prevent German armoured reinforcements from moving towards the beach. In case the intelligence proved to be wrong and there were unexpected minefields, these men were equipped with mine detectors and were to clear a route through the minefields and mark it with white tape.

The men of *Nelson* were finally to make contact with the navy and signal to the landing craft using radio beacons, and if necessary bright flares fired into the sky, when it was time to come ashore and carry out the evacuation. Captain Ross's men were to remain in position protecting the evacuation and were to be the last themselves to embark.

The second group of paratroopers were to drop five minutes later, at 0020 hours, about half a mile inland from the main site. Their objective was to capture the principal cliff-top radar installation. They were split into three parties. *Hardy* was a group of twenty men led by Major Frost himself. Their task was to launch the first round of the night raid, to capture the seaside villa known as Villa Gosset on the top of the cliffs that was thought to be the base for the radar operators and where many of the men would probably be sleeping. *Jellicoe*, led by Lieutenant Peter Young, was a party of ten men who would immediately afterwards seize and capture *Henry*, the Würzburg itself, and the dugouts and pits around it. They had to keep this area secure for the rest of the night's operation. The final group of ten men, codenamed *Drake* and under the command of Lieutenant Peter Naumoff, were to contain the enemy situated at the large rectangle of buildings to the north of the main site, known as Le Presbytère. The French underground agents had established that this was the base for about sixty Luftwaffe troops who were guarding the Freya radar installations further along the coast.

Just forward of this position was a farmhouse at Theuville. The planners at Combined Operations called this the *Rectangle* because that's what it was, a rectangular defensive position surrounded by a line of trees. It was anticipated that once the firing began, this was where the major German opposition to the raiders would come from. Aerial photography had identified machine-gun positions around the perimeter of the *Rectangle*, but it was still not certain if heavier weapons, such as mortars, were located here. *Drake* was to cause a distraction to divert fire from the *Rectangle*, allowing the vital work to take place at the Würzburg installation. When this had been completed, Naumoff was to withdraw his men to the beach with, as the orders put it, 'all possible speed'.

The final party of forty men were codenamed *Rodney*, led by Lieutenant John Timothy. He was excited to be going into action at last as part of this daring raid. The *Rodney* party were to drop five minutes after the other paratroopers and to form up to protect the eastern, landward side of the operation. They were to act as a sort of mobile reserve and provide support wherever it was most needed. If the Germans rallied any sort of substantial counter-attack, either from Le Presbytère or along the Bruneval road, *Rodney* was to oppose it and hold it up long enough for the rest of the raid to be carried out. Two more sappers with their anti-tank mines were attached to this group. Having fought off any counter-attack, *Rodney* was then to provide a rearguard defence of the evacuation if needed.

Cox and Vernon were attached to *Hardy* with two of the other trained sappers. After photographing the Würzburg they had to dismantle it and remove as many of the key parts as possible. They had a supply of pickaxes, jemmies, hacksaws, chisels, screwdrivers and spanners in order to carry out their task.[4] This core element of Operation Biting was only allocated thirty minutes in the schedule. If it took longer, if they had the wrong equipment, or if they came under fire and were unable to complete the process, the whole mission would have failed. Every aspect of Biting had to work like clockwork. Timing was critical.

The Whitleys of 51 Squadron under Wing Commander Pickard had to fly with pinpoint precision at night over a blacked-out countryside to ensure that the men landed exactly in their drop zones. There was bound to be anti-aircraft fire which might put the pilots off course. The RAF planned to carry out a series of bombing attacks on Paris, so that aircraft would cross the French coast in the general area between Le Havre and the Somme estuary every night during the week leading up to the raid. The local defenders would become accustomed to the presence of low-flying bombers at night. On the night of the raid itself, further bomber diversions were to be mounted in the Le Havre area to distract the local defences from the parachute drop. The Whitleys carrying the raiding party were to fly north–south about one mile out to sea and then turn inland near Le Havre and fly north again up to the drop zones.

The final stage of Operation Biting was the evacuation organised by the navy. HMS *Prinz Albert* had travelled south from Loch Fyne to act as the co-ordinating headquarters for the operation. It would set sail from Portsmouth in the afternoon before the raid and head towards the Bruneval coast accompanied by a flotilla of six motor gunboats (MGBs) for defence. Commander Cook would be on board leading the naval operation. When it had taken up its position off the French coast, the *Prinz Albert* would launch its six ALCs and two Support Landing Craft. It would be too large a target to remain so close to the French coastline and so was then to withdraw to Portsmouth. Cook would transfer to one of the landing craft that had to locate the beach at Bruneval.

This was what had proved so difficult in the rehearsals. Cook's 'biggest worry by far' was finding the tiny three-hundred-yard-wide beach between the towering cliffs after travelling by dead reckoning merely on a compass reading, a hundred miles across the Channel.[5] And this stretch of coast was full of tiny beaches between high chalk cliffs. If the wind got up and was blowing at anything more than Force 2 or 3, the whole naval operation, from lowering the landing craft from the *Prinz Albert* to finding the beach itself, would be put at serious risk.

According to the plan, the landing craft would come ashore when the signal was given, load up with the paratroopers and their stolen cargo of electronic radar components, and depart. All this would take place before dawn under cover of darkness.

To add to the limited firepower that the raiders possessed, each landing craft contained five soldiers armed with a Bren gun. If fighting was still taking place on land, they would be tasked with firing up into the cliffs or wherever there were German defensive positions that had not been overpowered. This would keep the heads of the enemy down while the delicate operation of embarkation took place.

In addition, a medical officer and twenty medical orderlies would be on the landing craft to deal with any seriously wounded. Finally, Donald Preist, the radar engineer, commissioned for the duration of the raid as a flight lieutenant in the RAF, was to be on board one of the landing craft, with two men to protect him. His party was codenamed *Noah*. He was only to land and assist in the technical assessment and dismantling of *Henry* if Major Frost had confirmed that the whole area around the Würzburg was secure. The operational order stated in block capitals: 'IT IS OF THE UTMOST IMPORTANCE THAT FL.-LT. PREIST SHOULD NOT FALL INTO THE ENEMY'S HANDS'.

The landing craft were to withdraw as soon as they could, with the Bren gunners still firing, if required, to distract the enemy. They did not have the fuel to cross the Channel under their own power, so the Paras and their cargo were to be transferred on to the faster MGBs, which would tow the landing craft back to Portsmouth. As dawn broke these vessels would be highly vulnerable to air attack, and so RAF fighters were to provide an escort to the armada of little ships as it crossed the Channel. Finally an escort of naval destroyers was to accompany the ships back into Portsmouth.

As this was to be the first raid of the newly formed Airborne Division, the men were acting as guinea pigs for all sorts of new ideas and gadgets. It was important for the future of the division to learn as much as possible about how men would react in a real night-time raid and to discover precisely how to meet the needs of those carrying out a raid of this sort. In addition to being equipped with the new Sten gun and radio system, some of the men were issued with morphine to administer. A potent analgesic drug used to relieve severe or agonising pain, morphine was usually administered through a syringe applied near the point in the body where the injury was causing pain.

In the British Army at this time, only medical officers or orderlies usually administered morphine. However, because of the restricted numbers that could be taken on the mission, limited by the fact that there were only twelve aircraft available and each aircraft could carry no more than ten men, the planners decided that there was no spare capacity to drop medical orderlies. For the assault, one in every ten men taking part in the raid was given special medical training to provide emergency field relief, which included administering prepared syringes of morphine if required. The medical officers of the Airborne Division realised they were setting a precedent and waited with great interest to see how it would work out.

The Paras were given all sorts of other new bits of kit to try out on the raid. Since, during the training exercises, the landing craft had found it so difficult to locate the correct beaches, the signallers in the raiding party were given a new radio transmitting beacon called *Rebecca*. Signallers in the landing craft were provided with a matching receiver, *Eureka*. As soon as the beach had been captured the operators were to turn on the *Rebecca* transmitters and it was hoped the *Eureka* receivers would lock in to the signals and guide the landing craft in to the right beach. But the technology was new and after all the fiascos in training no one was totally confident in it. In case of disaster, the transmitters were fitted with explosive charges and the signallers were instructed to blow them up to prevent them falling into the hands of the enemy.

All company communications were to be carried out on the same frequency on the new radio sets. The company commander, Major Frost, would normally go into battle supported by a full headquarters team to co-ordinate communications between his officers and across the company. He was told to use the 38 radio sets instead, to keep in touch with what was happening and to issue his orders as the raid unfolded.

The raid also provided the chance to trial a new method of labelling the containers of equipment dropped by parachute. A light attached to each container was set off when it was thrown out of the aircraft so it could be quickly identified in the dark. Containers with arms and weapons had red lights. Containers carrying signals equipment had green lights. Containers with equipment for the engineers had purple lights. Three specially constructed trolleys would be parachuted in with the function of carrying down the cliff to the beach any electronic equipment seized. The containers holding the trolleys had orange lights. Everything was designed to work smoothly and efficiently in the limited time available.

The final days leading up to the operation were hectic. After the last exercise in the Solent on Sunday 22 February, Cox noted that the men were cold, wet and 'browned off' by yet another foul-up.[6] They then returned to their camp at Tilshead. For two busy days the equipment for the raid was handed out and had to be checked. Weapons were issued and ammunition loaded into magazines. The engineers had to check their mine detectors, wire cutters and anti-tank mines, as well as the jemmies, chisels and explosives needed to dismantle *Henry*. The trolleys were assembled and tested, then folded up again. Everything had to be packed into containers for the parachute drop.

Only at this point did the officers explain to the men the full nature of their mission. During the last two days before the raid everyone was shown models of the site and its surroundings, based on aerial photographs and made at Medmenham by the model-making department. These terrain models were extraordinary.[7] They were made exactly to scale and with great accuracy. The contours were laid out using hardboard cutouts, mounted layer by layer on the baseboard. A mosaic of aerial photos was laid over the outline of the contours to provide a precise 3D landscape model, and the surface was then painted to show fields, rivers, hedgerows and trees. Tiny models of significant buildings were constructed, also to scale, and placed in situ.

One of the models of the Bruneval cliffs, made to a precise scale of 1:2000, was carefully brought down from Medmenham and assembled at Tilshead.[8] First the officers, then the NCOs and finally the men studied the models. Everyone had time to locate their drop zone, their assembly point, and to memorise the landscape and the local terrain. They could look at the beaches and see where all the known defences were. Finally, those who would be operating on the top of the cliffs could see the steep downward route they would have to follow to evacuate from the beaches.

Everything had been planned down to the last detail. Or so it seemed to many of the men taking part in the raid. The reality, of course, was that dozens of things could go horribly wrong. The success of the operation would depend upon the men being dropped in exactly the right place, being able to carry out the plan without too many distractions, and then being able to evacuate with their precious cargo on time and without any of the fiascos that had marred their training exercises. But more than anything, its success would depend upon the raiders' ability to overwhelm the local defenders and carry out the mission before the nearby garrisons could rally to hit back at them. Although a great deal was known about the defenders of this small stretch of French coast, it was still one of the biggest question marks hanging over the whole enterprise. How many and how good were the German troops stationed around Bruneval?

14

The Defenders

Ever since the German army had rolled across France in the lightning war of May and June 1940, the occupiers had been building up their defences along the north French coast against possible incursions. The whole coastal strip was a closed area to anyone other than residents or those with special permits – like Charlemagne, who had a permit to travel in the Département of Seine-Inferieure as he owned a local garage for the repair of vehicles. Later in the war, by 1944, the coastal defences along northern France would form what was called the Atlantic Wall, a huge defensive barrier of machine-gun nests, artillery positions and anti-tank and anti-personnel defences running for hundreds of miles, and intended to defeat any invading force on the beaches.

In early 1942 there was nothing as co-ordinated or well designed as this. Nevertheless, the Germans had good forces available and were determined to protect their precious equipment, like the sophisticated radar stations scattered along the north French coastline.

The intelligence available about the German defenders was partly based on an extensive study of the aerial photos by the specialist interpreters at Medmenham, and partly on information gathered by the agents of the French underground. This intelligence continued to arrive after Pol and Charlemagne's visit to Bruneval, and it made up a highly detailed picture of the organisation and layout of the German defences. For instance, it was known that a team of nine radar operators manned the principal target, the Würzburg radar on the top of the cliff at Bruneval, on shifts around the clock. Allied Intelligence assumed these men were specialist Luftwaffe engineers who lived in the Villa Gosset alongside. The sergeant in charge of this group was named Gerhard Wenzel. British Intelligence knew that, nearly half a mile further up the coast at Cap d'Antifer, there were another thirty operators manning the twinned Freya radar station, the site that had initially attracted the photo interpreters at Medmenham to look at this area in more detail.

The men working on the two radar stations were kept apart as much as possible and were forbidden to discuss their work. So the Würzburg operators had no idea what the Freya team was up to, and vice versa. They were all, however, part of the Luftwaffe Air Intelligence Branch, the unit that provided the signallers and operators for the specialist radar stations across France. These were the advanced 'eyes' of the German air defence system, linked by telephone with a direct line to the coastal defence centre at Octeville-sur-Mer, just outside Le Havre. From here the anti-aircraft batteries at Le Havre and along the coast at the towns of Étretat and Fécamp were alerted and the complex fire control systems were put into action.

Between the two radar outposts at Bruneval and Cap d'Antifer was the wooded area of Le Presbytère and the farmhouse at Theuville, known as the *Rectangle*. The photo interpreters had estimated from the size of the barracks that about sixty men were stationed here, and according to the information from the owners of the hotel nearby, they knew they were Luftwaffe troops. The Luftwaffe had its own ground-based field troops. Most of these men operated the anti-aircraft guns that protected every airfield. Another section of Luftwaffe ground troops was the German equivalent of the airborne paratrooper forces, the *Fallschirmjäger*, elite troops armed with some of the best weapons in the German arsenal. But there were also soldiers trained simply to guard airfields or other positions, like those who guarded the specialist radar outposts near Bruneval. They wore uniforms very similar to conventional German infantry-men and were armed with similar weaponry. But they had a Luftwaffe wing emblem on their collar tabs. And they lacked the training or experience of troops in the Wehrmacht, the regular army.

The men on the cliff-top plateau at Bruneval were part of the 2nd Reconnaissance Company of the 23rd Luftwaffe Air Reconnaissance Regiment. The commanding officer at Le Presbytère was Oberleutnant Hans Melches. The aerial photos suggested that these soldiers were armed with nothing heavier than light machine guns, equivalent to the weapon carried by just a few of the paratroopers, the Bren gun. Any bigger weapons would probably be mortars, but there was no sign of these in the aerial photographs. If they had them they did not seem to use them much.

The coast of northern France was guarded against attack from the sea by troops of the Wehrmacht. The intelligence section at Combined Operations knew that the forty-five-mile stretch of coast from Le Havre north-east to Sotteville-sur-Mer was guarded by the German 336th Infantry Division, largely recruited from Saxony, under the command of Lieutenant General Johann Joachim Stever. A Prussian, upright, formal and strict, a professional officer not a committed Nazi, Stever had been in the army since before the First World War. In 1940 he had led a Panzer division in the assault on France and Belgium, but it was thought he had not been a success as a Panzer commander and so in late 1940 he was put in command of the 336th Infantry Division. This would have been seen as a severe demotion.

A German infantry division was made up of several regiments and the unit based around Bruneval was the 685th Infantry Regiment, a new regiment formed at the end of 1940 to provide garrison troops for occupied France. In command of the 685th was another experienced professional officer, Colonel von Eisenhart-Rothe. The soldiers at Bruneval were part of the 1st Battalion of the 685th and the battalion was charged with the defence of a twelve-mile stretch of coast from Criquebeuf-en-Caux, to the north-east, to just south of Bruneval. The commander of this battalion was Major Paschke.

Down the steep slope from the cliff-top radar site, where the road came out to the sea, there was a network of German defences, as the underground agents had reported on their recce. Here the old villa known as Stella Maris and the road heading inland was surrounded by barbed wire approximately ten feet deep. The garrison consisted of a platoon of thirty men under the command of a sergeant. Five of these men slept in the villa, which had become a guard post manned twenty-four hours a day. The remainder were based at the Hotel Beau-Minet, which was about five hundred yards back up the road heading inland. The troops stationed at the Hotel Beau-Minet and the Stella Maris were from the 1st Company of the 1st Battalion under the command of Oberleutnant Huhn.

Above and behind the Stella Maris were a series of machine-gun positions and pillboxes facing out to sea and across the beaches. This was the defensive position called *Beach Fort* in the British plan. There were the two positions halfway up the cliff on either side of the road that Pol and Charlemagne had spotted. On aerial photographs, interpreters had sighted further machine-gun nests along and above the road heading inland. In addition to the open machine-gun positions there were a small number of concrete pillboxes that were still under construction. Most of these overlooked the beach and the road, and communication trenches linking them were being dug. But the photo interpreters had noted that in recent weeks a pillbox had been built on the shoulder of the cliff opposite the Stella Maris. This was a single, powerful position with a commanding view of both the beach and the valley inland. The intelligence team called this the *Redoubt*.

It was clear that a heavier defensive shield was under construction to prevent an enemy force from advancing up the road. As the pillboxes were roofed over it was obviously impossible to identify from aerial photos what guns were stationed inside. But from their size, the photo interpreters concluded that they contained nothing larger than machine guns. It was even possible that, as the defensive line was so recent and was still under construction, weapons had not yet been brought in.

British Intelligence knew that there was a further garrison from the 1st Company in the small village of La Poterie, only two and a half miles from Bruneval. The garrison amounted to the rest of the company, seventy men, and was Major Paschke's headquarters. The problem for these men was that they had no vehicular transport and so would be expected to march to the coast to provide assistance. By the time they had been alerted, in the middle of the night, had rallied and marched up the coast road, it was likely that they would not arrive on the scene for a couple of hours.

Further afield, at Étretat, a seaside town about six miles up the coast, there was another company of regular German infantry. Again, it was critical to estimate how quickly they could be expected to arrive on the scene. The planners at Combined Operations concluded that even if they were accommodated in barracks or in billets over a very small area, 'they cannot be expected to arrive on the scene of action within one hour of a warning being received, and it is highly probable that three hours would elapse before their arrival.'[1] Finally, British Intelligence knew that there was a reconnaissance battalion based at Yport, about sixteen miles away. This unit was equipped with armoured cars and it was possible that one or two of these vehicles, if alerted early enough, could arrive on the scene within about an hour. However, it would take much longer for a larger force to reach Bruneval and organise itself. The intelligence report for the Bruneval raid concluded with words that no doubt greatly relieved Major Frost and his lightly armed force: 'No tanks have yet been located in the neighbourhood.'[2]

The headquarters of the 1st Battalion of the 685th Infantry Regiment was about seven miles by road from Bruneval in a village called Bordeaux-St-Clair. From here the battalion commander kept in touch with his various outposts by field telephone. The Combined Operations planners thought there was a strong possibility that failures of communication would occur between the Wehrmacht units and the Luftwaffe soldiers, no doubt knowing how such failures frequently occurred between different elements of the British armed services. But it seems that on this stretch of coast, the local Luftwaffe commander, Oberleutnant Melches, and the senior army commander, Major Paschke, had met as recently as mid January to divide up and agree their respective defensive responsibilities. At the time of the British raid, co-operation between the two German military services was excellent.

Although there was no reason to doubt the determination of the German troops, British Intelligence did not know much about the quality of the soldiers the raiders would face, or about their morale. Overall, life for the troops defending this stretch of coast was reasonably good. Haute Normandy was a prosperous, farming region and there were all sorts of farm produce to be traded from the locals. Like all soldiers on garrison duty, the principal problem they had to fight was sheer boredom. Their guard rosters were long and passed slowly. It was easy for a rather sleepy atmosphere to prevail. To keep them alert, the regular soldiers made frequent patrols across the region, but never at predictable or regular times. They would appear out of the blue and challenge the local sentries.

Passwords would change daily and those guarding the facilities would be put on a charge if they got that day's password wrong. As the radar installations themselves were top secret Luftwaffe installations, the army patrols were never allowed to enter them and probably had no idea what they were for. But overall, at this stage of the war, the soldiers guarding the French coast had a pretty easy life, certainly by comparison to their colleagues fighting the Red Army on the Eastern Front.

The German soldiers did not mix much with French civilians, although as with all occupying armies, some liaisons with local girls developed. There were few problems from the Resistance at this time. And most of the soldiers knew that even with the Americans now in the war, the Allies did not have the capacity to mount any sort of invasion. The garrison soldiers, like troops anywhere, longed for a break or a visit home to Germany to see their wives, families and loved ones. The food they ate, the music they listened to and the papers and books they read were mostly imported from home, and each outpost brought a little bit of Germany to occupied France.

No matter how reassuring the intelligence reports and briefings sent to Frost and his team, it was possible that units could be changed during the course of a day. As the Allies would find two and a half years later, on D-Day, relatively weak units were swapped with hardened troops at a moment's notice and the Allied troops found themselves up against much tougher defenders than they had anticipated. Nevertheless, the analysis of enemy positions and reinforcements in the area had been extremely thorough and Major Frost and his officers felt that they were going into battle with an immense amount of information about their enemy. Frost reflected that rarely had men been given so much information about the enemy they were coming up against: 'the strength, the billets, the weapons and even the names of some of the Germans were known.'[3]

The conclusion of the intelligence assessments was that the troops in the immediate vicinity of the drop zone were a mixture of radar and communication specialists defended by relatively lightly armed soldiers. But the machine-gun nests were clearly an issue, and although primarily positioned to fire across the beaches it was clear that they could also be used to fire across the valley and along the road that would be one of the vital routes for the *Nelson* group. The Wehrmacht units were scattered across the countryside and the possibility of their quick response underlined the need for speed throughout the raid. If the paratroopers were held up at any point in the mission it would give critical minutes for large numbers of German reinforcements to arrive. Of course, it was not known how determined any of these defenders would be, or how well they would fight when surprised by British paratroopers in the middle of the night. Only during the raid itself would the real combat calibre of the enemy forces become apparent.

In the week before the raid on Bruneval was due, as called for in the plan, the RAF began to fly more and more raids across the coastal region between Le Havre and Dieppe. Every time RAF aircraft crossed the Channel in this area the Freya radar operators would pick them up and sound the alarm. When they were twenty-five miles off the coast the Würzburg team would begin to track them. The RAF raids took place throughout the night. They put immense strain on the radar operators, who telephoned their information as to the sightings of the enemy aircraft as soon as they had fixed on an identification. The generally rather lazy atmosphere grew more fervent. It was clear that something was up and that the RAF were now hitting hard at targets across northern France.

15

The Drop

There were only three nights in which conditions needed for the raid, a full moon with a high tide, were ideal – the nights of Tuesday 24 to Thursday 26 February. The final exercise had only finished on the Sunday before. Having checked their weapons and packed their equipment, on the morning of 24 February the men nervously waited to hear that the mission was on. The containers were then taken off to the airfield, and the men were told to rest and get some sleep if they could. They would be driven the few miles across Salisbury Plain to the airfield at Thruxton in the late afternoon for emplaning. Weather conditions had to be just right for the RAF to fly its sorties, for the parachute forces to jump and for the navy to get the men off the beaches.

Tuesday had dawned stormy and blowy. Gale force winds were reported in the Channel. With all the containers packed, a call came through from divisional HQ in mid afternoon. The high winds over the north French coast meant that conditions were not suitable for a parachute drop. The operation was postponed for twenty-four hours.

In the preceding rush of activity, the men had been focused on last-minute preparations, using their time to study the maps, photographs and models in order to imprint in their minds what lay ahead of them. Now, in the hours following the postponement, they had an opportunity for the first time to reflect on all that might go wrong. It was not a good few hours. Nevertheless, on Wednesday morning, the men of C Company went through the whole process again: checking weapons, packing containers and studying their operational orders. Then, again, in the middle of the afternoon a call came through from headquarters. The strong winds in northern France meant that the navy could not guarantee that the landing craft would be able to get in to the beach successfully. The mission was postponed for another twenty-four hours. This time it was worse. Not only the men but their officers, Major Frost included, became broody. Having reached a pitch of preparedness, all this time to think was definitely not good for morale.

On the morning of Thursday 26 February, for the third time, the men packed the containers and checked their weapons, while the officers carried out inspections. This morning the rumour went around that a further postponement would involve missing the necessary combination of moon and tide, and the whole raid would almost certainly be postponed for at least a month until the conditions were propitious once again. The men were convinced that the divisional commanders would do anything to avoid this, and so would probably take a risk and launch the raid even if the weather was less than perfect. This meant that they would probably be jumping in dangerous conditions. But once again, in mid afternoon, the call came through and the raid was postponed. Everyone was downcast and thoroughly miserable. After all their training and preparation, they had been defeated by the weather.

On the following morning, Friday 27 February, the men awoke to a bitterly cold but bright, clear winter's day. For the first time that week, the wind had died down. Anyone who knew about weather conditions could see that the south of England was under an area of high pressure. Major Frost thought that at any moment he would be ordered to stand the company down, send the men on leave with plans to reorganise and recommence training in a couple of weeks. But then a messenger arrived from Airborne HQ saying that they had decided to keep open the window of opportunity for the raid for one more night. Everyone was instructed to repeat one final time the whole procedure they had carried out three times already. The men grudgingly packed the containers and prepared their weapons once more. But few did so with much heart. Listlessly and without enthusiasm they went through the motions. Only Company Sergeant-Major Gerry Strachan exuded confidence, telling everyone he was convinced that this was the night. As he bounded about encouraging them, no doubt most of the men thought this was just an act to get them to complete their preparations for a fourth, fruitless time.

That morning a meeting took place in Portsmouth between Commander Cook and Admiral James, the commander of the operation. James had been bombed out of his old office and had moved on to HMS *Victory*, which was in dry dock. In the bizarre setting of Nelson's historic cabin, Cook and James reviewed the latest weather forecast delivered by the RAF meteorological team. Aircraft from Coastal Command flew regular sorties out in the Atlantic to take readings of wind speed and direction, air pressure, temperature and humidity. From this data future weather conditions could be predicted in some detail.[1] Even though the ideal moon and tide conditions had passed, the forecast predicted good weather that night with calm seas and little wind, for the first time that week.

James was still hesitant, as he feared that by the time the landing craft came in the tide would be going out, making embarkation difficult. Cook, eager to avoid the crashing disappointment of a postponement of the operation, produced what he described as his 'trump card'. He had found a pre-war picture postcard of the beach at Bruneval showing a lady bather in summertime standing near the sea. From this it was possible to see that the beach on which the embarkation was to take place was less steep than they had imagined, and so the change in tidal conditions would be less critical. As a result James was persuaded that the raid should definitely go ahead.[2] But first he rang Group Captain Norman and General Browning to get their views. Both were keen to commit to the raid. James needed to decide before lunchtime, as the *Prinz Albert* had to depart on its Channel crossing in the afternoon in order to be in position, with the landing craft standing by, in the early hours. He hesitated only briefly and then sent out the signal: 'Proceed with Operation Biting.'

Once again, soon after lunch, Major Frost was called to the telephone at Tilshead camp. He was sure that he would be told to stand down. But this time he was given a different instruction.

The mission was on and the men were to prepare for transport to the aerodrome. Immediately, as the news rapidly spread, everyone was galvanised. As the men rushed around finalising their own personal affairs and checking their identity tags, some of the doubters were still saying that the whole thing would be cancelled once again. But, as if to confirm everything was now set to go, a selection of the men were issued with French currency, ten-franc notes, in case they were left in France and needed cash, while a few of the Paras received handkerchiefs with a map of France printed on them. Then, in his immaculate uniform and looking every inch the commander of men in battle, General Browning himself appeared at Tilshead to wish the men luck and give them a final pep talk about the importance of the mission they were about to undertake. There was no doubting now. This was it.

The men were given a hot meal at Tilshead, and soon after tea time vehicles arrived to ferry them the few miles to the airfield at Thruxton. Frost had his meal with officers from the Glider Regiment with whom he was sharing the billet. The glider troops were still blissfully ignorant about what their colleagues in C Company were up to. Frost had to remain silent about the raid and remembered thinking as he looked at the other officers around the table, 'You have no idea. In two or three hours I'll be flying off to France. I have a rather exciting appointment.' However, at the end of the meal, his mood changed and as the officers from the Glider Regiment settled down in the mess for a quiet doze around the fire, Frost thought, 'Lucky devils, soon going off to bed in a warm little hut while we'll be shivering and miserable somewhere up above, going to goodness knows what.'[3] With these thoughts in mind, he and his batman boarded their vehicle and headed off for Thruxton.

The paratroopers were taken to three blacked-out Nissen huts around the perimeter of the airfield. Inside, they found their parachutes, neatly packed and in lines of ten, laid out for each of the twelve aircraft that would fly that night. The men were offered sandwiches and cups of tea. Chatting nervously, they checked each other's parachute straps, told jokes and tried to keep cheerful. Some blacked their faces so they would not stand out at night. A reporter later noted that 'even their teeth' had been blacked up.[4] They only wanted one thing now, to get on with it.

Major Frost and Sergeant-Major Strachan went from hut to hut to talk with their men and give out any final instructions. They wished them luck and generally gave off a sense of optimism and confidence. It was just what men about to go into combat needed. They had been given their detailed briefings and knew the landscape they were to operate in, but only now were they informed that the location of Operation Biting was the cliffs of northern France. As the target was just on the other side of the Channel, it would be a relatively short flight to the drop zone.

Frost was outside one of the huts when Group Captain Norman appeared. He had come down to Thruxton to wish Frost and his men good luck. But Norman had also just received the latest weather report from an RAF aircraft over the coast at Bruneval. He told Frost that conditions were excellent. The sea was calm, visibility was good, at least three to four miles, the cloud was thick at a little under 2000 feet, so it would be easy to see the ground from the aircraft and identify the DZs.

Norman finished by telling Frost, 'The latest news is that there is snow on the other side and I'm afraid the flak seems to be lively.'[5] Then he wished him good luck, turned and departed for Portsmouth, where he would sit out the night following the news of the raid in Admiral James's command post.

Frost's heart dropped. He thought about all the RAF aircraft that were supposedly carrying out their diversionary raids but had in effect awoken a hornet's nest along the French coast. Maybe every anti-aircraft gunner in northern France would be alerted and waiting for the squadron of Whitleys when they finally made it over there later that night. He was also irritated to hear of the snow. There was no snow in southern England and he had expected none in France. He fretted about the fact they had left their white smocks back at Tilshead. Maybe they would be highly visible in dark gear crossing the expanse of white and an easy target for the local defenders. But it was too late to do anything about that now. Frost went around the men for one final visit to tell them the latest news. He tried to be encouraging and not to show the qualms he was now feeling about the mission ahead.

In the middle of the evening, soon after 2130, in the darkness, the Paras of C Company finally marched from their Nissen huts out on to the tarmac of the apron to the waiting aircraft. The company piper, Piper Ewing, piped them out, playing the regimental marches of each of the Scottish units from which the men had been drawn. There was nothing like the sound of bagpipes to send men into battle. As on so many occasions in the years before when Scottish troops had prepared for combat, the bagpipes had the effect of steeling the men and instilling them with a fighting spirit. Added to this was the relaxed bravado of the RAF crews who met the men at their aircraft. Flying over occupied Europe at night was routine for them. Their business-as-usual attitude helped to provide extra courage.

All that is, except Wing Commander Charles Pickard. This evening the dashing pilot and famous film veteran felt less than sure about the whole mission. Before getting into his plane, he took Frost aside and expressed his fears to him, saying that carrying all these paratroopers into action made him 'feel like a bloody murderer'.[6] It was an extraordinary thing for an experienced pilot to say to the leader of the men he was flying into action. In many ways it was quite unforgivable. Fortunately, it had little effect on Frost, who was too busy thinking about his men and the problems ahead to be seriously upset.

There was one final task before the men climbed up into the aircraft. The Elsan lavatories had been removed from each plane to reduce weight. Anticipating the consequence, the orders stated that 'troops should relieve themselves last thing before emplaning.'[7] After all the tea they had nervously drunk in the last few hours this was a wise move. Had anyone been watching, they would have seen in the darkness dozens of men laden with parachute packs on their backs, drawn up alongside each Whitley bomber pausing to undo themselves and taking a final piss on to the Hampshire soil. Relieved, they then climbed into their aircraft, so heavily loaded up that each man had to shove the one in front into the fuselage. The last man had to be hauled in by his colleagues.

By 2200 all the men had emplaned. The first of the engines were started up, filling the quietness of the night with the roar of the Rolls-Royce Merlins. For most of the men it was the sound they had been praying to hear for four days. At 2215 the first of the Whitleys began to taxi out to the end of the runway. A few moments later it was airborne and the mission had at long last begun.

The paratroopers had precise positions for the take-off and most of the flight. With a load of ten men, along with the canisters of weapons and other equipment in the bomb bays, each of the Whitleys would be fully loaded. There were no seats in the aircraft and the men had all been weighed in their kit. Frost, for instance, weighed in at 93 kg fully laden. Everyone had been allocated positions to balance the aircraft, most of them lying out and spread across the ribs of the fuselage.

Even though the Whitleys would not be flying at a high altitude, it would be freezing cold in the unheated body of the aeroplane. So the Paras were given kapok sleeping bags and a pair of silk gloves to help them keep warm. This was RAF kit and seemed strange to the tough fighting men of the elite Para force. But the men were told that they had to take up their exact pre-assigned positions. The orders made it alarmingly clear by stating that 'with troops aboard the pilot will be unable to control the aircraft unless "TAKE-OFF POSITION" is correctly taken up. The alternative is a crash.'[8] No one wanted to risk that and the big, tough paratroopers obediently crawled into their correct positions.

At roughly sixty-second intervals, each of the remaining eleven Whitley bombers took off. By just after 2230 the last of the bombers was airborne. They flew along the English coast past the RAF fighter station at Tangmere to the rendezvous for their coastal departure point over Selsey Bill. The first aircraft to take off circled over this easily identifiable landmark until all the remaining aircraft in the squadron had arrived. There were no stragglers, so at 2315, precisely on schedule, they headed out across the Channel at 125 mph flying on a direct route for Fécamp, a fishing port on the French coast a few miles north-east of the drop zone. They flew low, just below a thin layer of cloud.[9]

Paratroopers on board aircraft heading for their drop zone experienced a range of emotions. They knew that within a couple of hours they might be fighting for their lives behind enemy lines. Or they might be stranded or isolated, having been dropped in the wrong place. The intelligence itself might prove to be wrong and a reception committee of heavily armed enemy troops might be waiting for them. Worse still, they might be shot down before they even arrived at the drop zone, sending the whole aircraft plummeting in flames. Or their parachute could fail to open and they would plunge to a certain death on the ground below.

This uncertainty was something that all paratroopers faced, whether commanding officers or humble privates. It was unique to parachute forces. The jump out of an aircraft behind enemy lines was something that brought them together in a sort of equality that ground troops never experienced. Several of the men in C Company would go through this many times before the war's end and the veterans would help the newcomers with the inevitable tension that everyone felt. But the night raid at Bruneval was the first time that any of the men had been through this experience. They were all new to the emotions in what seemed to everyone like a long haul as the Whitleys droned on across the Channel, heading for France.

Everyone had a different way of coping with the tension. Some men sang songs to keep their spirits up and to help them feel they were all members of a 'band of brothers' facing the same fate. Others played cards. A few read books or magazines they had brought with them. One or two even managed to doze off, or at least to shut their eyes for a couple of hours of rest and relaxation. Most thought that anyone who could still their nerves, sit quietly and go to sleep on the flight before a combat jump was super-cool. In fact this was not the case. People respond differently to tension and for some it was easier to be calm, collected and self-possessed than it was to take part in communal singing or games. There was not a single man who deep down did not feel fear of what lay ahead. Even if, wanting to appear cool to their mates, they pretended to be unconcerned, it would have been extraordinary not to be anxious. Paratroopers would often say later, 'if you weren't afraid you weren't human'.

On Frost's aircraft the ten men were cheerful. They sang songs and played cards, mostly pontoon. Frost wrote in his report, 'Spirits were high; indeed, I can describe them as terrific.'[10] He later told a reporter that on every aircraft it was as though the men were 'having a concert party'.[11] In one of the aircraft, a group played cards for money. Corporal Stewart, the company gambler, already had a full wallet from previous winnings. He won again and, with his wallet bulging even more, he pointed out that if anything happened to him, whoever was nearby would 'find himself in luck's way'.[12]

Lieutenant Charteris discovered that the man next to him in his aircraft was one day older than he was and they would both be celebrating their twenty-first birthday in a few days' time. They swore they would get through the mission and celebrate together. Again, the men in this aircraft were in high spirits, singing and joking. The only tension that the young officer observed was that the men kept asking him what the time was and how long there was to go. He never gave a precise answer.[13] Clearly, the four-day delay and resulting emotional roller-coaster had not seriously upset the men. They were fully primed and ready for action.

A few hours before and several miles south, on the cliff tops at Bruneval, the nine men on the night shift of the Würzburg had left their billets at Le Presbytère and walked across the field to the radar station. At exactly 1900 hours they had begun to arrive for duty, relieving the day shift. Theirs was the long night shift that would last until 0800 the following morning. Throughout the night, at least two men would be on duty at the radar at any one time. The others would be on lookout duty, or be resting in a dugout next to the site. The small lookout post was a short distance away and contained a machine gun, binoculars and a telephone. Every night the radar men knew that the defence of key German strongpoints in France depended on their vigilance.

As the evening progressed, the radar operators had a busy shift. In the middle of the evening an alert came through from the Freya radar operators of British bombers approaching the port of Le Havre. This was one of the diversionary raids mounted that evening. Accordingly, the power supply was turned on in the nearby dugout and the Würzburg started up. This was a slow business: it always took a few minutes for the equipment to become usable and the cathode ray tube at the centre of the machine needed at least two minutes to warm up. The operators then calibrated their apparatus. This had to be done each time the equipment was started up and was carried out by picking up a return signal from a point at a known distance and direction. The team at Bruneval used an echo point on the cliffs at Étretat about six miles away. They then started to take readings of the height and direction of the bombers, which were about twenty-five miles out to sea, and phoned the readings through to their control headquarters near Le Havre every couple of minutes. After a while the aircraft flew out of range and the Würzburg was turned off.

The whole process was repeated a little later when another group of bombers were spotted off the coast. Instead of getting a little sleep in the dugout, the team remained on alert throughout the evening. But none of them on duty that night had any idea of what was coming their way next.

By contrast, a few hundred yards away, in the old seaside villa Stella Maris down below the cliffs, the night was passing slowly. The sound of anti-aircraft fire against the far-off bombers could barely be heard. And the task of the soldiers here was to guard the beach from possible enemy raiders. They were not concerned with distant air raids. At 2120 the guard changed and those who had been on alert in a dugout looking out to sea came inside and a fresh shift went out to keep watch. The men who had been on duty were relieved to be indoors out of the cold. They kicked off their boots, took off their greatcoats and lay down to rest, as they were allowed to do. Within minutes, most of them were dozing, although the telephone orderly, Corporal Georg Schmidt, remained awake to answer any calls that came in from company or battalion headquarters. For these soldiers it looked like being another long, cold, quiet night.

After a little less than two hours' flying time the Whitleys approached the French coast. The order was shouted down from the cockpit to the men, 'Prepare for action,' and the hole in the base of the aircraft was opened. Immediately the fuselage was filled with freezing night air from outside. The parachute force now gathered themselves for action. Each man connected the static line of his parachute to the cable that ran along the fuselage. Every man checked that the line of the man next to him was fully secured. The men nearest the hole could look out and see the calm sea below.

As predicted, when they approached the French coast the anti-aircraft gunners opened up. Frost looked out and saw the tracers of the anti-aircraft fire coming up towards them, mostly orange with a little red. He thought it looked like 'a pleasant firework show'. But there was nothing pleasant about the heavy fire aimed towards the squadron of bombers. Lieutenant Charteris thought the flak sounded as if 'a man was hammering on a piece of tin below us'.[14] The lucky ones were those inside the aircraft who could not see out. Sergeant Macleod Forsyth was at the back of his Whitley but remembered that the face of the corporal who was sitting at the hole waiting to jump turned a ghastly white. He thought the man was going to be sick. When Forsyth later had a chance to ask him why he had turned so pale, the corporal said, 'So would you if you had seen that tracer coming up at you.'[15]

The pilots started to take evasive action. The risk was that this would throw the aircraft off course and the navigators would get lost, with the consequence that the pilots would drop their cargo in the wrong place. Two and a half years later, this was exactly what would happen on the night before D-Day. On that occasion, the pilots broke formation and rushed to give the signal to jump, in order to get the men out as soon as possible. As a consequence, paratroopers were scattered across tens of miles of countryside, many of them miles from their objectives.

The Whitley bombers flew in a line south-west along the French coast about half a mile out to sea at between 1000 and 1500 feet. The pilots and navigators could clearly see the French cliffs and were able to take a bearing from the Cap d'Antifer lighthouse, the only one along this stretch of coastline. Then, as planned, just before Le Havre the Whitleys turned to port and flew inland for five hundred yards or so. They then turned again to port and flew north-east on a reverse parallel line to that which they had just travelled.

On the ground below, the Würzburg operators grew more alarmed. It looked as though the British aircraft were heading straight for them. There seemed no alternative. They were the target for that night. They were going to be bombed. The sirens rang out and the men in the nearby garrison at Le Presbytère rushed to their dugouts.

As the bombers made their final turn to port the red warning light came on inside the aircraft. The men on board knew that they were only seconds away from the order to jump. Some of them could see the familiar sites of the valleys and woods near the drop zone. The planes were now flying low, at about 400 feet. As the navigator and the pilot spotted the deep valley containing the Bruneval road they pressed the green light. This was the signal for the paratroopers to jump. They should all be out by the time the aircraft had passed the line of trees on the other side of the road.

This was the moment the men had trained so hard for. They had to get out of the aircraft through the hole in the base of the fuselage as quickly as possible without smashing their faces on the side of the hole, the 'Whitley kiss'. As the first men jumped into the cold night air their adrenalin kicked in. The mission was on. There was no turning back now.

16

Attack

Lieutenant Charteris, 'Junior', leading the *Nelson* detachment, jumped from the very first aircraft, which was piloted by Wing Commander Pickard. They were scheduled to jump at precisely 0015. Charteris remembered sitting by the hole and waiting to jump, looking out and seeing every house and every tree passing below. He felt it was unreal, as though he were acting in a play. As soon as the light went green he jumped. It was a lovely drop and he came down 'like a feather' in about ten seconds to make a perfect landing in a field. There was no wind and it was easy to cut away the rigging lines of his parachute. He saw the other nine of his stick landing nearby.

They went straight into the prepared plan, quickly gathering the containers and emptying them. While they were doing this, Charteris was supposed to check out the route to the beach. But almost immediately he realised that something was wrong. There was not a row of trees at the end of the valley as there should have been. For a few seconds he was completely baffled. Where were the trees? Had the model been wrong? Then the horrible truth dawned on him. He and his men had been dropped in the wrong valley. It looked roughly right, but the slopes on either side were not steep enough. The wood they were due to form up against was not where it was supposed to be. But if he and his men weren't where they should be, where on earth were they? Charteris had no idea in what direction the beach was, or how far away. He had a moment of panic. He was behind enemy lines with no idea where he was. He later wrote in his report, 'I don't mind saying that was a nasty moment. I felt very lost.'[1]

As nineteen men from two aircraft gathered around their young officer, fully kitted with all the equipment from the containers, they looked to him for direction. But he had no idea which way to lead them. The valley was completely unfamiliar and the landscape bore no relation to the countryside they had studied so carefully on maps, models and aerial photographs. Moreover, Captain Ross and his team of nineteen men were not there with them. Had they been dropped at the correct drop zone or were they miles away as well, trying to work out what to do? As the men struggled to come to grips with what had happened, the next wave of four Whitleys passed overhead. Charteris knew they would be flying in a north-easterly direction. So at least he knew which direction north was. The problem was, had they been dropped too soon, in which case they would have to go north to find Bruneval and complete their mission? Or too late, and would have to go in the opposite direction to join up with the rest of the party? Charteris took a gamble and calculated that it was most likely he had been dropped too soon. He told the men that they should head north, but they had to move at speed as they might be several miles from Bruneval.

He worried to himself that he was wrong, that they would get so far and then have to turn around, retrace their steps and head off in the opposite direction. He knew this would be disastrous for morale. Trying not to show his concerns, he ordered his men to spread out in a rough diamond shape. He led from the front and the men set off in what he desperately hoped was the right direction. With speed of the essence, he led his men in a slow run and they jogged off to the north at what Charteris reckoned was about 6 mph. The fact that Charteris had been dropped in the wrong place and didn't even know if he was heading in the right direction was not a good start to the raid.

The German soldiers in the vicinity had been roused by the sound of the low-flying aircraft. The sergeant in charge of the platoon at the Hotel Beau-Minet had seen in the distance further inland what looked like British paratroopers dropping to the ground. At precisely 0015 he called his company headquarters at La Poterie to report that he believed the enemy had dropped parachute troops in the vicinity. Company commander Oberleutnant Huhn was immediately alerted. It so happened that the company had been carrying out an exercise that night and about thirty men had just returned to base. Huhn immediately ordered them to march to Le Presbytère to reinforce the Luftwaffe troops there. This was not good for the British raiding party. They had anticipated that it would take at least two hours for any troops from La Poterie to arrive on the scene, but the first platoon were on their way within minutes of the first Para landing.

Huhn also ordered the sergeant at the Beau-Minet to alert the guard at the Stella Maris. The NCO in charge was told to take a section and man the machine-gun positions above the villa and on the other side of the cliff. At this point the German commander still had no idea of what was going on, how many men might have landed or what their objective could possibly be. But, thanks to his quick response, the German defenders were rallying far more rapidly and efficiently than the British had hoped.

Five minutes after Charteris and the first contingent had jumped, at 0020, Major Frost and his party of men arrived over their DZ. Frost was the fifth out of his aircraft and had the responsibility of tugging on the cord that released the containers from the Whitley's bomb bay. As he went down he had time to look around him, and in the bright moonlight he recognised the terrain exactly as the model had shown it, with a row of trees by a steep gully. Frost and his party, the forty men of *Jellicoe*, *Hardy* and *Drake*, were dropped right into the centre of their intended DZ. This was a fantastic feat of flying by the pilots and navigators of the relatively slow-moving, heavily loaded bombers, who for the last few minutes had been flying under continuous anti-aircraft fire. The RAF crews with their cool heads had dropped this group of men perfectly on target.

For Frost and his men, the night's work was now beginning. He landed softly in the snow after a perfect descent. Then, partly due to nerves, partly as a consequence of suddenly hitting the cold night air, and partly because of all the cups of tea he had drunk before emplaning, Frost felt an urgent call of nature. The first thing he did on landing in occupied Europe behind enemy lines after removing his parachute was to relieve himself. He realised this was 'not good drill', as paratroopers are at their most vulnerable in the moments after landing, but he later rather proudly described it as a 'gesture of defiance'.[2]

Sergeant-Major Strachan soon appeared in order to check that his commanding officer was all right, then led the men in gathering up their containers, unpacking the equipment and forming up in their allotted positions by the line of trees. With everyone present and correct they quickly moved off, silently and stealthily, towards the plateau on the cliffs. They saw no evidence of any German alarm and after only about ten minutes they had covered the required six hundred yards and reached the Villa Gosset. There was no sign of any reception party waiting for them. Relieved that the security of the mission had apparently been preserved, Frost gave the order for the men to pan out as planned. By about 0040 the villa and the Würzburg radar apparatus was surrounded. So far, everything for Frost's men had gone exactly to plan, and not a single bullet had been fired.

Imagining that the Villa Gosset was the headquarters of the Luftwaffe radar platoon and their associated signallers and defenders, it was written into the plan that the attack on this building would mark the formal start of the raid. There had been much debate about how to enter the villa, but Frost was surprised to find the door wide open. When everyone was in position he went up to the door and at the last minute remembered to blow his whistle, the signal the paratroopers had been waiting for. He blew a long, hard blast. On the sound of it, the night raid began in earnest.

Frost and six men charged into the ground floor through the open door. Frost fired eight rounds from his pistol. Another group of men burst in through windows on the other side of the house. They threw grenades into each of the four rooms on the ground floor but each room was completely empty. The paratroopers charged up the stairs, yelling at the top of their voices in English 'Surrender' and in German '*Hände hoch*'. Along with this they screamed out obscenities ... in English. It was enough to get their blood up and to terrify any enemy soldiers.

They burst into a room on the first floor where a single German soldier with a rifle was looking out the window towards the Würzburg. The poor man did not stand a chance. The first Para into the room killed him with a burst from his Sten gun.

To Frost's surprise, there were no other Germans in the villa. It was completely empty except for this single man. There was not even any furniture in any of the rooms. What they did not know was that the RAF had bombed the conspicuous looking building about six months earlier and an incendiary had dropped on the bed belonging to the sergeant in charge. From that point on, the German soldiers had avoided using the villa, thinking it was safer to sleep outside in the dugouts. In all their planning the Paras had anticipated an intense fire fight to gain control of the villa. But now in minutes it was theirs. It all seemed to be too easy.

As he surveyed the villa's bare rooms, Frost heard firing and the sound of grenades being thrown around the radar installation itself, a hundred yards away outside. After a few more shots had been fired everything went quiet. He told his men to wait on guard in the villa. Everyone was in a state of heightened tension but they maintained strict order. Frost and another soldier went outside and ran across the grass the short distance to the radar installation. Here there had certainly been a skirmish. The Paras' orders had been to take as prisoners only men who appeared to be radar experts or operators. Lieutenant Peter Young followed this to the letter. The Germans had been in their dugouts around the radar installation when the firing began. They were soon overwhelmed. Everyone had been killed or had run away into the dark. Young moved through the dugouts to ensure that there were no survivors and said he would have shot anyone who was not a radar operator. Even Sergeant McKenzie, his hardened NCO, had been shocked by this and had called him a 'cruel bastard'. But orders were orders.

Young later reported that all the Germans had been killed in the skirmish; after the first sentry to challenge the Paras had been shot dead, 'we hunted them [the rest of the Germans in the dugouts around the Würzburg] out of the cellars, trenches and rooms with hand grenades, automatic weapons, revolvers and knives. Most were killed, but some ran away.' He described how one of those who had tried to run away had fallen about ten feet down the side of the cliff. The Paras quickly found him and ordered him back up the cliff side with his hands up. Young remembered, 'At the time I thought I had never seen anything funnier than a German trying to scramble up the lip of a cliff with his hands up.'[3]

When Frost arrived, Young told him that five Germans were dead. At that moment the Paras appeared with the prisoner who had fallen over the edge of the cliff. They had retrieved him and now he stood before the British Paras, petrified. They must have looked a terrifying sight, their faces blacked up and 'with their blood up', as it was said at the time. They could see he had Luftwaffe markings on his uniform. He clearly had something to do with the radar. Frost called for the interpreter, Nagel, the man known as Private Newman. He immediately went up to the prisoner and with his bare hands ripped the Luftwaffe badge off his lapel. A soldier asked, 'Why did you do that?'

'For my personal satisfaction,' replied Nagel. It was the first time the German-born Jew had seen a German soldier in uniform and the hatred he felt erupted in this spontaneous act.

Frost wanted to try to find out from the terrified prisoner the strength of the local German garrison. Through Nagel, he asked the prisoner how many Germans there were in the immediate vicinity. With a sudden swell of courage, the German replied defiantly, 'One thousand.' Sergeant McKenzie struck him hard across his jaw with the butt of his rifle. Another man made it clear that he thought they should kill the prisoner now. Stunned and near to tears, the prisoner's courage collapsed and he rapidly started to tell his captors that there were only a hundred Germans in the neighbourhood. This was exactly what the intelligence reports had predicted.

Alarmingly, however, the prisoner said they had all been warned an hour ago that British parachutists had landed in the vicinity. It appeared that the prisoner's name was Heller. He admitted that he was from a Luftwaffe signals regiment and he explained that he operated the big radar they were standing next to. This was just the sort of prisoner that the Paras wanted. He could be a valuable addition to the night's work. Frost instructed his men to keep the German under guard. Delighted with how the raid was progressing so far, Frost then turned his attention to the radar. The engineers had been kept in the shadows up to now. It was time for them to come forward and fulfil their part of the mission.

Flight Sergeant Charles Cox, whose task it was to dismantle the Würzburg, had been in the same Whitley as Major Frost and had joined the men in the singing as they flew over the Channel. Reputed to have a good voice, Cox bellowed out a solo of 'The Rose of Tralee', trying hard to make himself heard above the engine noise, and was mightily cheered by the others when he finished the song. Cox remembered that when they were a few minutes from jumping Frost passed around a flask of tea mixed with rum and he had a couple of small sips from it. Like for everyone else, the next few minutes passed quickly in a blur. Cox jumped as number seven from the plane. He remembered hearing the command 'Number Seven – Go!' and recalled dropping through the hole. He remembered the tug as his parachute opened and then landing softly in the snow. He gathered in his parachute and felt a strong sense of loneliness, standing there in the silence of a French field, far from home. Then the others began to appear in the darkness and Cox ran to the canisters, which were easy to spot with their flashing coloured lights. He and the other Paras unpacked the elaborate trolleys they had brought to carry off the radar apparatus. Some of the men now headed off with Frost to attack the villa and the radar. Cox was told to remain in the rear until the location was secure.

The RAF sergeant loaded up the trolleys with all the other equipment, and he and a couple of sappers moved off towards the forming-up position, where they would meet Lieutenant Vernon and the rest of the engineers. This was to the left of the main group, just above the steep slope that ran down to the road and the small village of Bruneval. It was tough going pulling the loaded trolleys across the snow and at one point they had to pull them over a barbed wire fence. Cox cut his hands doing this, and thought 'First blood to Jerry.' But at about 0040 he met up with Vernon, who had also had a good jump and with the rest of the engineers had arrived at the rendezvous in perfect time.

The men lay for some time in the snow listening to the sound of the fighting around the villa and the Würzburg. Then it fell silent. After a few minutes they heard grenades going off in the valley below. Cox thought to himself that there must be a battle taking place for the village. Vernon told Cox and the other sappers to stay where they were as he crawled forward to see if they had the all-clear to approach the Würzburg.

When he reached the installation there was still some confusion among the Paras around the site. Vernon made contact with Lieutenant Young, who told him they had found nothing in the dugouts and trenches of any interest and that the villa appeared to be empty of equipment or papers of any sort. Vernon tried to make contact with Frost but couldn't find him in the dark. Frost was told that the engineer was there but couldn't locate him either. 'Vernon, Vernon, where are you?' he called out urgently. Vernon was only a few yards away as it turned out. Frost told him the site was secure and he could now start his work.

About ten minutes had passed, and Vernon sent a runner back to tell Cox to come forward with the trolleys. Soon after 0100 Cox rejoined Vernon at the radar apparatus. The paratroopers were kneeling and in position all around the Würzburg. This was what they had come for. The target of the mission was there in front of them. The lives of thousands of aircrew could be saved if the components they took now helped the boffins back home to understand how this device operated.

Cox began to size up the apparatus. Just as he had expected, it consisted of a big conical transmitter aerial about ten feet in diameter, supported on a chassis. Behind this was a cupboard or cabin about four feet high by three and a half feet wide and a few feet deep. In addition to this was the unit containing the electrical operating gear. The whole radar installation was in a pit with a two-foot wall running around the side of it. Vernon started to take photographs of the apparatus with his Leica. But the flashes immediately provoked a response from the enemy. From the copse at Theuville known as the *Rectangle* the enemy opened fire.

The Wehrmacht infantry platoon that had been out on exercises had now joined up with the Luftwaffe ground troops at Le Presbytère. Together these men had moved forward to the tree line between the Freyas and the Würzburg on the cliff plateau. Their immediate response was to think that the Freyas had come under attack, as this was a bigger installation, older and more established. But it did not take them long to realise that the British paratroopers appeared to have occupied the Villa Gosset and had attacked the Würzburg installation instead. Although these were mainly Luftwaffe ground troops, most of them were armed with rifles and they had with them two light machine guns. As soon as they had surveyed the situation and lined up behind the trees they opened fire. The British parachute troops were only about four hundred yards away and were clearly visible in the bright moonlight against the snow.

The final party of British paratroopers, the group known as *Rodney* commanded by Lieutenant Timothy, had been third to jump, five minutes after Frost and his men. Everything went smoothly for the first of the four aircraft and the men jumped at 0024 right into their correct DZ. It was another instance of masterly flying by the RAF. The second aircraft, however, dropped its stick short of Bruneval. They took some time to form up with the rest of the section on the ground. There was a further problem in the third aircraft. The first group of men were again dropped in the wrong valley. Then, the number five paratrooper caught his foot in the static lines of the men who had already jumped. He was somehow thrown forward and found himself suspended head first, with his feet caught in the lines, three-quarters out of the hole in the base of the aircraft. It was a terrifying position to be in. The remaining men managed to haul him back in. The pilot, with steely nerves despite the anti-aircraft fire, agreed to fly in a circuit out over the sea and come around again. When they were over their DZ, the rest of the men jumped, including the brave man who had nearly been thrown out of the plane on his first attempt.[4] It was the one jumping mishap that night and it only delayed the forming up of the men who had reached the correct DZ by about five minutes.

Their job completed, the pilots turned for home and headed back across the Channel. The first aircraft landed back at Thruxton at 0140 and the remainder over the next fifty minutes. Although three of the Whitleys had been hit by flak, none of the damage was serious and no one had been injured. For Pickard and his men, their night's work was done.

Once they had organised themselves on the ground, the

Rodney team took up their position behind the main assault party, to defend the rear of Frost's men from any significant counter-attack from La Poterie or any of the other German troops known to be in the area. But the men who were missing from the first batch of the third aircraft included two of the radio operators with their invaluable 38 radio sets.

Major Frost was not surprised that he and his men were now coming under fire from the *Rectangle*. That had been anticipated. But he was alarmed at how quickly the German troops seemed to have got themselves into position and opened fire. Frost ordered the men he had left at the Villa Gosset to withdraw from what was too clear a target and to join the rest of them around the Würzburg. It was while the men were leaving the villa that, in an early salvo fired from the *Rectangle*, Private McIntyre buckled and went down. He was the first British soldier killed in the raid. Frost ordered Lieutenant Naumoff, who was in charge of the *Drake* party, to deploy to the right of his men and to return fire into the *Rectangle*. Suddenly, the area around the Würzburg had become none too healthy.

Vernon continued to take photos and Cox began the well-drilled process of dismantling the gear. Sapper Stan Halliwell leapt up on to the concrete wall with a hacksaw and prepared to cut the radio cable. He paused for a moment, wondering if the power supply had been turned off. If not, he knew he was in for 'a shocking experience'. But there was no problem and his hacksaw sliced through the cable in seconds.[5]

Then Cox went around to the back of the big metal cabin and severed the cable connecting it to the aerial. They managed to break in to the cabin, which contained several smaller units in closed boxes: the transmitter, the oscillator, the amplifier, the cathode ray tubes and the pulse generator. This was the heart of the machine and the key zone that the engineers had been told to search for. It had been switched off but was still warm from earlier use that evening. Cox and Corporal Jones, another sapper, began trying to unscrew the panels with the various screwdrivers and spanners they had with them. It would have been difficult work in any circumstances but in the dark and under fire it was a real struggle, and it seemed desperately slow going. Cox wrote later that 'bullets were flying much too close to be pleasant', but working behind the cabin and the aerial they at least had some protection. He remembered calmly in his report that 'Two bullets hit the apparatus, but most of the machine gun fire went high.'[6]

As Cox and Jones continued to try to unscrew the key units, Vernon carried on taking photos with his flashlight. Each flash seemed to attract more fire from the German soldiers in the *Rectangle*. And all the time their fire seemed to get more accurate. Every time Vernon used his flashbulb the paratroopers kneeling or lying around the Würzburg cursed and swore at him. Their loud protests made the task of the dismantling squad even more difficult.

Despite the return fire from Naumoff and the *Drake* party, the German soldiers in the *Rectangle* were becoming more organised and more determined. A few had moved out from behind the trees and taken up positions in the open space between Theuville and the villa. Oberleutnant Huhn was still at his headquarters at La Poterie trying to piece together the disparate fragments of information that were coming in, attempting to understand what was happening and how many of the enemy had landed in his area. But more German troops were heading for the fire fight that was taking place on the cliff plateau.

If Huhn was having difficulty making sense of what was going on around Bruneval, Frost had his own problems. By now, he knew that Charteris and his *Nelson* party had been dropped in the wrong place and had not yet taken control of the beach. He didn't know where they were or how long it would take them to arrive, or if they would arrive at all. This was disastrous for the raiding party on the cliff top as they had no route along which to withdraw with their precious cargo. Some of the radio operators were missing and in any case the new radios were not working properly. As a consequence Frost had no clear communications with parts of his company. He cursed the fact that he and his party had been organised into an assault group for the attack and he now had no sort of company organisation around him through which to receive information and issue orders. Men who would otherwise be runners, and his company sergeant-major, Strachan, were dispersed and totally occupied with their own tasks. Meanwhile, as the Germans kept up their fire against the main operation at the Würzburg, Vernon, Cox and Jones were still bravely attempting to dismantle the apparatus.

Cox and Vernon were aware that they had hit a problem. Although a sapper had removed many of the labels, which showed that most of the equipment was made by Telefunken, they were unable to unscrew the boxes containing the main components. They took a decision to try to smash their way into the boxes. Using jemmies, hammers and axes they started to attack the solidly constructed units with brute force. They realised they might damage some of the equipment in so doing but at this point it was a risk that seemed reasonable to take. With Corporal Jones providing leverage on a large crowbar, part of the frame came away with a tearing sound. It turned out not to be just the casing of the cabin but the switching unit that allowed both the transmitter and the receiver to use the single aerial. It was a vital part of the Würzburg's design.

Vernon took one last photograph and the flashbulb lit up what would have seemed a very strange scene. A group of heavily armed Paras with blackened faces, in full kit, were kneeling or lying holding Sten guns alongside a team of what looked like burglars with jemmies and a crowbar standing around a small cabinet and a large radar bowl on the top of a cliff in northern France.

Frost now had to make a decision. The German fire was becoming ever more determined and more accurate. But his exit route to the beach was still not open. It looked as if the men on the cliffs would have to fight their way down. While he was still weighing this up, a paratrooper alerted him to the fact that in the distance three vehicles appeared to be approaching Le Presbytère. Were these reinforcements, or were they armoured vehicles that had arrived far sooner than expected? The co-ordination of the German response seemed to be far better than the planners had anticipated. The Paras could probably withstand the small-arms fire and the machine guns for a bit longer, but if reinforcements with mortars or artillery pieces were now arriving they would become easy targets. The men around the Würzburg were getting impatient with the process of dismantling the gear. Vernon and Cox grew increasingly heavy-handed, smashing at boxes and pulling out whatever bits of electronic gear they could.

Frost made up his mind. He ordered the engineers to stop work and the men to pull out and head towards the beach. The Paras had rehearsed this many times and each man knew what he had to do. But what they didn't know was what they would find 300 feet below them on the road.

17

Fire Fight

Captain Ross, C Company's second-in-command, was part of the *Nelson* group that had jumped in the first wave that night. But unlike the twenty men of that group who had been dropped in the wrong place, Ross and his men jumped on target into the correct DZ. They soon realised that the rest of *Nelson* were not with them. They waited for a few minutes at the forming-up position to see if Charteris and the others would arrive, but when they didn't show Ross decided he had to carry on regardless.

The original plan to attack the beach defenders called for one section to assault the machine-gun position and the casemates on the north side of the beach road. These were the German positions that lay between the beach and Frost's party on the cliff plateau. On the other slope, Charteris was to lead the main assault on the Stella Maris and the network of defences just above it called *Beach Fort*. Ross and his section was to provide covering fire and prevent any troops stationed at the Hotel Beau-Minet from coming up to give support to the German positions on the beach. This plan had now to be seriously reassessed. Ross had only half of the men he should have had to carry out the assault. So he split them into three groups. Sergeant Tasker was to take a group to attack the casemates on the northern cliff. Sergeant Sharp was told to move down that slope towards the wire on the beach. Ross himself, with a small group, would try to clear the enemy from the defensive positions above the Stella Maris.

Early that evening everything had seemed very quiet and normal at the Stella Maris, despite the sound of the distant air raids. The raids had become so frequent that they ceased to bother the men guarding this small stretch of beach. The section that had changed shifts at 2120 had come in and settled down for some rest. There were nine men with a sergeant in charge. Then, soon after 0015, Corporal Schmidt had been startled by the ringing telephone. It was the company headquarters at La Poterie calling to say that there were reports that enemy parachutists had been dropped in the area.

The telephone orderly woke the sergeant in charge, who was told to man his defences around the villa in case British paratroopers came his way. He ordered his men to wake up and prepare for action. He grew annoyed at how long it took some of them to get ready. For many, no doubt, it felt like yet another exercise dreamed up by their officers to test their response in the middle of the night. Even if it was not an exercise, it would no doubt prove to be a false alarm. As the men grudgingly got themselves organised, the sergeant distributed hand grenades. The machine gun positioned at the front of the villa overlooking the beach was removed and taken to be installed in the defences above, overlooking the road and the steep slope running up the cliff opposite.

By 0030 the men at the Stella Maris were in position and waiting to see what would happen next. Only Corporal Schmidt, the telephone orderly, had been left behind to keep in touch with company and battalion headquarters in order to relay any further messages that came through.

Initially, things went well for Ross and his men. Tasker's squad started to move on the casemates and Sharp and his team moved down towards the wire across the entry point to the beach. But then, in the bright moonlight, the sergeant from the Stella Maris, on full alert, spotted Sharp and his men moving across the hill on the far side of the road. He could not see who they were but was immediately suspicious. He fired a white Very light into the sky above where he saw movement, which lit up the whole area. If they were German troops they would fire a different-coloured flare in response. But no response came. So the sergeant fired his automatic pistol across the valley towards the moving figures. In the moonlight he could see men scattering across the ground opposite. A new fire fight now began down in the valley by the sea. This would be a much tougher and longer fight than the one that had taken place on the top of the cliff.

The sergeant had spotted Ross's men as they moved down the gully towards the beach road. They immediately returned the fire and directed their weapons towards the old villa, the outline of which they could clearly see across the valley. However, the sergeant at the beach post ordered the rest of his men into the defensive positions above the villa at *Beach Fort* where he had already positioned his machine gun. This gun now opened fire on the Paras on the slope opposite, forcing them to lie low. But then Tasker's men, higher up the side of the cliff and overlooking *Beach Fort*, opened fire on the German troops, spraying the whole area with bullets from their Sten guns. Now it was the turn of the German defenders to get their heads down.

Before long Sharp's men joined in the firing. The Germans were surprised at the intensity of the fire that was now coming at them and had no idea how many British paratroopers they were up against. But they were well dug in. Their defensive positions, identified in the aerial photographs, had only been completed about two weeks before. The Germans now threw their grenades as well. A full-scale battle erupted along the road to the beach. But neither side showed any sign of giving way.

From the cliffs above, Frost could hear the sound of a fierce fire fight taking place in the valley. The commander of the raid was continuing to regret the failure of the radio communications and began increasingly to feel that he simply did not know enough about what was going on, who was where, and who was firing on whom. He gave the order for Lieutenant Young and the *Jellicoe* section to move down from the cliff plateau to give support to Ross and his men. They started to slowly descend the cliff towards the gully. Frost made contact with Lieutenant Timothy and instructed him to keep watch on Le Presbytère, but to send men up the valley towards the beach to help in the assault on the German positions up there.

Inside the Stella Maris there was intense activity. Men were rushing in from the positions above to collect ammunition, grenades and more Very flares to light up the area. With the sound of battle echoing up the valley, the phone kept ringing and the telephone orderly was kept busy. Before long the battalion commander from Bordeaux-St-Clair, Major Paschke, came on the phone. He asked what was going on and Corporal Schmidt explained they were in a fight with British paratroopers. Paschke sounded as though he didn't believe what he was being told and asked to speak to the sergeant. The orderly went outside to try to call him to the phone, but immediately came under fire from the other side of the valley. Major Paschke never got to speak to the sergeant. The fire fight continued to rage across the valley by the entrance to the beach.

The Royal Navy was of course to provide the third element of the raid that night, the evacuation from the beach. But they were having their own problems that night. HMS *Prinz Albert* had left Portsmouth in the afternoon of the day before and sailed without incident to a point about fifteen miles north of Bruneval. Accompanying her were the six fast-moving MGBs. Weather conditions were near perfect, with no wind, a calm sea and a bright moon with only a very slight haze. At precisely 2152 she offloaded the six Assault Landing Craft and two further Support Landing Craft. They were to wait off the beach until requested to come in and embark the whole paratrooper force. On board each of the ALCs were the men from the South Wales Borderers and the Royal Fusiliers, armed with Bren guns to fire up at the cliff defences if there was still fighting going on when they arrived at the beach. In one of the landing craft was the *Noah* party, with Donald Preist, the TRE radar specialist.

The small flotilla moved away and assembled off the coast at 0025 to wait for the signal from the paratroopers to come ashore. Not far away, the lighthouse at Cap d'Antifer suddenly turned its light on and gave a couple of flashes as it rotated. It was a form of reassurance for the men in the landing craft, suggesting that nothing unusual was happening. The ships' navigators were delighted to take a bearing from the lighthouse and confirm their precise location. It seemed a stroke of good luck. But not for long.

The ALCs were about a mile and a half offshore when suddenly the lookouts sounded the alert. The lighthouse beam had been turned on to assist a line of larger ships that came into view moving rapidly down the coast from north to south about a mile further out to sea. The men on board knew they had to be enemy ships. They identified two German single-funnel destroyers and two E-boats, fast, deadly, torpedo-carrying motor boats. Had someone given their position away? Commander Cook told the vessels to cut their engines and to maintain silence. The men on board the landing craft could do nothing but hold their breath and pray.[1] They would be easy targets for the German ships. The British sailors now cursed the clear light of the moon brightening up the sea. The MGB crews prepared for action but knew that they would be totally outgunned by the German vessels. Sergeant Eric Gould waiting on his landing craft was 'scared to death' at the sight of the enemy ships and overheard one of the sailors say, 'God, I hope they don't see us or they'll blow us out of the water.'[2]

The German vessels sailed on by, but then they slowed up. Had they spotted the ALCs and their escorts? The German ships seemed to be altering course. Then, to the immense relief of the crews watching from the landing craft and the MGBs, the German vessels moved on towards Le Havre. It seemed that they had been waiting for clearance to enter the harbour.

As the German vessels disappeared towards Le Havre, the British sailors gave an immense sigh of relief. Because they had been between the German vessels and the land the British vessels had been disguised and had not been spotted, even though it was such a clear night. It would have been the end of the whole operation if the German destroyers and E-boats had got in among the evacuation fleet. But the incident underlined the huge risks that were being taken by having such a tiny flotilla of small British vessels off the coast of occupied France in waters that the Kriegsmarine regarded as its own. As the men recovered their composure, some of the sailors detected a freshening wind blowing up from the south-west. If it strengthened it could blow everything off course.

Back in the valley leading down to the beach, the fire fight had reached stalemate. The German soldiers in their well dug in defensive positions were spraying the area where the British paratroopers were thought to be with machine-gun fire. The Paras were returning the fire from at least three positions, but there were too few of them to carry the day.

It was at around this time, at 0115, up on the cliff plateau, that Frost and his men found themselves under ever-increasing fire from the German troops in the copse four hundred yards to their north. Cox and Vernon had barely been allowed ten of the thirty minutes allocated to them to take apart the Würzburg. But Frost could not hold on any longer. The Germans had rallied too quickly and the Paras were impatient to move. And he had already sent Young and his section down to assist Ross's men. On hearing the order to withdraw, Cox gathered up everything he and Vernon had pulled out of the Würzburg cabin. Together they placed it on the trolleys, barely aware of what they were taking with them and what they were leaving behind. They started to haul the cumbersome trolleys along the plateau to the edge of the cliff. It was no easy task but everyone gave a hand. Behind him, Cox heard an explosion as the engineers blew up what was left of the Würzburg.

When they reached the top of the steep descent to the beach they found the pillbox that they knew as the *Redoubt*. Fortunately, it was not manned. The Germans had been taken by surprise to the extent that they had not had time to fortify all their positions. As the Paras moved around the pillbox Frost heard a voice coming up from the valley below that seemed to say, 'The boats are here. It's all right. Come on down.' With a great sense of relief, he led his men forward over the crest to start their descent down the steep 370-foot slope. Just at that moment the machine gunner that had been pinning the men down at the bottom of the valley spotted the British paratroopers clearly silhouetted as they came over the top of the cliff. The gunner instantly opened fire. Sergeant-Major Strachan, who was about five yards behind Frost, dropped in a hail of gunfire. He had stopped seven bullets, three in his stomach.

Frost immediately went back to help him. He could barely believe that this heavyweight brute of a man was lying there in agony in front of him. He pulled him into some cover behind the pillbox. Remembering that some of the men had morphine on them, he called one of them over to give Strachan an injection. It gave some rapid relief, but it was clear that Strachan was in a bad way and might not survive for long without serious medical attention.

Just as he was considering this, Frost heard another shout

from the valley below. This time he recognised it as Ross, who he knew was down in the valley somewhere leading the assault on the beach defences. Ross shouted up, 'Don't come down. The beach has not yet been taken.' Having reached this point, however, Frost had no alternative. He told Cox, Vernon and the other sappers to dump the radar equipment near the pillbox and ordered everyone to lie down and take cover. Another hail of gunfire came up from the machine gun below. One of the bullets grazed Cox's boot, but fortunately he was not hurt. They would have to remain on the shoulder of the cliff. They were stuck up there, for now.

Lieutenant Euan Charteris and the other nineteen men from *Nelson* who had been dropped into the wrong valley had travelled about three-quarters of a mile when he saw through the trees the Cap d'Antifer lighthouse in the distance. It was a great relief to the young officer, as he knew now that he was heading in the right direction. It turned out that he had been dropped about two and a half miles south of the intended DZ. He was now moving up a track in a valley and thought that if he continued he would probably come out into the village of Bruneval before long. Aware that there was a platoon of men stationed at the Hotel Beau-Minet in the centre of the village, he nevertheless knew how critical his part of the operation was and how much every delayed minute cost the mission, so he decided to continue regardless. He spread his men out in the wood at either side of the road and carried on at a jog, hoping that if they circuited the village silently they would manage to reach the beach and carry out the assault they were there to lead.

The soldiers based at the Hotel Beau-Minet were utterly confused by what was happening around them. They knew that

British parachutists were in the area but they had no idea how many, where they were or what they were trying to do. They heard firing from the cliff top, and then the sound of battle coming up from the beach about five hundred yards away. But they had received no clear orders as to what they should do. So the sergeant sent out small patrols to reconnoitre and bring back information as to what was going on. It so happened that one of the patrols went south in the direction of Charteris and his men, who were advancing towards them.

Moving quickly through the woods on either side of the steep little valleys it was dark and confusing, and the German patrol became split. One man separated from the rest saw the familiar sight of soldiers moving through the woods and fell in behind them, trailing them for some minutes. It's not clear who spotted whom first, but the British Paras realised that the man at the rear of their squad was not one of their own when he suddenly called out to them in German. At pretty much the same time the German realised his dreadful mistake and screamed out. Charteris, near the rear of the group, turned and pulled out his revolver to shoot the man at about five yards, almost point blank. But in the flurry and speed of the incident he forgot to release one of the safety catches of his pistol and the weapon did not fire. The terrified German soldier fired his rifle but was too distraught to take proper aim and missed.[3]

Sergeant Gibbon, who was at the front of the group with his Sten gun, span around in a flash. Private Tom Hill, at the rear next to the man with whom he had been advancing through the woods, was amazed to find he was a German. He saw the sergeant move and threw himself to the ground.[4] Gibbon fired his Sten gun over Hill at the German, who dropped instantly.

The scare was over, but the men had been shaken and Charteris, even more determined now to catch up with the others, ordered his men to continue. It later became part of the mythology of Bruneval that the Paras had used their knives to kill the German in complete silence. But this was not what happened, and the sound of the shooting had given away the presence of Charteris and his section moving up towards the village.

In no time the Paras reached the road heading west into Bruneval and down the valley to the beach. Charteris told his Bren gun team to cover him while he and a group of men crossed the road and advanced through some scrubby land to the north. After a while, all twenty men went forward towards the village. By now the NCOs were calling out orders to the men as they advanced through woods and shrubs and were making quite a bit of noise. Charteris wrote in his report, 'I was sure, however, that speed was more important than silence,' and he told his men to carry on. It was now that they came under fire from the soldiers based at the hotel. One man, Private Sutherland, was badly wounded in the shoulder and the arm.

The situation now became even more confusing for Charteris. Under fire he took cover in the scrub, while most of the men disappeared into the woods. At least four got separated from the rest. Charteris sent a corporal to try to find the missing men, but he returned having been unable to do so.

At around this time he made contact with men from the *Rodney* group, who were acting as the reserve to prevent German reinforcements from coming up the main road. Having laid their two mines, they were already involved in skirmishes and had suffered casualties, with two more men wounded. Since the radios had gone missing in the drop, the commander of *Rodney*, Lieutenant John Timothy, was using runners to keep in touch with Frost. Timothy was able to tell Charteris that the operation at the radar station had been a complete success and that Frost had started to move off the plateau but that the beach had still not been captured. This news no doubt spurred Charteris on. It had been his task, after all, to take the beach.

Charteris and the few men he could muster moved off, again running, in the direction of the road to the beach. They came under sporadic fire but in the darkness they were able to keep moving forward. There were now men spread across the cliffs and hillsides and the valleys surrounding Bruneval firing at each other. Some groups were in positions they were familiar with and could just about see their enemy. Others were lost or waiting to move, unsure who was where and what they should do next. The German commanders, miles away in their headquarters, were still trying to make sense of the many reports of firing they were receiving, still struggling to assess the strength of the force they were up against and what its objective was. Meanwhile, Frost was stuck on the shoulder of the cliff, unable to move off without coming under fire from a machine-gun position on the valley opposite, and unable to communicate with most of the men in his company. The fog of war had truly descended on Bruneval.

Frost had another problem to worry about. Somewhere out to sea, hopefully not far away, were the landing craft of the Royal Navy, waiting for the order that the beach was secure and that they should come in to take the men away. But the signallers around Frost could not make contact. The new model 38 radios did not appear to function correctly. Frost himself repeatedly flashed from the cliff top a blue signal from a bright torch. But he received no response. This was beginning to cause some alarm.

In fact, the tiny flotilla of landing craft was on station about a mile and a half away. The men in the vessels could see flashes and tracer rounds on the coast where the cliffs came down into the valley. They were also aware of the occasional flare going up ashore. But they too could make no contact with Major Frost or the Paras. They had no idea whether the raid was a success or if the British troops were being massacred on the cliffs. It was now approaching 0200, nearly two hours since the first Paras had jumped.

It was at this point that Charteris and the men who had kept up with him finally approached the villa Stella Maris where the German defenders were keeping the rest of the Para force at bay. The men with Charteris were exhausted. They had been moving quickly through woods and valleys for about ninety minutes, knowing that the enemy were in the trees and buildings around them. Some of them had been carrying heavy equipment and ammunition supplies. Charteris let his men rest up for a moment. He took one man's rifle and gave him his revolver instead.

But he and some of his group had now reached their objective, the Stella Maris, the base for the German beach defence. He wrote afterwards, 'I had thought for a month how best to attack this house. I had examined all the photographs and worked out all possible plans but when I came to do so the reality was quite different from the expectation.'[5]

The men from the various sections were all mixed up but Charteris got together a group of men and they crawled down the slope of the cliff towards the Stella Maris. When they were within range they threw two volleys of grenades at the villa, while Sergeant Tasker and his squad kept up a constant covering fire towards the German positions. As the grenades were going off Charteris and a few men made a dash for it into the road that ran up to the villa. This was their most vulnerable moment. If the German defenders had rallied quickly and lobbed a couple of grenades down into the road they would be dead men. But the Germans too were tiring. It had been a long and confusing fire fight for them. The defenders kept their heads down while the British grenades exploded.

Screaming and shouting, Charteris and his men charged towards the villa itself. Some of the men with him were Seaforth Highlanders, an old regiment with a proud military tradition. As they charged, Sergeant David Grieve, who was right behind Charteris, screamed the regimental war cry, 'Caber Feidh'.[6] As the others joined in, the cry echoed across the valley warming the hearts of every Scotsman nearby. It almost certainly had the opposite effect on the enemy in their defensive positions.

Charteris was first to reach the villa and threw some more grenades into the building. He charged around the corner to a terrace overlooking the sea. There was no one there. He could not find the front door, so he went around to the back of the building where he saw an open door and charged in. The room was dark but beyond it was a door leading to a lit passage. He yelled out loudly 'Hände hoch', 'Komm hier', and various other German phrases he had learnt for the occasion. He threw another grenade and, with Sergeant Grieve behind him, again went forward.

Inside the villa, Corporal Schmidt the telephone orderly was still dutifully taking and sending messages. At the moment that Charteris approached, Schmidt happened to be on the phone once again to Major Paschke at his headquarters in Bordeaux-St-Clair. Grenades were going off in the building around him and the major was getting more and more angry, asking time and again what all the noise was. Finally there was a few seconds' pause and the orderly managed to get it out that the noise was from British grenades. With some disbelief that British soldiers were so near, Paschke told the man he must withdraw and abruptly put the phone down.

At that moment Charteris and Sergeant Grieve charged into the telephone room firing their Sten guns. As they came in they were clearly lit up and silhouetted by the passageway. The orderly could see them but for a moment they could not see him. Schmidt had the opportunity to open fire and would almost certainly have killed both men. But he could not bring himself to fire into a man's body at just a few yards' range. Obeying Charteris's randomly shouted instructions, he threw his hands into the air, came forward out of the shadows and surrendered.

Adrenalin pumping hard, Charteris in turn could easily have fired a couple of rounds into the German standing in front of him. Instead he grabbed the corporal's weapons and screamed loudly at him, 'Where are the rest of you?' When he repeated this in a form of German, Schmidt pointed to another door and said, 'Zwei.'

Leaving the German prisoner with the sergeant, Charteris

charged through the door screaming loudly. But he could not find the two other Germans and soon worked his way up to the roof. From there he spotted the entrance to the trenches that formed the principal German defensive positions. He threw another grenade, but it failed to go off. By now the German machine gun not far away had stopped firing. Charteris paused to draw breath. He was now by himself on the perimeter of the German defences.

Within seconds Captain Ross appeared from the road below. He and his men had pressed forward into the German defensive positions. Private Tom Hill took part in this assault and rolled a grenade into one end of the defensive dugouts. As a German soldier appeared hurriedly from the other end, Hill fired at him and he ran away.[7] All the other defenders now disappeared and *Beach Fort* was finally in British hands.

Charteris's action in storming the Stella Maris had been the turning point of the night's action. The Germans had at last ceased firing and appeared to have fled up into the woods above the road. More and more Paras now arrived on the scene. When Lieutenant Young, who with his section had been sent down from the cliff by Frost, also appeared at the villa, Ross dispatched him to check out the beach defences to see if there was any further resistance to overcome. But all the Germans appeared to have left. However, as he moved cautiously into one of the pillboxes, Young found a German who had been slightly wounded and had crawled into the pillbox for cover. The young soldier was only too keen to give himself up to the British Para officer, and Young had no alternative but to accept the man's surrender. His name was Fusilier Tewes.

One of those wounded in the skirmish at *Beach Fort* was

Corporal Stewart, the company gambler. He had been hit in the head. After the fighting was over, lying on the ground with blood oozing from under his helmet, he turned to the man nearest to him, Lance-Corporal Freeman, and said mournfully, 'I've had it. Here's my wallet.' And he handed it over, packed with weeks' worth of takings at cards.

Freeman took the wallet enthusiastically, before turning to examine Stewart. In the bright moonlight he could see him clearly and realised that he had been only grazed. 'You've only got a scalp wound,' he said. Stewart cheered up immediately and retorted, 'Gie us my bluidy wallet back, then!'[8]

It was now 0225 and the beach was at last under British control. But the south-westerly wind in the Channel was getting stronger. And as the wind got up, so the sea haze worsened, with visibility decreasing minute by minute. Time was running out for the navy to get the men off the beach.

18

The Ruddy Navy

Flight Sergeant Charles Cox lay on the ground at the top of the cliff by the pillbox, next to the valuable pieces of radar equipment on the trolleys. He listened to the battle raging below, even hearing what he described as 'Scottish war cries'. But he could do nothing but wait. He thought he was lying there for about thirty minutes. Meanwhile, behind Cox and the others, German troops around the *Rectangle* were still firing in their direction. Cox wrote later that he 'did not feel unduly worried'.[1] If this was true, he was probably the only man who was not worried at this point.

While Cox was waiting a new alarm was raised. The soldiers from Le Presbytère had moved forward and reoccupied the Villa Gosset, which was only about three hundred yards behind the men at the pillbox. Frost decided there was no alternative but to take a squad back and evict them. He only had a few Paras left with him and rounded up all the weapons he could find. Lieutenant Vernon joined the group, changing roles from an engineer to being a soldier.

Frost led the men back across the plateau and charged towards the Villa Gosset, all guns blazing. Astonished, the German soldiers withdrew quickly and retreated to the *Rectangle*. Probably these were Luftwaffe soldiers without the combat experience of the Wehrmacht troops. In any case, few defenders hold firm when a group of determined paratroopers charge at them in a frenzy. With the German soldiers pulling back, Frost had at least averted this threat to his rear.

Frost returned to the small group sheltering around the pillbox. As he did so, silence finally fell down in the valley. There was a lot of shouting from below and Major Frost gave the order that they should now move down the steep slope of the cliff. This was no easy matter when dragging trolleys laden with heavy electronic equipment. Cox, Corporal Jones and the other sappers manhandled the trolleys part way down the slope, but it was very icy and the trolleys slipped and were difficult to control. After a while they gave up and abandoned the trolleys and many of the heavy tools they still had with them, carrying the vital apparatus on their shoulders for the rest of the descent.

Frost's party also included the prisoner, Heller, from the Würzburg and the badly wounded Sergeant-Major Strachan. Somehow, Strachan managed to part walk, part slide down the slope with the aid of the other men. Frost deduced that the rapid use of morphine had a beneficial effect. But Strachan was slowly becoming delirious: when he reached the bottom of the cliff he started giving out orders rapidly but with little coherence. The others could barely understand what he was saying and took no notice. But he was a difficult man to ignore and kept demanding their attention.

Lieutenant Timothy now joined the party coming down the cliff and he gave Strachan a cricket sweater he had brought with him in the aircraft, to help keep the wounded man warm.[2] No doubt it was good for Strachan to keep talking; it kept his mind active and prevented him from falling into unconsciousness, even if to the others he was talking nonsense. But his condition was clearly deteriorating.

As they reached the bottom of the slope they had to pass through a patch of trees and bushes, and when they emerged they were surprised to be challenged by a sentry. But it was a British voice that called out, 'Halt, who goes there?' They responded with the password 'Biting' and were allowed to carry on to the road, which was now open to the beach.

Cox was surprised by the strange scene he now found in front of him. Everywhere there were signs of the aftermath of a major fire fight. There were two German soldiers with their hands up standing against a wall, guarded by a semi-circle of Paras. Charteris was going from dugout to dugout calling on any surviving Germans to come out with their hands up. A sapper with a mine detector moved about on the beach, making sure that the intelligence brought back by the French underground agents was correct and that the *Achtung Minen* signs really were for show only. More and more Paras were drifting on to the beach from the various sections that had been involved in the fire fight at the villa. After a short while the sapper with the mine detector called Cox and the others over to tell them the beach was clear. They went forward with their booty and sat down with it under the cliff.

With all the drama of the last hour now over, Cox had time to reflect for almost the first time that night. Although the beach was a hive of activity, there was obviously something wrong. There was no sign of the Royal Navy. Where were the landing craft? He grew concerned and started to question what would happen if they did not turn up, wondering 'if we should be killed or taken prisoners'.[3]

Lieutenant Euan Charteris had no time to enjoy his moment of glory. Growing more agitated, he assigned a Bren gunner to take up position where the German machine gun had been, with its commanding view across the valley and the exit to the beach, telling the gunner to keep careful watch on the woods on the slope behind him in case the Germans who had fled in that direction tried to return.

Charteris positioned other men in the German slit trenches to guard the approach to the beach. He was annoyed with the group standing around the prisoners. They looked far too casual, he thought, as though the show was over, they were still on an exercise and an army transport would be turning up any minute to take them back to camp. He ordered some of them to deploy into defensive positions, leaving only one man to search and guard the prisoners. Corporal Campbell turned up and said he had been sent by Sergeant Lumb, who was part of the *Rodney* party. Apparently, Lumb had been in the aircraft where the man had been caught in the static lines. Lumb had jumped before the incident occurred and he and his group of paratroopers had landed south of Bruneval, along with some of the radio equipment and two of the signallers. Making its second run after the man had been freed, the aircraft had dropped the remaining Paras at the correct DZ, but without the radios. Now

Lumb had made it with the radios but was still somewhere in the woods behind Bruneval under heavy fire from the enemy based at the hotel.

Cursing, Charteris told Campbell to go and get Lumb and the radio operators down to the beach and to report to Captain Ross as soon as possible. Charteris also spent a moment looking out to sea, hoping desperately to see the landing craft appear. He realised that the situation was getting serious. They were about an hour behind schedule.

Having reached the foot of the cliff and quickly surveyed the scene to see that Charteris and Young were doing a good job in positioning the men, Frost met up with his second-in-command, Captain Ross, whom he had not seen since emplaning at Thruxton airfield. They had one overriding concern now, to contact the navy and bring in the landing craft. Ross had a radio operator in his party and Frost ordered him to start sending out the agreed signal immediately.

After a few minutes he reported back that he was getting no return signal. Frost himself started signalling, using his torch with the blue light. Still he got no response. The sappers with the Eureka system started sending the signal from the beacon out to sea. But again there was no response. By now it was 0230 and the Germans had had more than two hours to mobilise a force to counter-attack the beach.

A mile and a half out to sea and a little north of Bruneval, Commander Frederick Cook was equally puzzled. After the drama of the passing German warships, everything had gone quiet for the small flotilla. When no signal had been received from the beach, at 0145 flotilla commander William Everitt had used his radio to try to make contact with the paratroopers. But he had received no response. He assumed that either the battle for the beach was still raging or that something had gone wrong with the radio communications. In his landing craft, Preist grew more and more worried. The lookouts strained to pick up the agreed signal from the Para commanding officer's blue torch or any other sign that the beach had been secured. The sea haze had by now reduced visibility to less than half a mile, and they were further than that from the beach.

There was nothing Cook could do but wait. He could not risk sending the craft into the beach if it was not secure. But how much longer should he wait before withdrawing? The boats must be well away from the French coast by daylight.

Back on the beach, Major Frost was beginning to despair. He reviewed the situation. The mission had achieved its objectives. The Paras had seized and dismantled the Würzburg radar and the key components were now on the beach waiting to be taken off. They had given the Germans a 'good hammering' and so far the enemy had not responded with overwhelming counter-measures. They had suffered a few casualties but had fared better than Frost had expected. The men of *Rodney* who had been providing the defensive perimeter had now mostly come in, although a few men were still defending the rear of the Para force. But there was no sign of the navy. It looked as though they were going to be left high and dry to fight it out until their ammunition ran out. Then they would have to surrender and spend the rest of the war in captivity. Frost found the thought of this 'hard to bear'.

Frost instructed Nagel to interrogate the three prisoners and find out where enemy reinforcements were likely to come from. But they were too frightened to provide any useful information.

As a last measure, someone suggested that green flares should be fired from both ends of the beach. Frost agreed and the flares were fired. But still there was no response.

Frost reluctantly gathered his officers around him, and decided with a sinking heart they must start to prepare a perimeter defence. Some men would have to go back up the cliff to fend off any counter-attack from Le Presbytère. Others would have to return to the village and take up positions to fight off an assault down the main road. They had found a small fishing boat and Frost ordered that the radar equipment should be loaded into it, along with the wounded, and that it should be sent off to sea. It would carry eight men with difficulty and might just make it across the Channel back to England. Frost stated in his report that he was feeling thoroughly 'fed up'.[4] If he was willing to admit this much to his superiors, he must in reality have been feeling a hell of a lot worse.

The officers had just finished their meeting and were about to order the men into defensive positions when a shout echoed across the beach. Someone called to Frost, 'Sir, the boats are coming in! The boats are here! God bless the ruddy navy, Sir!' Frost looked up and saw a set of black shapes approaching, gliding across the sea towards the beach. The commander of the flotilla had ordered the landing craft to move into a position about three hundred yards off the beach, where they were to turn off their engines and wait. Fortunately, at this distance, one of the lookouts had seen the green flares through the haze and Everitt had ordered the landing craft to go in. A sense of 'relief unbounded' spread rapidly amongst the Paras as the men called out to each other, 'The boats are here!' 'The Navy's here!'[5]

The plan had been for the landing craft to come in two at a time and for an orderly evacuation to take place in three waves, with the embarkation of the radar equipment and the wounded the first priority. Then officers were to oversee each member of their section as he embarked in the remaining landing craft. But just as the lookout saw the flares through the mist, the radio operator on one of the landing craft picked up the signal requesting all the boats to come into the beach as soon as possible. So all six landing craft came in at the same time, preparing to beach and drop their ramps. The consequence was a free-for-all.

The chaos of the next few minutes was increased when a German machine-gunner up in the cliffs spotted the landing craft approaching and opened fire on them. The sailors in the tiny vessels saw tracer coming down towards them but fortunately none of the fire was accurate. The Bren gunners on the landing craft opened fire up into the cliffs with a furious burst when the boats were about fifty yards off the coast. Frost desperately tried to tell them to cease fire, as there were still Paras up on the cliff slopes. But the noise made by the gunners as the sound of up to twenty Bren guns echoed around the small bay made it difficult for Frost to make himself heard.

Everyone knew they were running out of time. Naval officers yelled orders from megaphones. The Para officers were also trying to be heard above the din. Between them, with a great deal of shouting and calling, they managed to get the wounded, the prisoners and all the pieces of radar equipment on to a landing craft. Cox and the sappers had to wade out into the sea with the water up to their thighs carrying the equipment above their heads. They got to the landing craft, climbed in and were told to go forward and sit down.

The craft was just about to pull away when the German machine-gunner opened up from the top of the cliff again. Most likely soldiers from Le Presbytère had now ventured forward towards the pillbox on the shoulder of the cliff. At once the Bren guns in the landing craft returned fire at the site of the machine gun. The sound of gunfire was deafening, but there was no further fire from the German machine-gunner.

The first landing craft was now ready to pull off the beach, but had got stuck on the shingle. With everything running late, the tide had turned and was going out. This was what the naval commanders had most dreaded. For a moment it looked as if the fiasco of the rehearsals on the Dorset coast would be repeated. But there were too many men on this first landing craft, so some of them were told to get out and on to the next vessel. A naval lieutenant, D.J. Quick, jumped into the sea and managed to attach a line from the landing craft to another one that was not stuck, while a group of soldiers jumped overboard and, after much heaving and pushing, managed to free the landing craft. They clambered back in and the craft headed out to sea. Seeing that the wounded and the radar cargo were away, Frost gave the order for a general withdrawal.

The same sequence was repeated on the other five landing craft. Men piled aboard. Naval officers shouted instructions. On one boat there were nearly sixty men at one point and several were told to get back on the beach and find another boat. In the plan, *Hardy* and *Jellicoe* were supposed to be the first sections to embark. But in the chaos on the beach men from every section threw themselves on to any boat they could reach. To add to the mêlée, German soldiers now appeared from hiding places on the cliff slopes and the woods and threw hand grenades down to the beach. But any German soldier who made the mistake of firing a weapon was met by a hail of gunfire from the Bren gunners on the landing craft.

The officers tried vainly to control what was going on. But the desperation to get away among both the Paras and the sailors, combined with the ear-splitting noise and the gunfire and grenades coming out of the darkness on to the beach, prevented anyone from taking control. Frost admitted that the 'checking out system' for the Paras 'had gone west'. He put this down more than anything to 'the noise made by the barrage' put up by the Bren gunners.[6] Charteris had to wade out into the sea to get into a boat. He tried to count his men, but so many of them had made for other boats that he was unable to tell who was where. Sergeant Forsyth from *Rodney* section was another who had to physically push his landing craft off the shingle amid shouting and yelling from the sailors and while bullets from the top of the cliff ricocheted off the boat around him.[7]

On Sergeant Gould's boat another disaster now occurred. After the landing craft filled up with paratroopers, the sailors hastily hauled it off the shingle but as it headed out to sea the front ramps opened and water began to pour in. The boat took in between two and three feet of water before the sailors managed to close the ramps. Gould told the Paras on board to start baling out using their helmets. Frantic action prevented the boat from going down but then, to make matters worse, the engine broke down. Another landing craft came by and threw a line across, towing the stricken craft out to sea while the Paras were still madly throwing water over the side with their helmets. Sergeant Gould was relieved to be out of danger, but all the guns had been on the floor of the boat and were now flooded. They would be defenceless if they were attacked by German aircraft.[8]

Frost was the last to embark on the final boat. He had to wade about five yards out until he was nearly fully immersed to climb on board. He told the boat crew to wait while he shouted to ensure that no one was still left on the beach. There was no reply so the boat reversed, hauling on its anchor chain until it freed itself from the shingle and moved off into the darkness. Frost was sure that no one had been left behind. It was 0315. The raid had lasted almost exactly three hours.

Donald Preist was waiting on the landing craft in which the radar equipment had been loaded. He took a first look at the bits and pieces as soon as he could. According to plan, the landing craft headed out to sea and after a short while, out of sight from the shore, made a rendezvous with the MGBs, to which the Paras and the captured equipment were then to be transferred. But with the wind now up and quite a swell, it was not easy to transfer the radar gear. Preist boarded MGB 312 and reached down to take the pieces of the radar one by one. But as the MGB rose in the choppy water, the landing craft descended.

Fearing that he would drop the cargo into the sea, Preist began to panic. 'I visualised with horror the consequences. After all the hard work, the preparations and the battle itself, we looked like dropping the stuff in the drink.'[9] But after a few anxious minutes everything was loaded successfully, and Cox and the sappers clambered aboard. MGB 312 turned on its powerful engines, lined up in the direction of Portsmouth and sped off at twenty knots.

Preist wanted to hear from Cox what he had seen and done at the Würzburg while it was all still fresh in his mind. But Cox began to go pale and started to feel dreadful. Perhaps it was a reaction to the fact that the danger was now largely over, and everything started to catch up with him. He turned to Preist and said, 'Please sir, I'm feeling seasick. I want to be sick.' Preist had visions of Cox being incapacitated for hours, exhausted, in a daze and unable to remember anything about the night's events. He was merciless. 'Sorry, old man,' he said. 'Come down below and tell me the story. Then you can be sick.' He led Cox down to the cabin below decks. Cox gave a short but detailed and very clear report, telling him how impressively he thought the German radar had been engineered. Preist told him he agreed, but that for now he had better keep this 'under his hat'. Having given Preist the information he needed, Cox went back up on deck and was violently and repeatedly sick. Eventually the captain of the MGB insisted Cox go below and use his own cabin. There, utterly exhausted, he quickly fell asleep.

Meanwhile another more serious drama was taking place. The last of the landing craft, with Frost on board, had made contact with its MGB, and the major clambered up from the ALC on to the faster vessel. There he was told that two signallers had made contact with the naval flotilla. They had been in the group with Sergeant Lumb, in pursuit of whom Charteris had sent Corporal Campbell when the battle at the Stella Maris was over. But, pinned down by heavy fire, they had been unable to get to the beach while the landing craft were there.

They arrived on the beach as the last vessels were pulling away, and sent a message pleading with the navy to come back to get them.

Frost immediately volunteered to return in a boat to look for them. But Commander Cook forbade this. Telling Frost about the two German destroyers and the E-boats that had very nearly spotted them, he explained that for the safety of the whole party, sailors and Paras alike, they had to get out quickly before dawn. The party could not split up and leave one of the boats at the beach. Frost reluctantly accepted Cook's decision. But he hated the idea of leaving men behind.

In fact, in the chaos of the beach embarkation, six men had been abandoned, one of whom was badly wounded. Remarkably only two Paras had been killed in the raid, Privates McIntyre and Scott. Their bodies were left in France.[10] Eight others had been wounded, the most serious of whom was Sergeant-Major Strachan, and they were all successfully evacuated. No RAF or Royal Navy personnel were killed, wounded or missing. In his estimate, after he had had time to speak to all his officers and do a tally, Frost concluded that they must have killed at least forty Germans – although, it turned out later that this was a major exaggeration.

Out in the Channel, it was time for the small flotilla to make its escape. The transfer on to the gunboats was complete by 0326. The faster MGBs now began to tow the slow-moving landing craft. But by this time the south-westerly wind had reached about Force 5 and they could make only a relatively slow six knots in the choppy sea. The landing craft started to take on water, slowing things even further. Two of the craft broke their tow ropes, which had to be repaired mid-Channel.

By dawn they were still only about fifteen miles from the French coast. They would have a long trip ahead. MGB 312, with Cox, Preist, twenty other men and the radar apparatus aboard, had been dispatched directly to return to Portsmouth, where it arrived safely at 1000 on Saturday morning.

After the intense drama of the last few hours, most of the men were able to take it easy on the journey home. The lucky ones on the MGBs had gone below deck. The naval crews made a real fuss of their passengers, who were given blankets or duffle coats brought out specially for them. There were portions of bully beef and sweet biscuits with pots of tea available. And on more than one boat the crew generously distributed a good dose of naval rum. Although the small MGBs tossed and turned in the rough seas, the men could dry out and keep warm. Some of them dozed, though many were still high on adrenalin and chatted away endlessly to each other. Most of the men were badly seasick during the journey back. Sergeant Forsyth remembered one man having so much of the navy's rum that he was blind drunk when he got back and could barely walk.[11] On one of the boats, the ship's doctor gave Strachan much-needed medical attention.

Charteris, the hero of the night's action, found himself on a boat with Nagel, the German-speaking private, and Corporal Georg Schmidt, the telephone orderly whom he had taken prisoner. Charteris spent much of the journey back talking with the prisoner and learning about life for the German sentries at Bruneval. On Cook's boat another German prisoner, Tewes, was violently sick over the side of the vessel. Cook went up on deck to find a paratrooper clinging on to the PoW's leg as he threw up to prevent him from falling over the side rail. Asked what he was doing, the Scottish paratrooper replied, 'Sir, I've come a long way to get a Hun prisoner and I'm damned if I'm going to let this bastard get awa' the noo.'[12]

Frost on his boat felt that he did not deserve the fuss that the naval crew were making of him. Increasingly worried about the men they had left behind, he blamed himself for not double and triple checking that everyone was on board the landing craft. The reality was that in the circumstances this had just not been possible. It had been a case of every man for himself. It was almost inevitable that with the communication failures that had plagued the operation from the moment the Paras landed, combined with the wide dispersal of the force over cliffs and woods, some men would miss the order to withdraw. But in the few hours of the Channel crossing, Frost grew more and more annoyed with himself. For a while he completely lost sight of the fact that the operation had been a success.

As they neared the English coast, however, he got a message from Preist on board MGB 312 that the radar equipment they had brought back was in good shape and was going to reveal almost everything the scientists wanted to know. When he heard that, Frost snapped out of his gloom and was considerably cheered. He was in a much better mood by the time he got back to Portsmouth.

About an hour after dawn the men on the returning flotilla of little ships heard a welcome sound. A squadron of Spitfires flew low over the ships. It was the escort provided by the RAF to ensure that enemy aircraft could not attack the vessels coming back to England. Flying around in a wide circuit, the Spitfires covered the rest of their journey, providing in the words of one of the naval officers a 'lane of fighters' to welcome them back.[13] Not long after, four French naval corvettes sailing out of Portsmouth appeared in order to provide the flotilla with a naval escort. It was a nice touch for the French navy to welcome back a raiding party from occupied France. And finally two British destroyers, HMS *Blencathra* and HMS *Fernie*, came out to accompany the MGBs and the landing craft into Portsmouth harbour.

Word had got around that men from a successful raid were returning and most of the boats in the harbour tooted their whistles loudly, while some played 'Rule Britannia' over their loudspeakers. As they approached the *Prinz Albert*, one of the Spitfires dived low and dipped his wings in the traditional RAF salute for a job well done. It was by now 1630 on Saturday 28 February and it was proving to be quite a welcome for the returning Paras. Photographers and a newsreel film cameraman were waiting to record their arrival. Wing Commander Pickard and most of the pilots who had flown the Paras from Thruxton the night before had come down to welcome them home and to hear first hand what had happened to them. Smiling and cheerful, they were on board the *Prinz Albert* within the hour, enjoying the hospitality and comforts of this spacious ex-passenger ship. Frost remembered that in the bar that night there was 'some serious drinking to be done'.[14]

There was one other important person waiting to meet the Paras on the *Prinz Albert*. Alan Humphreys, a journalist from Reuters who had been accredited by the Admiralty and the War Office to Operation Biting, was a bright young reporter who had covered a couple of commando raids before and was thought by the military authorities to have done a good job and to be thoroughly reliable.[15] Humphreys had been, in today's parlance, 'embedded' with the Royal Navy for the operation. Based on the *Prinz Albert* for about ten days, he had been briefed in detail and had lived through the anxious period when the weather had caused a postponement for several days. He sailed out with the *Prinz Albert* on 27 February and saw the landing craft being disembarked at night to go in to pick up the paratroopers. He then returned to Portsmouth with the *Prinz Albert* to await the outcome of the raid.

When the men from C Company came back on board, he spoke to many of them and started to write up a report of the raid, stressing, as he had been briefed to do, that the operation was 'combined'. He wrote that the RAF had taken the parachute troops to France, the navy had brought them back, and the infantry had provided vital support from the landing craft as they came under attack from the cliffs. He stressed the Scottish element in the Para force and the regional balance of the other men who had taken part.

Humphreys' report was passed on to the BBC and over the next couple of days was syndicated to all the major newspapers. Within hours of their return, the Paras of C Company would be heroes.

19

Aftermath

If the Paras who had come home to Britain were seen as returning heroes, those left behind at Bruneval were treated very
differently. Throughout the night the Germans had been active
in the whole area. At 0445 the official message had gone out,
'The enemy attack is over.' But several units mobilised along
the coast continued to converge on Bruneval and La Poterie.
They included light artillery and motorised infantry, while soon
after 0600 a Panzer unit arrived on the scene. These were the
troops, well equipped and raring for action, that the Paras
would have had to face if the raid had gone wrong or if the
navy had not collected them in the nick of time.

Also arriving at La Poterie in the early hours of the morning
were the two senior German officers with responsibility for
the area around Bruneval, Lieutenant General Joachim Stever,
commander-in-chief of the 336th Infantry Division, and Colonel

von Eisenhart-Rothe, commander of the 685th Infantry Regiment. They began an immediate investigation of what had happened and what the British raid had been about. Confronted with a variety of confusing and contradictory reports, one of which strangely claimed that the Freya radar station had been entirely destroyed, the first thing they did was to organise patrols to search the fields, valleys and farms around Bruneval as soon as dawn came up.

Private Donald Sutherland, a member of Charteris's section, had been wounded as the men moved up through the woods towards Bruneval. Having sustained five bullet wounds, three in his left shoulder, one in his elbow and one in his wrist, he had been left behind near a farm in the woods called Des Echos with a small supply of morphine that helped him get through the night. Early in the morning, German soldiers had visited the farm and searched every room. From the wood nearby, Sutherland heard the sound of the Germans in the farmhouse.

After they had gone, the seriously wounded Para, cold, hungry and in pain, decided to come out from his hiding place. He went up and knocked on the door, which was opened by the farmer's wife, Madame Delamere. She spoke no English and the young Scottish soldier spoke no French; 'Tommy, Anglo,' he said, waving his identity discs. Seeing that he was frozen and in a bad way, she took him inside. Her husband soon appeared in the farmhouse kitchen, where they gave him some hot coffee and a swig of the local apple brandy, calvados, to revive him.

Realising how badly wounded the young soldier was, his left arm heavily swollen and the morphine he had been taking for the pain now beginning to wear off, they knew he desperately needed medical care. But the nearest hospital was ten miles away and the area was crawling with Germans. The punishment for hiding an enemy soldier was death for the male householder and imprisonment for the rest of the family. Towards 0900 they heard the German soldiers returning. Sutherland insisted he wanted to surrender and they must hand him over so he could be taken to a doctor. This they did, but not before he had torn off the airborne wings from his shoulders and had given them to the family. They hid them and kept them for the duration of the war. The German soldiers were delighted to have found a prisoner and took Sutherland away to the Hotel Beau-Minet, where a German doctor examined him and patched his wounds.[1]

Privates David Thomas and John Willoughby and Lance-Corporal John McCallum were part of a small group from *Nelson* that, pinned down by German fire, had become detached from the others during the advance through the woods towards Bruneval. When the shooting ceased they managed to get down to the beach, but to their amazement they saw the last of the landing craft departing. They had not heard any call to withdraw. Willoughby started to wave and shout out. McCallum used his radio to send a signal that there were men left behind, but no one responded. Before long enemy soldiers descended to the beach and the three Paras took refuge in a small cave. The enemy soldiers did not stay long and the three men ventured out once again on to the beach.

There, to their surprise, they met two more Paras, Frank

Embury and George Cornell, from Sergeant Lumb's group. They had got lost earlier in the combat, and Charteris had sent men to try to find them after the battle for the Stella Maris. They too had arrived on the beach to see the landing craft departing. The five men huddled together and, realising that the navy were not coming back for them, discussed what they should do next. They were aware it would be too difficult to survive inside enemy-occupied territory as a group of five. Embury and Cornell decided to head inland and try to escape into the southern, unoccupied zone of France. The others thought they were better off staying on the coast. They agreed to split into two groups and went their separate ways.

McCallum, Willoughby and Thomas headed south along the pebbles. Before long they found another cave and decided to wait there until dawn. At about 0830 a Luftwaffe patrol, tasked with trying to find the missing radar operator, Heller, came down on to the beach. It was feared that Heller had fallen down the cliff edge and might be in trouble. As the Luftwaffe soldiers searched the beach they found a body, but it was not that of the German radar operator, it was a British paratrooper who appeared to have fallen down the cliff and had died of his injuries during the night. This was the second Para to die as a result of the raid. His identity tags showed that his name was Private Alan Scott.

As the Luftwaffe soldiers continued their search, they approached the cave the three Paras were hiding in. The men, freezing cold and exhausted, decided to give themselves up. To the astonishment of the Luftwaffe patrol three British paratroopers emerged from the bottom of the cliff with their hands up. The surprised officer took their surrender. The three were told to collect Scott's body and the small group were led back up the road from the beach.

At this point the Luftwaffe patrol met with another patrol led by Oberleutnant Huhn, commander of the 1st Company. To the surprise of the British, an argument then erupted between the Luftwaffe and Wehrmacht officers as to who should take responsibility for the prisoners. As the defence of the beach had been the responsibility of Huhn and his men, he insisted on taking charge of the prisoners. Eventually the Wehrmacht prevailed and Huhn took them back to the Hotel Beau-Minet.

Back at the hotel the senior German officers were still eager to find out what the raid had been all about. General Stever, who spoke fluent English, had a conversation with Private Sutherland after he had received medical attention. The general was courteous and patient and entirely correct in his questioning, but the Para was defiant and refused to say anything other than to give his name, rank and serial number.

After a few minutes Stever decided he would get no further with the wounded Para. As he went to depart, Sutherland thought he ought at least to show some mark of respect to the most senior officer he had probably ever met, so he stood to attention and saluted the general with his healthy arm. When the other three Paras arrived there was a happy reunion with Sutherland before he was taken away by ambulance to a military hospital at St-Romain-de-Colbosc near Le Havre. He later made a good recovery.

The German officers now began to interview the three new prisoners, but again they would only provide the most basic information to their captors. Passing in and out of the rooms of the hotel, Madame Vennier, who had helped the French underground six weeks before, was impressed with the demeanour of the British prisoners and made clandestine signs of support to them when the Germans were not looking.

Eventually the three men were taken away. Waiting for transport at La Poterie, a group of French schoolchildren passed the prisoners, who made secret V-signs to the youths with their fingers. The three were taken to Étretat and then to Paris. At each place they were treated well but were questioned further. Then they were taken on to Frankfurt and finally to Berlin, where they were interrogated again at Luftwaffe headquarters. The men were of particular interest as they were the first British Paras captured by the Germans.

The Luftwaffe officers were surprised that unlike the German *Fallschirmjäger*, the British Paras were part of the army and not the RAF. General Martini himself, head of the Luftwaffe's signals division, interrogated the three Paras, as he assumed that, having been sent on a raid to seize German radar, they would be radar specialists. He must have been disappointed to find that they knew remarkably little about either British or German radar.[2]

Having left the others, George Cornell and Frank Embury found the going very slow. Neither had a map, but one of them had a compass in a button of his coat. They made their way only about two miles inland to a nearby village called Tilleul, where they hid out in a barn for the rest of the night. The French farmer, named Charles Canu, found them in the morning and gave them a meal, along with coffee and calvados. But he knew the punishment for hiding them, and so he told them they had to leave, sending them off towards the hamlet of Pierrefiques.

He then went in to Étretat and reported to the gendarmerie that he had seen the British, claiming they had gone off in the opposite direction.

Realising there were more British Paras in the area, the Germans launched a full-scale search across the countryside. The two fugitives began an adventure that continued for several days. Their survival relied upon the covert support of dozens of French civilians who provided food or helped to direct them, or who simply turned a blind eye on seeing them. At Pierrefiques an English-speaking couple named Monsieur and Madame Duflo kitted them out in the blue overalls of French farm workers, a disguise which helped them to travel across the countryside more easily.

As the search continued, the Germans stuck up 'Wanted' posters, warning the populace that anyone aiding Allied servicemen would be sent to a military court martial and that the penalty was death. The two fugitive Paras spent several days in the care of André Lechevallier, who eventually, on 6 March, assisted them in getting to Le Havre, where they were introduced to the French underground network that aided escaping members of RAF crews that had been shot down. Maurice Lajoye, who, it so happened, lived in the same street as Charles Chauveau, 'Charlemagne', now took control of the two fugitives. Lajoye and his fiancée, Mademoiselle Regnier, smuggled the two men by train to Tours.

However, having got so far, on 9 March, when crossing a bridge over the Cher river to the unoccupied zone and freedom, Embury and Cornell's luck ran out. An alert German sentry stopped them and began asking questions. Unable to reply in either French or German, they acted dumb. The sentry started to grow suspicious and pulled them in for further questioning. The papers the French underground had given them were in order, but they were repeatedly questioned for some days.

Realising the game was up, Embury confessed that they were British paratroopers and the two men were arrested. They were interrogated in France and were eventually sent on to Berlin, where they rejoined their mates from C Company in the Luftwaffe interrogation centre. The French couple who had shown such bravery in helping them were also arrested at the bridge and were imprisoned. Maurice Lajoye was eventually sent to Buchenwald concentration camp and then transferred to Dachau. Mademoiselle Regnier was sent to Ravensbrück. In such camps life was harsh, brutal and short, far worse than in the military prisoner-of-war camps. The pair paid a high price for trying to help the British soldiers. But both Lajoye and Regnier survived the war and eventually returned to France, where later they married. None of the others who had helped the fugitives were ever named or incriminated for their contribution to the near escape.[3]

Finally, all six British prisoners from Bruneval were sent on to a PoW camp at Lamsdorf in Upper Silesia, Poland. Lamsdorf, also known as Stalag VIIIB, was huge. More than a hundred thousand prisoners from many Allied countries passed through the camp during the war.[4] The British paratroopers spent the rest of the war there. Other captured British Paras would later join them. In early 1945, before the Red Army arrived at the camp, the men were marched west as part of a huge convoy of prisoners and finally they were liberated by American troops in April 1945. All six men captured

from the Bruneval raid returned to Britain at the end of the
war.

The Wehrmacht carried out an investigation into the Para
raid at Bruneval and a short official report was written within
days of the action. The Germans still believed that the purpose
of the raid after having captured the Würzburg was to attack
the Freya radar station, and that it was only the heavy fire from
Le Presbytère that prevented the Paras from moving on to their
next, possibly their main, objective. But by this time it was
realised that before blowing up the Würzburg, the Paras had
photographed it and removed parts of it.

The report praised the sergeant and the nine men based at
the Stella Maris for fighting off the Para attack for ninety minutes before being overpowered by the British fire from the
woods. It noted that because the defences along the hillside
above the Stella Maris had been constructed to prevent an
attack from the sea, they were less well suited to defending an
attack from inland. The report also recorded that 'The commandos embarked just as strong German reinforcements
reached Bruneval.' Had the arrival of the navy been delayed
further even by minutes, it is clear that, as Frost had feared, it
would have been a disaster for the Paras.

Frost had claimed, after consulting with his officers, that
about forty Germans had been killed or wounded during the
course of the raid. But there was always a tendency in combat
to exaggerate the scale of the losses inflicted on the enemy,
and in fact the numbers were much smaller. The German
report cited their losses as a total of five killed (two infantrymen around the Stella Maris; three Luftwaffe men up at the
Würzburg and in the Villa Gosset) and two wounded (one in

the Wehrmacht and one in the Luftwaffe). It also listed five as missing. Only three prisoners were taken by the Paras (two Wehrmacht and one Luftwaffe), so it is not known what happened to the other two missing men. Perhaps they had been killed at the Würzburg but for some reason were not listed. The German report correctly lists the British as having lost two men killed and, at the time of writing, four men captured. Embury and Cornell were still at large when the report was written.

While applauding the actions of the defenders, the German report paid a big compliment to the British Paras, stating that the operation 'was well planned and was executed with great daring'. It went on to say that 'For a full thirty minutes one group did not fire a shot, then suddenly at the sound of a whistle they went into action.' The report concluded: 'During the operation the British displayed exemplary discipline under fire. Although attacked by German soldiers they concentrated entirely on their primary task [of attacking the radar installation].'[5] This was generous praise indeed and is an interesting observation from the first time German troops engaged with British Paras. In the following year in North Africa the German army was to develop a very healthy respect for the courage and determination of the Paras.

Back in Britain, Frost had just returned from Portsmouth to Tilshead and was about to take a bath when he was told to report to London early on the following morning, as the Prime Minister wanted to see him urgently. On the Monday a staff car arrived early and took him to Downing Street, where he was ushered around the corner, through a building and down some steps to a set of underground meeting rooms. There, the model of Bruneval had been laid out and General Browning soon arrived, along with Mountbatten. A group gathered including most of the Chiefs of Staff and the War Cabinet. Frost was still being introduced to the dignitaries when Churchill appeared, wearing his siren suit and puffing a large cigar. Frost, in his Cameronian major's uniform, was very conspicuous. Churchill came across and said, 'Bravo, Frost, bravo, and now we must hear all about it.'

Before Frost was able to utter a word, Mountbatten stepped forward and provided a clear and compelling narrative of the whole raid. He had been well briefed and the official communiqués, which he had read and approved, had been thorough. At one point Churchill interrupted and asked Frost about the accuracy of the intelligence he had received before the raid. Frost replied that it had been excellent, to the extent that they had known the names of the local German officers. Churchill was told that Mountbatten's intelligence chief, Wing Commander Marquis de Casa Maury, was present in the group. The PM turned to him with a beatific smile before telling Mountbatten to continue.

Delighted with the report and evidently cheered by the success of the raid, Churchill turned to Air Chief Marshal Portal, the Chief of the Air Staff, and asked what the RAF had got out of it. Portal began to describe the technical details of the Würzburg radar but before long, an impatient Churchill interrupted, telling him to carry on 'in language that ordinary normal mortals can understand'. Portal quickly summarised the position, that when the scientists had got to work they would soon know a great deal about German radar and how to jam it. Churchill went across to study the model of Bruneval.

He ran his finger along the beach and up the cliffs. 'Now about these raids,' he said slowly. 'There must be more of them. Let there be no doubt about that.' With that he turned around and departed.[6]

By this time, everyone in Britain knew about the success of the Bruneval raid. The military commands had not wasted any time in releasing a communiqué about the brilliant success of the Para raid.

20

Good News

Britain's war effort needed some good news. After the disasters of the last month, from the defeat in North Africa to the surrender of Singapore, from German and Japanese advances to the humiliation of the 'Channel Dash' by the *Scharnhorst* and *Gneisenau*, the military wanted to obtain maximum value from the Bruneval raid. It was the first ever successful use of British parachute forces and in promoting the Bruneval story the War Office was making public that it now had at its disposal a new arm of warfare, the Paras.

BBC radio was the principal means by which the British people received their daily diet of news and information about the progress of the war. The BBC had launched a television service in 1936, but only a few thousand householders had invested in the expensive and bulky cathode ray tube television sets.[1] The service was suspended at the outbreak of war in case its high frequency transmitters were used for navigation purposes by enemy aircraft, or its signals interfered with Britain's then secret radar network. That left the radio, universally known as the 'wireless'. Up to 23 million Britons (out of a total UK population of 48 million) listened to the main news bulletin at 9 p.m. each day. In pubs, clubs and military installations people would gather around the wireless at nine o'clock each evening. Even more heard some of the most important wartime speeches, which attracted an audience of up to two-thirds of the adult population.[2] Most Britons thought that BBC news was objective, impartial and fair, although in many working-class districts listeners regarded the Home Service as horribly middle class, posh and distant. They pre-ferred the Forces Programme, a network created in 1940 to cater for the younger members of the armed forces, and broadcasting a lighter fare of music, record requests, comedy, entertainment and sport.

However, most people were sophisticated enough to realise that when they bought a newspaper they got the slant on the news dictated by the politics of that paper. They knew the *Daily Mirror* would have a different agenda from the *Daily Telegraph*. Polls by Mass Observation revealed that three out of four people believed that the BBC was giving them the truth and was more reliable than the newspapers.[3]

In fact the relationship between the government and the BBC was a complex one. BBC managers were keen to stress their independence and not to be seen as a 'state broadcaster'.[4] On the other hand, they were happy to accept a degree of govern-ment control during wartime. The Ministry of Information had total control over news output when it came to military matters and could direct BBC correspondents to one story rather than another. They further encouraged BBC news editors not to dwell on bad news by, for instance, beginning bulletins with a list of ships that had been sunk, and requested them to spare listeners 'unnecessary frightening details' when reporting the bombing of British cities or military engagements overseas.[5] As a last resort, the Director of Radio Relations within the Ministry could censor the news when he felt that issues of 'national security' were at stake, and could prevent the BBC from reporting anything the government did not want the public to know about. The system for reporting news of military activities with its various contradictions had started the war awkwardly, but was working reasonably well by 1942. And, having broadcast a chronicle of tragedies and disasters for several weeks, the news editors at the BBC were as keen as anyone to put out good news when they had a genuine opportunity.

And so, after a communiqué was released jointly by the Admiralty, the War Office and the Air Ministry on the morning of Saturday 28 February, BBC radio news was the first to break the story of the success of the Bruneval raid in its 1 p.m. lunchtime news bulletin with the words 'British parachute troops have been in action in northern France, where they have destroyed an important radiolocation post.'[6] After weeks of secrecy that had surrounded everything they had been doing, the Paras returning to Portsmouth after the raid would have been astonished to know that the BBC had already begun broadcasting news of the successful raid while most of them and their supporting troops were still in mid-Channel. It was a risk to report the raid so early, but such was the enthusiasm to generate good news that the communiqué had been released before the men were safely back home. The BBC news report noted that the raid was the second use of British parachute troops after a drop in southern Italy just over a year ago. It did not remind listeners that this had been a disaster.

The BBC news editors also noted the official communiqué's recognition 'that the enemy is now using radiolocation – the method of detecting the approach of aircraft by means of ether waves – which was used so successfully by us in the Battle of Britain'. The existence of British radiolocation, as the new science of radar was still referred to at the time, had been made public in June 1941. But this reference acknowledging the German use of the technology had to be passed by the Ministry of Information, and an official signed the script in pencil specifically to approve it. Air Ministry Intelligence was also consulted before the announcement was made.[7]

It was otherwise a day full of daunting and gloomy news from the fighting fronts in Burma, Libya and Russia, and depressing reports about fuel shortages and new coal restrictions in the London area. More single women were to be called up for war work and a new fund-raising campaign had been set up to call for loans for building new warships. In the 6 p.m. news that evening the story of the raid was still therefore the leading item, with the BBC reporting that 'our forces are now understood to be home again'. But they had no further news to add, other than that the Germans had admitted that a raid had been carried out but were playing it down by saying that British parachutists had done no more than to 'overcome a weak coastal-defence position' and that 'they withdrew by sea after two hours'.[8]

By the midnight news bulletin, a longer official communiqué had been released, and the BBC were able to report then and throughout the following Sunday that 'the radiolocation post was destroyed, some German prisoners taken, and casualties inflicted.' Quoting from the official communiqué, reports made it very clear that this was a combined operation and that 'The Royal Navy, the Army and Royal Air Force each played an equally important and interdependent part in the raid.' This was the message that Mountbatten's Combined Operations team was so keen to get across. Leading individuals were named, including Wing Commander Pickard, who the BBC was sure its listeners would know as 'F for Freddie's pilot in *Target for Tonight*'. Major Frost and Commander Cook were also both referred to in person.

It was reported that 'the moonlight raid ... went off with complete success', and that after this 'small-scale but successful combined operation none of our aircraft was missing and our casualties were very light. The next of kin are being informed.' Interestingly, the news team at the BBC had amended the official communiqué to lighten it and make it easier to read. Again, an official from the Ministry marked the typed script in pencil as 'Approved', noting that the script 'is more broadcastable than the communiqué'.[9]

By midnight the BBC was also quoting a first, short account from Alan Humphreys, the Reuters journalist on HMS *Prinz Albert*. Humphreys reported that the paratroopers, whose faces were 'blacked', had landed 'in the early hours of the morning' and had covered more than half a mile to reach the radiolocation post 'before a shot was fired at them'. He went on, 'It was after the main part of their job was done that they came up against the serious opposition. They overcame and silenced the beach defences, sent out a signal to the naval craft waiting a little offshore and in a matter of minutes were heading across Channel back home.' There was of course no mention of the delay and confusion over the embarkation. There was no need for the public, or the enemy, to know about that.

The BBC report continued: 'One of the parachutists told the correspondent they'd got away just in time. The Germans had an armoured division about fifty miles away, he said; as he left the beach he saw a column of headlights coming towards them, although it was still some way off.' This vivid account soon entered the popular mythology associated with the Bruneval raid, although it is difficult to understand how anyone on the beach could have seen lights inland over the cliff tops.

One key piece of information was kept out of all the news coverage of the raid. None of the reports admitted that parts of the German radar apparatus had been removed and brought back for examination in Britain. That aspect of the mission was to remain top secret.

In addition to the popularity of the radio news at home, the BBC had built up an immense reputation throughout Europe and overseas for providing people with an accurate account of what was happening in the war. BBC News became known as 'the voice of freedom'. And in contrast to the constant barrage of overt propaganda sent out from Berlin or Rome, the BBC was indeed the voice of objectivity and accuracy. By 1942, the BBC was broadcasting out of Bush House in Aldwych in twenty-six different languages.[10] In most of occupied Europe it was illegal to listen to BBC broadcasts from London and the punishments for being caught were severe. At some stages of the war the occupying German military authorities threatened men and women with execution if caught doing so. But people continued to listen in large numbers, regarding the broadcasts as their only link with what was really happening in the outside world.

The BBC also provided a beacon of hope and a reminder that not all of Europe lived under the Nazi yoke. Many operatives in the French underground first heard of the success of the Bruneval raid on radio bulletins over the weekend. Men like Chaveau and Dumont were delighted to hear they had contributed to such a successful and daring venture. Gilbert Renault, Rémy, had been brought out of occupied France by an RAF Lysander which had picked him and a colleague up from a field in the countryside north of Rouen on the very night of the raid. He was now planning the next stage of the underground war with intelligence chiefs in London. Rémy read the news of the raid in the headlines of a London newspaper. 'Such words make wonderful reading to an intelligence agent,' he wrote later.[11]

Like the BBC, the press were subject to censorship from a Chief Press Censor working within the Ministry of Information who had final control over what could be printed.[12] But again the press needed no encouragement in picking up the official communiqué issued by the military authorities on 28 February. The Sunday papers on 1 March were full of news of the raid, and most of the front pages were given over to it. The papers described Major Frost and his men as heroes, and Britain needed its heroes at this point of the war.

The *Sunday Times'* headline was 'Full Story of a Paratroop Raid' and the paper spoke of the 'brilliant success of Friday night's combined raid by British paratroops, infantry and naval forces on an important German radiolocation post on the

French coast'. The report continued, 'Overcoming strong enemy opposition, the paratroops destroyed the apparatus, inflicting heavy casualties and capturing prisoners, some of whom they brought back with them.' It then told how 'Having completed their task, they overcame the beach defences from the rear and, under cover of fire from light naval forces, embarked safely. Not a single plane or ship was lost and our casualties were "very light".'[13]

The other Sunday papers, too, splashed the story over their front pages. The *Observer* lauded the role of the paratroopers, all of whom the paper noted were 'volunteers who after being accepted by the Selection Board, are given an intensive course of athletic training'. The paper went on, 'The men were selected for their exceptional physique and also for their courage and determination.'[14]

By Monday 2 March, the full report by Alan Humphreys for Reuters had been syndicated to the press, providing a lot more colour that gave the story new momentum. Again, the front pages were full of the Bruneval raid. The *Guardian* quoted Captain John Ross, who said that although the Germans fought well, 'when it came to fighting at close quarters they gave in'. Major Frost was quoted as congratulating the RAF, who 'put us down ten yards from where we wanted to be ... within two minutes of leaving the plane the troops were armed, organised and ready to fight'. He went on to say that the 'real hero' was the youngest officer 'commanding a section which was dropped away from the bulk of the troops' and had to find his way back into the action to 'lead the battle for the beach'.

Lieutenant Peter Young was quoted as saying that when the German sentry at the radiolocation post opened fire on them, the Paras 'rubbed him out'. After that they hunted down the other defenders 'with hand grenades, automatic weapons, revolvers and knives. Most were killed but some ran away.'[15] Accompanying these vivid stories were photographs taken by the official War Office photographer of the men in training and returning to Portsmouth on the MGBs.

One of the stories fed to the press in the days following the raid was that Stanley Morgan and Cyril Tooze, two of the infantrymen who came in, guns blazing, on the ALCs, were professional footballers. They had been groundsmen at Arsenal before the war and were now playing for Brighton and Hove Albion. When they came on to the pitch before the match against Millwall on the Saturday a week after the raid, the press made much of the fact that these Bruneval heroes were now playing a different kind of sport. According to the *Daily Sketch*, the Brighton team were enhanced by two of the 'intrepid band who smashed the Nazi radio location post at Bruneval'. The reporter quoted a Brighton official as saying, 'The other lads will get the shock of their lives when they know. We never see the pair until shortly before kick-off and never know what they do between matches.'[16] It was an early example of feeding the press with stories to keep an incident in the mind of newspaper readers.

Suddenly, everyone knew about the paratroopers. The news of the daring night raid did immense good for the reputation of this elite new arm of the fighting services. Sergeant Macleod Forsyth from *Rodney* section remembered a paratrooper friend from another unit telling him after the raid that every time he went into a pub, people wanted to buy him a drink as soon as they saw the airborne wings on his shoulder. 'But I wasn't on that raid,' Forsyth's friend would protest. But everyone said, 'Never mind mate, you're a paratrooper and that's all that matters.'[17] When Private Tom Hill arrived home on leave after Bruneval everyone in the village knew all about the raid and a reporter from the local paper came out and wrote an article about their local hero.[18]

Forsyth remembered the raid as a great morale booster, because 'we were losing everywhere and now the papers said "we can do it"'. At that time, he recalled, everyone in Britain thought the Germans were so clever: 'they can do this and that but they weren't so clever and we caught them with their trousers down around their ankles'.[19]

The guiding force behind the sophisticated orchestration of news about the Bruneval raid was none other than Lord Louis Mountbatten. Taking a very modern view of how an army or a navy should fight, Mountbatten was keen to embrace the media, and to seize every opportunity to promote the work of the armed services. During the early months of 1942, he devoted a lot of his own personal time to the media portrayal of his then most famous exploit. In the summer of 1941 Mountbatten had told his friend Noel Coward the story of the sinking off Crete of HMS *Kelly*, of which Mountbatten was captain. Captivated by Mountbatten's account of the event and of the speech he had made to the survivors, the playwright and theatrical star decided to write and produce a film about the subject in which he would himself play the role of the captain. The Admiralty were at first opposed to the project, as they did not like the idea of a popular film that centred on the sinking of one of their warships. However, Mountbatten personally introduced Coward to Sir Dudley

Pound, the First Sea Lord, and to Brendan Bracken, the Minister of Information. Under pressure from this joint charm offensive, the authorities came around. Two Cities, one of the big British film production companies of the 1940s, decided to make the movie.

Mountbatten remained closely involved in the production of the film, going through draft scripts and discussing the plot with Coward. He was even consulted in the casting of some of the minor parts. Despite his hectic schedule he found time to make frequent visits to Denham Studios, where the production was based, and arranged for the King and Queen to make an extremely rare visit to the studios.[20]

Released in late 1942 and entitled *In Which We Serve*, the film was an immense hit with the cinema-going public and rapidly became one of British cinema's great wartime classics.[21] For nearly a year, it was the highest grossing film at the British cinema box office and Noel Coward won an honorary Oscar for it. Although in the movie the ship was renamed HMS *Torrin* and was only loosely based on the *Kelly*, most people realised where the story came from. And the film did Mountbatten's career no harm.

Mountbatten was equally keen to promote the work of his Combined Operations unit, and was happy to employ the press and the media to do so. Not only had he been in favour of placing Alan Humphreys on the *Prinz Albert* when more conservative commanders had doubted the wisdom of having a civilian on board, but he had also encouraged the photographing and filming of the many exercises and rehearsals that had taken place during the weeks leading up to the raid. These photographs now provided a perfect accompaniment to the yards of newsprint that were produced about the raid. In addition, Mountbatten authorised a film cameraman to record the training and the return of the paratroopers to Portsmouth harbour.

Eddie Edmonds was an experienced cameraman who had worked for Gaumont British News, one of the five main newsreel companies, since before the First World War. In addition to his wartime experience in filming the London Blitz, in 1941 he had filmed the commando raid on the Lofoten Islands. Like Reuters correspondent Alan Humphreys, he was known and trusted by the military and so in February 1942 they invited him, on terms of the strictest secrecy, to film with C Company and the naval teams training for Bruneval. He was 'embedded' with the navy for more than two weeks, making a film record of the preparatory exercises and of the return of the Paras from Bruneval.[22]

The cinema newsreel was a form of news that before the war had usually combined bouncy silliness and trivia with brief headlines of one or two major news stories. The newsreels came out twice a week and were shown in cinemas across the country as part of the programme that preceded the main film. Since it always took a few days for the news footage of an event to be dispatched to a film laboratory and developed, processed, then cut into a short story and distributed to the cinemas, the newsreels never contained the latest news in a way we are familiar with today, in the era of digital twenty-four-hour news. But during wartime, when up to 22 million people visited one of the 4500 cinemas in Britain every week, the newsreels provided a rare opportunity for audiences to see moving film of the events that were shaping their lives.

Inside a Whitley bomber, Paras wait to jump. They had to pack themselves in. It was dark and uncomfortable.

A Para can be seen here jumping from a Whitley bomber. A static line to the right is pulling a parachute open; another man has just jumped through the hole.

An exercise in an ALC on the Dorset coast. The approach to the beach at Bruneval would have looked very similar.

Returning heroes. A motor gunboat (MGB) at Portsmouth harbour loaded with Paras coming back from the raid. Major Frost is on the bridge, second from the left.

Infantrymen coming ashore from an ALC at Portsmouth after the raid.

Major John Frost (wearing a helmet), commanding officer of C
Company, talking to Lieutenant-Colonel Alexander Goschen, the
Quartermaster of the Airborne Division at Portsmouth. Frost is still
in the smock he had worn during the raid; Goschen wears the new
maroon beret that was just coming into use.

Group Captain Sir Nigel Norman talking with Flight Sergeant Charles Cox on the deck of HMS *Prinz Albert* at Portsmouth. Corporal Jones is next to Cox, on the left.

Donald Preist (in glasses) talking to Captain Peate on the *Prinz Albert* after the raid. Corporal Jones can be seen in the background.

Two of the German prisoners being searched at Portsmouth harbour. Heller the radar operator is on the right. His Luftwaffe badge was torn off his jacket by Nagel. Tewes (who had been wounded) is on the left.

Wing Commander Percy Charles Pickard surrounded by the Paras he flew to Bruneval. They are admiring some booty, a captured German helmet.

MAR 1942.

THE TIMES

THE RAID ON FRANCE

WING COMMANDER P. C. PICKARD, leader of the carrying force of R.A.F. bombers, and members of the parachute force. Wing Commander Pickard is seen examining an enemy steel helmet captured during the raid.

AFTER THE RAID.—Some of the parachute troops who took part in the successful raid on an enemy radiolocation station near Havre are seen on their return in the left-hand photograph. The other illustration shows German prisoners captured in the raid, one an airman and the other an infantryman, being searched on board a returning vessel. The Navy, the Army, and the R.A.F. each played an equally important part in the raid.

RETURNING TO PORT.—One of the craft used for the operation on the French coast returning to port with men engaged in the raid. The embarcation was completed in good order, and all our naval craft returned safely to their base.

PILOT'S ADVENTURE.—Pilot Officer J. J. Lynch while flying over enemy territory hit a telegraph pole, but his Spitfire cut through the pole and was flown safely to its base. A piece of the pole is seen sticking to the wing.

The Times, Monday 2 March 1942, making good use of the photographs taken of the returning Paras and prisoners.

A Para reading one of the newspaper reports of the raid. His girlfriend looks over his shoulder. The Paras became famous thanks to the coverage of the raid.

Stanley Morgan (left) and Cyril Tooze (centre) talk with their fellow teammates at Brighton & Hove Albion Football Club after the raid.

Above: Men from C Company pose in front of their wooden barracks at Tilshead camp after the raid; 'V' is for Victory.

RALPH RICHARDSON

RAYMOND HUNTLEY
RICHARD ATTENBOROUGH
MARJORIE RHODES
JOHN LAURIE
PAMELA MATTHEWS

SCHOOL FOR SECRETS

Q Two Cities Film

Written and Directed by
PETER USTINOV

Produced By
GEORGE H. BROWN & PETER USTINOV

EAGLE-LION DISTRIBUTION

The poster for *School for Secrets*, the 1946 feature film that helped to celebrate the Bruneval story.

Some of the Paras were issued with ten-franc notes in case they were left behind. This one came back with its owner and the other men in his squad signed it. He obviously didn't think he would be going back to France for a while.

In reality, the newsreels were more a part of the entertainment industry than they were of the news business. They were tabloid in tone and as much about celebrity as about politics or the war, once being described by the American comedian, Oscar Levant, as 'a series of catastrophes ending in a fashion show'.[23] But during the war, the Ministry of Information strictly controlled the content of the newsreels, like that of the press and the BBC. After months of bad news, the Ministry was keen to get the good news of Bruneval across to a mass cinema audience.

Edmonds with his film camera had been invited up to Inveraray to film the paratroopers as they practised boarding landing craft from HMS *Prinz Albert* on the banks of Loch Fyne. It was no accident that he had been present on 12 February when Mountbatten arrived to meet and talk to the paratroopers and the sailors. Mountbatten was always very happy to be filmed for the newsreels.

Edmonds had filmed him inspecting the troops on the foredeck of the *Prinz Albert*, although he had not filmed the speech in which the admiral had let the cat out of the bag that the men were likely to be training for a military mission rather than for a demonstration to politicians. Newsreel cameramen rarely filmed speeches. They were too long, as anything more than a brief soundbite would slow up the fast-paced newsreel, and they used up too much precious film stock. In any case, a newsreel cameraman like Edmonds rarely travelled with cumbersome sound recording equipment that would have needed an additional team to operate. All his footage was mute, without sound.

Over the next two weeks, Edmonds filmed the various exercises on the Dorset coast. He filmed the infantrymen cleaning and loading their Bren guns before going in with the landing craft. And, most importantly, he filmed the jubilant scenes on Saturday 28 February, when the Paras arrived back at Portsmouth on the MGBs and re-boarded the *Prinz Albert*.

Edmonds' film was pooled for syndication to the five major newsreel companies: British Paramount News, Pathé News, Movietone News, Universal News and his own company, Gaumont British News. All five companies edited the footage into a major up-beat story, three placing it as the lead story in their issues on Thursday 5 March.[24] Gaumont British News devoted nearly half of its ten-minute newsreel to the story of the Bruneval raid,[25] a sign of how important the event was thought to be. By then, everyone in the cinema audience would have heard about the raid and would probably have seen some of the photos in the press. These, though, would be the first moving pictures they had seen.

The newsreel began, as always, with a split-screen title sequence, a musical fanfare and a newsreader announcing, 'This is the Gaumont British News presenting the truth to the free peoples of the world.' Then came a title that read 'Britain's Paratroops Raid France'. In the rather hyped-up style common to the newsreels, the commentator read the following words to Edmonds' edited film of the Paras and the navy in training:

Perfect training and rehearsal down to the last detail were the secrets of the great success of the British paratroop raid near Le Havre which destroyed the radiolocation station at Bruneval. The actual raid of course took place at night making photography impossible, so the record brought back by the Gaumont British cameraman who went with the invading troops across the Channel is limited to events before and after the actual assault.

Mountbatten and the War Office were keen to emphasise that Britain's force of paratroopers was a new elite. So the commentary went on, with magnificent hyperbole, over shots of the Paras training:

> This is the type of man who volunteered for the most hazardous work of the war, parachute troops – more physically perfect than any other body of men on earth. Quick, resourceful and courageous and super efficient in the use of arms, the perfect partner in a rough house.

Over shots of Captain Peate of the *Prinz Albert*, Commander Cook and Major Bromley-Martin on deck rather self-consciously looking at maps, the commentary continued: 'Now last-minute details are discussed by the officers in charge of operations.' No newsreel can avoid a bit of light relief, and Edmonds had filmed the mascot of the *Prinz Albert*, a dog, running about on deck with a lifebelt dangling around its neck: 'On this trip even the ship's mascot dog wears a lifebelt.'

After explaining the success of the mission and using the film that Edmonds had shot of the Paras returning to the *Prinz Albert* at Portsmouth, the newsreel built up to its climax, delighted to explain that these men had just raided occupied France: 'This is the real thing. These men who are coming aboard have just returned from enemy territory. They have surprised the German garrison and overcome it.' There is much cheering on the soundtrack at this point. But over shots of Sergeant-Major

Strachan being brought aboard the *Prinz Albert* on a Robertson stretcher, the commentary continues: 'Casualties were light but not all came through unhurt.'

With the shots of Wing Commander Pickard talking to the Paras, the newsreel got the RAF into the show as well: 'On board the parent ship the wing commander who led the troop carrying aircraft had a chat with the troops. He had returned to his aerodrome and came back with the navy to see the finish.'

The newsreel finally reached its climax, providing its own bullish take on what the success of the raid meant: 'It does your heart good to hear that somewhere we're hitting out, not just being hit. None of us ever believed that we are in danger of losing the war but we are in deadly danger of doing too little to win it.' This was the nearest Gaumont British News dared go towards criticising the country's political and military leadership.

Despite the bombast, and the silliness of showing the ship's mascot dog (which no doubt provoked a loud 'Aaaah' from the pet-loving audience), the newsreel encapsulated several key messages about the raid. It talked about the training, efficiency and daring, about the strength and capability of the new force of paratroopers, and about the success of hitting the enemy with a surprise blow. It celebrated the co-operation of the Royal Navy and RAF in the raid and the combined ability of the military to hit back at the enemy. If Mountbatten ever saw the newsreel he would have been delighted at how strongly these messages came across. But he would also no doubt have been greatly disappointed that the film of him on the *Prinz Albert* in Loch Fyne had ended up on the cutting-room floor. Sadly, he did not play the starring role in this newsreel version of the raid.

Promoting the success of the raid at home was one thing. But showing off Britain's ability to strike and surprise the enemy was also an important objective of overseas news, especially for Britain's allies in the US and the Soviet Union. Again, the news story of the Bruneval raid was fed to the foreign press, and in the United States it was picked up with particular enthusiasm. The USA was developing its own parachute forces in what would become two separate elite airborne divisions, but neither had yet been deployed in combat. American and Canadian readers relished the news from Bruneval and after the news coverage had been absorbed, photo magazines devoted whole features to the story of the development of Para forces. Two weeks after the raid, on 14 March, the *Toronto Star Weekly* devoted several pages to photos and descriptions of how the British paratroopers had won a splendid victory at Bruneval. Edmonds' footage was again used in April 1942 in the War Pictorial News, an official newsreel produced by the Cairo branch of the Ministry of Information for circulation through-out the Middle East.[26] In addition to screenings to Allied troops in the Middle East, the newsreel was translated into Arabic and French and shown as widely as possible to local audiences.

Overall, the press and media co-ordination for Bruneval had been masterly. Of course, newspaper readers and cinema audiences wanted to be told good news at this dreadfully low point. And newspaper and newsreel editors were equally keen to tell of a British triumph. But the way in which the press and the newsreels at home and abroad eagerly took up the key messages that the Royal Navy, the army and the RAF wanted to get across about the raid must have pleased the military chiefs enormously. This was another of the many ways in which the Bruneval raid was a turning point. When the suggestion of 'embedding' journalists on ships or planes or with military units came up again, the armed forces were more likely to look on it favourably after the success of the Bruneval experience had shown how a good news story could be controlled.

This was not a case of manipulating the press. Everyone wanted to read the story. But the news media were fed the precise spin the military wanted to give. And it never slipped out that the Paras had brought some vital booty back with them for scientific analysis. There would be countless more examples over the next few years of reporters flying on operational missions, of journalists travelling on naval vessels and within military units, and by the end of the war reporters were even jumping behind enemy lines with the Paras. A new example had been set.

The Bruneval raid had entered the consciousness of the British public. Later raids and incursions were not always so successful, but the memory of Bruneval would remain as a heroic episode in Britain's wartime story. Soon after the war was over, a movie was made about the backroom boys and the radar story, in which a dramatisation of the Bruneval raid would play an important part. *School for Secrets* was written and directed by Peter Ustinov for Two Cities Films.[27] After *In Which We Serve* in 1942, Two Cities had made another Noel Coward epic in 1944, this time about a family living in the suburbs between the wars and called *This Happy Breed*. And in the same year the company had made Laurence Olivier's epic rallying cry for the nation when he directed and starred in *Henry V*. Unlike these other titles, *School for Secrets* is no film classic and is largely forgotten today. But it includes many features pertinent to the Bruneval story.

The film presents itself as the story of 'a handful of boffins', the word which had come to define the quiet, self-effacing backroom scientists whose work was by 1946 beginning to be recognised for its contribution towards victory. They were usually seen as rather eccentric and whacky, as indeed were the group in *School for Secrets*. The film tells of a group of five boffins who are sent out of London to carry on their top secret work and are billeted in the same house, with a Mrs Arnold to look after them. Here they begin a desperate race to develop a form of radar that helps to save Britain in the summer of 1940 during the Battle of Britain.

Mrs Arnold, however, is suspicious of her guests and believes they are a group of conscientious objectors. Her son, a pilot in Bomber Command played by a young Richard Attenborough, thinks otherwise and eventually meets some of them carrying out radar experiments on his RAF station. One after another, the inventions come tumbling from the minds of the brilliant but weird scientists. As the wife of one of them says when he drops all the plates while trying to help with the washing up, he is 'more theoretical than practical'!

The film ends with a sequence based on the Bruneval raid in which a group of commando-paratroopers are instructed to go and capture an enemy Würzburg radar. In this version of the raid the Paras take with them one of the radar experts, Professor Heatherville (played by Ralph Richardson), who gets stuck in a tree with his parachute. He has to dismantle the German radar under fire and is given twelve minutes to do the job. All this is done quite realistically. Indeed, Lieutenant John

Timothy was assigned by the Airborne Division to act as technical consultant for this part of the film. Timothy was awaiting his demobilisation and spent a few happy weeks at Denham Studios rubbing shoulders with movie stars. Ustinov offered him a cameo role in the film but the actors' union Equity blocked his appearance.[28] Timothy did not record what he thought of the final version of the film.

School for Secrets was all part of the myth-building about Britain's war record that the British cinema indulged in through the late 1940s, the 1950s, and even into the 1960s. The film helped to shape some strong interpretations of the wartime experience. For instance, most of the RAF officers are shown as being dismissive of the WAAFs operating the radar. Nevertheless, the glamorous WAAFs bravely rise to the challenge of reading the radar screens even when being bombed by the Luftwaffe, showing how important was the role played by women in the war, despite the chauvinism of the men around them. The film contains another popular cultural stereotype – that of the Paras, who are portrayed as a particularly bloodthirsty and ruthless bunch who kill the Germans with their knives when they can. But it is clearly intended as a celebration of one of Britain's great wartime achievements, the development of radar, and as a tribute to the backroom scientists whose genius and hard work helped to bring victory in the war.

Ultimately, though, the success of the Bruneval raid would be judged not on the damage it inflicted, nor on the boost to morale it generated, but on the value of the material that had been brought back to Britain. What would the scientists make of the parts that Cox and Vernon had brought back?

21

The Scientific War

It did not take long for the scientists who had suggested the Bruneval raid to get their hands on the booty that had been brought back from France. R.V. Jones, like most other people in Britain, heard over the weekend of 28 February that the raid had been a success. He was telephoned on the Sunday and told that the equipment that had been seized would be at the Air Ministry on the afternoon of Monday 2 March.

Jones was absolutely delighted by what he found. Only one significant component had been left behind in France and that was the display screen, probably the least important feature. Vernon and Cox had done a magnificent job in dismantling the equipment and carrying it down the cliff for transportation back to England. Jones was even more impressed to hear that they had only had ten minutes to take the Würzburg to pieces rather than the half-hour originally allotted, and that the dismantling had taken place under enemy fire.

Jones's first impression when he started to examine the Würzburg was how much better engineered it was than British radar equipment. It was possible to remove faulty parts and install new ones with ease. As Jones went through the components he realised that many of them had been replaced, each new part containing a works number and the date of manufacture. The thoroughness of the German engineering industry in marking every component turned out to be a great help.

From these details Jones was able to work out the name of every factory building parts for the Würzburg. By looking at the dates of manufacture, he was able to paint a clear picture of how many parts were being produced. And from this, he was able to calculate that the average rate of production was about 150 sets per month. Allowing for the production of a large percentage of spares, this suggested a total output of about a hundred Würzburgs each month. This was way beyond anything that had been anticipated beforehand, and clearly indicated the central role that the Würzburg system was going to play in the radar defence of occupied Europe and primarily of Germany itself.

Jones knew that the Bruneval Würzburg was already of an older type using a simple aerial, whereas the Giant Würzburgs that the photo interpreters had spotted on aerial photographs were not only larger but also had spinning aerials that would enable them to locate and identify a target far more accurately. But he suspected that the same electronic components could be used in both systems. And Jones now had these principal components on a bench in front of him.[1]

The stolen equipment was soon to be taken to TRE in Worth Matravers, where it could be analysed in detail. There it would be possible to calculate the limits of the wavelengths it could be tuned to. The scientists could come to a detailed understanding of how the electronics operated. And, most importantly of all, now that it was clear that the Würzburg was to be at the heart of the German night fighter defence system, ways of jamming it could be sought. But Jones knew that a radar operator had been captured and brought back to England. He was keen to meet this man and hopefully discover even more about how an operator used the Würzburg and what its full potential was. Jones gathered up the pieces and took them with him to the RAF prisoner interrogation centre at Cockfosters, where his old friend Wing Commander Denys Felkin was leading the interrogation of the prisoner.

To the British, Heller was an unlikely man to be operating a front-line radar system. He had very limited scientific knowledge. But the man was certainly willing to talk and had happily filled in his background for Felkin and the interrogation team. Heller told them that he had joined the Luftwaffe soon after its creation in the mid 1930s. But it was clear that he was not an ideal candidate and during his training, which took place in Augsburg, he was unable to learn Morse code. This basic communication system of dots and dashes was still a fundamental requirement for many grades in air force and army signalling units around the world. But Heller had never been able to master it.

Three days after war was declared in September 1939, Heller had applied for compassionate leave to return home, where his baby daughter was seriously ill. With the war just beginning, his request was refused. So he absented himself without leave. On 9 September he was arrested by the military police.

Tragically, his daughter died five days later. Heller was taken to Munich, where after an investigation lasting four weeks he was tried by court martial and sentenced to six months' imprisonment. After two months he was released on good behaviour and sent back to a Luftwaffe signals unit in Augsburg. But only two weeks later he went absent without leave once again and with some friends went on a two-day drinking spree. Arrested once more, this time he was sentenced to twelve months' imprisonment, with an additional two months remitted from the first sentence. He was sent to the well-known military prison at Torgau, where there were up to two thousand prisoners.

Later he worked as a prison labourer reclaiming land on the Baltic coast and then as a worker in the Volkswagen plant at Fallersleben. He stayed at the factory, even though his sentence had expired, until September 1941, when he rejoined his Luftwaffe unit in Augsburg. Towards the end of the year, his regiment was asked to provide ten men for Luftwaffe units in France. Heller was selected, possibly as a way of getting him out of trouble in Germany, and before long he was allocated to the Würzburg radar station at Bruneval.

No doubt Heller's low morale was due to the punishment that had been meted out to him and explained in part his willingness to talk to the RAF interrogators. But Felkin was amazed when the prisoner started to talk about the Würzburg, the machine he had been assigned to operate. He spoke with some pride about his machine having a 'magical eye'. Although he had spent two months on the radar, he still claimed that the Würzburg was able to 'see' enemy aircraft in some way. This, he claimed in all seriousness, was why the system was less effective in cloudy weather than when the sky was clear.

Felkin thought he must be trying to take the interrogators for a ride, to deceive them in some way. But as he spent more time with the prisoner he realised that this was a man with a low IQ and little training, who had not understood even the basic principles of radar. In his report, Felkin could barely contain his contempt for the prisoner; he wrote, 'P/W [prisoner of war] is very willing to impart all he knows, but is of limited intelligence ... even after two months' practical experience of the Würzburg apparatus, he still believes that the instrument "sees" the aircraft in some way.'[2]

Felkin was very dismissive of the prisoner when Jones arrived at Cockfosters with parts of the stolen equipment. Jones sat on the floor and observed Heller fitting different parts together, which he could clearly do very easily. As he did so, Jones asked him through a translator what the radar could do and what his job had been. Jones, like Felkin, was flabbergasted. The man had no idea of the complexity of the equipment he was using. He was no engineer and had none of the scientific training required of every radar operator in the RAF. In his almost childish way he chatted on about the magic eye. He even said at one point that on his last leave he had told his wife about the isolated outpost he had been assigned to, and that one day the British might raid the site and capture it. He wondered out loud if his wife was a fifth columnist and had passed these details on to British Intelligence.

However, Jones was learning an important lesson about the German radar technology. Although no scientist and no engineer, the prisoner was part of a team using cutting-edge technology. Not only was it supremely well engineered, it was clearly designed for use by operatives with a very low technical competency, people who would have been regarded as unsuitable in the RAF.

Jones later heard that the Luftwaffe had a very low priority in recruiting personnel for their radar and signals units, taking people thought not to be suitable for other duties. In Germany, Hitler had banned amateur radio before the war, fearing that opponents of the Nazi regime might use it to organise an opposition. And so there was no reserve of skilled and enthusiastic amateurs to draw upon, whereas in England men like Charles Cox, who had been assembling and dismantling wireless sets since their childhood, were ideal recruits to RAF radio and radar teams. As Jones now realised, the Germans had to ensure 'that the equipment was so well made, and so easily replaceable if any part broke down, that the system could be operated by relatively unskilled personnel'.[3] This was a revelation both to him and to the rest of the British scientific establishment.

Much had thus been learnt from the pieces brought back from Bruneval. The scientists had discovered the high quality of the design and engineering and the low grade of the operators that were using the equipment. Jones concluded that British scientists now had a 'first-hand knowledge of the state of German radar technology', especially as it was being applied to 'our principal objective, the German night fighter control system'.[4]

In addition to the technical knowledge gained, the raid had a variety of immediate consequences. Believing that the Villa Gosset was the headquarters of the German radar team at Bruneval, the planners had agreed that one objective of the raid should be to blow the building up. Finding the villa empty when they arrived there, however, Frost and his men left it standing. However, within days of the raid the Germans themselves destroyed the building, believing that it was this unusual structure that had attracted attention to the existence of the Würzburg. Of course, this was not the case. In fact it had nearly diverted the attention of the photo interpreters from the tiny path leading to the speck that was the first sighting of the Würzburg.

As a second consequence, the Germans decided that they must provide better defences for their radar installations along the northern French coastline, and so they constructed large rings of barbed wire entanglements around each installation. What they did not realise was that on black and white aerial photographs barbed wire stands out very clearly, as the grass grows beneath it and has a darker shade than surrounding grassland. The effect was like using an aerial marker pen to highlight every radar station in France. Before long Claude Wavell and his section at Medmenham had been able to identify all the installations along the coast, including several new Freyas and Würzburgs they had not spotted before.[5] This was a very welcome if unexpected consequence of the raid.

One further consequence was not so welcome to some. After Bruneval, the possibility of a retaliatory raid on a British radar installation seemed a high possibility. The obvious site for a reprisal would have been TRE – right on the coast, spread out over a large area and easy to identify on aerial photographs with its several masts, tall aerials and workshops. The Air Ministry suggested to Rowe that it was time to move, and some of those working at Worth Matravers began to grow nervous. There was only one road in and out of the site, and that was through the pretty little town of Corfe Castle. It would be easy for a raiding party to block this road, and so scientists and engineers started to take precious objects like the invaluable cavity magnetrons, and their top secret research papers, home with them of an evening in case there was a raid that night.[6] Many of the scientists nevertheless loved where they were working. It was in a beautiful stretch of Dorset countryside near the pretty seaside town of Swanage. They did not want to move.

The crunch came in late April 1942. Aerial photography spotted that a German parachute unit had moved to a position near the head of the Cherbourg peninsula, only seventy miles across the Channel from Worth Matravers. Perhaps a German Para raid was imminent. Still the scientists were reluctant to move from their seaside home. On a visit to the site to catch up on progress with research into the pieces captured at Bruneval, R.V. Jones ostentatiously wore a revolver strapped to his belt and carried a tin hat. Throughout his visit he made it clear that he wanted to get back to London as soon as possible. His behaviour no doubt added to the scientists' nervousness. The matter was resolved when in early May the War Cabinet instructed TRE to find a new home, its third move since leaving Bawdsey Manor at the beginning of the war. After a frantic search for alternative premises, the entire establishment was uprooted on 26 May and moved to the buildings of Malvern College in Worcestershire.

The transfer of men and materials had as many complications as the earlier moves. However, this move was its last. TRE stayed at Malvern for the rest of the war and remained there into the post-war era, when it changed its name to the Royal Radar Establishment. It was to become the centre of British radar research and the development of computers for use in guided missiles.

The capture of the radar at Bruneval had provided the final pieces the British needed in order to understand how the German defensive radar system worked. The Freyas could detect the approach of Allied bombers from about ninety miles out. As the bombers came within about twenty-five miles, the Würzburgs or Giant Würzburgs tuned in to them. With their centimetric radars they could even pick out individual aircraft flying within a formation of bombers. These installations constituted a vast defensive shield running from Denmark down through Holland, Belgium and north-eastern France, to the west of the German border. Commanded by General Josef Kammhuber, it was therefore known to the Allies as the Kammhuber Line. All bombers would have to cross this strip of territory in order to reach targets inside the Reich.

Along the Kammhuber Line the airspace was divided up into sector rectangles approximately 27 miles wide and 21 miles deep. By 1942, each sector was covered by a Freya for early warning and two Würzburgs, one of which tracked the movement of the Allied bombers while the second followed that of the intercepting German night fighters. The highly accurate information was sent back to command rooms, where two lights were shone on to a table map known as a Seeburg Table. A red light represented the movement of the bombers, a blue light that of the fighter. The controllers could then mark the angle at which to direct the fighters to target the bombers. During 1942, more and more bomber crews reported the intense activity of night fighters along the Kammhuber Line and losses were mounting.

At TRE, first in Worth Matravers and then in Malvern, a team under Robert Cockburn had been working on the jamming of enemy radar. The arrival of the stolen Würzburg parts was a huge boost to their work. They soon discovered the wavelengths to which the Würzburg could be tuned and found that it had no built-in counter to jamming.

Jones had suggested before the war, after a visit to Bawdsey Manor, that radar would always be vulnerable to what he called 'spurious reflectors', that is devices employed to mislead the radar receivers as to where or how extensive an approaching fleet of aircraft was. Robert Watson-Watt and his colleagues were reluctant to pursue this possibility, as they were committed to making radar work, rather than proving how it could be made not to work. As a consequence, when war came there were no plans to cope with German jamming of British radar, except the ability to switch to different frequencies.

However, the science of jamming had developed rapidly from the summer of 1940 onwards. The Royal Navy repeatedly jammed enemy naval radar stations along the French coast. The Germans had very effectively jammed British coastal radar when the *Scharnhorst* and *Gneisenau* made their dash up the Channel in February 1942. Now the British scientists had their hands on one of the most advanced pieces of German technology, they could look at different ways of jamming that too.

As well as being studied at TRE, the captured gear was also examined at the Royal Aircraft Establishment at Farnborough. Here engineers identified a weak spot in the design of the receiver. The wire from the mixer to the frequency amplifier was unshielded. If a signal was sent at the right frequency this would be picked up and would jam the Würzburg's output. Donald Preist later described this as 'very significant in terms of the radar war'.[7]

Cockburn and his team came up with a variety of suggestions. The TRE scientists realised that the Würzburg would be subject to the jamming or distortion caused by dropping dozens of strips of aluminium. They discovered that if these were roughly half the length of the wavelength of the radar, that is about 25 cm or 10 inches long and about half an inch wide, the aluminium would resonate or amplify the radio waves back to the Würzburg's receivers. Not only would it give the impression that there were many more bombers than were actually present, it would also prevent the operators from tracking individual aircraft and so guiding the night fighters to attack them. 'Window' was the name given by A.P. Rowe to this jamming system. Bundles of aluminium foil were prepared and were ready for use within two months of the Bruneval raid, in April 1942. The wireless operators and flight engineers of the heavy bombers were trained in throwing the aluminium pieces out through a special chute at two-minute intervals.

However, there was a strong argument against jamming enemy radar. Once they had realised what was being done, the enemy could devise or copy similar measures to jam British radar. Watson-Watt was particularly vocal in his objection to jamming, as he believed it would ultimately lead to the disabling of Britain's own radar systems. Churchill's friend and scientific adviser, Professor Frederick Lindemann, also argued this view. Just before Window was going to be used for the first time, in May 1942, Lindemann obtained a prohibition. He was concerned that if the British used aluminium foil, the Germans would retaliate by using a similar method to jam British radar. Fighter Command would be unable to function, leading to a massive loss of life from German bombers attacking Britain.

Jones was totally opposed to this argument. He believed that the Germans were inventive enough to have worked out a similar form of jamming themselves. In any case, he argued, the Luftwaffe were now mostly occupied on the Eastern Front and did not pose the threat they had done against Britain in the winter of 1940–1 during the Blitz. Knowing that Window was a means to defeat the formidable defences of the Kammhuber Line, Jones wanted to use it as soon as possible. As it turned out, he was correct in predicting the Germans' inventiveness. They tested a similar form of jamming over the Baltic, but Göring forbade its use in case the Allies retaliated with the same technique. Bizarrely, both sides had worked out the system but neither wanted to use it.

In the spring of 1942 Bomber Command launched a huge new offensive. New four-engined heavy bombers like the Halifax and the Lancaster were now available, new and more effective bombs had been designed and the Command had a new, bullish leader in Sir Arthur 'Bomber' Harris. He was convinced that bombing could win the war on its own by destroying the German war machine. With Stalin calling for a second front, a new bombing offensive was the only way Britain, and with it the United States, had at this point of the war of hitting back at the heartlands of German industry and wartime production. Accordingly, the first ever 'Thousand Bomber Raid' took place over Cologne on the night of 30 May.

Subsequently hundreds of British bombers flew almost

nightly over Germany, but the losses to German night fighters and to anti-aircraft fire were alarmingly high. Various techniques were used to try to reduce the effectiveness of the Kammhuber Line. The big four-engined bombers were told to take evasive action as they passed through the Line by corkscrewing and descending a few thousand feet. This confused the Würzburg operators, who temporarily lost the bombers' precise location. Another measure was to fly outside the Line, either to the north or the south. But such measures were short term and limited. Jamming remained the best way to defeat the Line. Nevertheless, the delay in the use of Window continued through-out 1942. On 4 November, Air Chief Marshal Portal called a meeting to reconsider its use. But, once again, under pressure from Lindemann and Watson-Watt supported by Fighter Command, who believed they would be the big losers, the use of Window was rejected.

Instead, the RAF chiefs decided to use another jamming system called 'Mandrel'. This was an airborne interception system carried by Defiant aircraft, which worked by creating a burst of noise that disrupted the wavelength on which the Freyas sent out their radio signals. This helped to incapacitate the Würzburgs by turning off the early warning system they relied upon. But the German engineers soon got around Mandrel by adjusting the wavelengths on which the Freyas operated. Another method, called 'Spoof', was also tried out in the summer of 1942. Instead of jamming the radar, this sent out radar-like pulses that told the Freyas that large fleets of enemy bombers were approaching. If these were used to distract from a real bombing raid taking place somewhere else, they could draw off the enemy fighters to the wrong area. This was used quite effectively for a few months to draw fighters away from the American daytime bombing raids. But before long the Germans installed more Freyas and were able to predict which was a Spoof attack and which was a real raid.

Everything came back to Window, but still its opponents held the floor. Finally, after most other techniques had been tried, the use of Window once more came up before the Chiefs of Staff on 23 June 1943. This time none other than the Prime Minister took the chair. Those for and those against lined up as before, and presented the same arguments as they had a year earlier. But this time the new head of Fighter Command, Air Marshal Sir Trafford Leigh Mallory, argued that even if his defences were neutralised by the German use of Window in retaliation, the case for saving the growing losses in Bomber Command was overwhelming. Mallory agreed to take responsibility for any consequences. Churchill weighed up the arguments and concluded, 'Very well, let us open the Window!'[8]

There was a further delay as the Chiefs of Staff did not want to use Window before the invasion of Sicily in case it was used in turn against the landing fleet. However, Window was finally dropped for the first time on the night of 24 July 1943 in a raid on Hamburg. Its use had a spectacular effect in disabling German radar and the use of their night fighters. Only 12 bombers were lost out of 791 that took part in the raid – a loss rate of 1.5 per cent compared with 6.1 per cent for the previous six raids. On the following nights it was used in raids on Essen, and then again on Hamburg. Radio interceptors in Kent listened in to the confusion of the Würzburg operators as they struggled to identify the British bombers and guide the night fighters anywhere near them. At long last the Kammhuber Line had been blinded and the German night fighter menace muted.

The raids on Hamburg set off huge firestorms that raged across the city. Whole districts were engulfed in flames. Buildings simply disappeared. Bodies were incinerated. It was later estimated that about 42,000 people had lost their lives. More than a million had fled. Twenty-two square kilometres of the city had been razed to the ground. Albert Speer, the Minister of War Production, told Hitler that if the Allies launched similar attacks against six cities in swift succession, German war production might collapse.[9] The scale of destruction unleashed by the use of Window was of a new order. But its use had been delayed for seventeen months after the stealing of the Würzburg pieces from the cliff top at Bruneval.

German scientists were of course quick to respond to jamming devices. *Würzlaus* was a radar system capable of distinguishing between aircraft and at least a light scattering of foil. The Germans also found ways of using weather reports across Germany to guess where the Allied bombers were heading. Combined with the monitoring of Allied radio activity, this enabled them to predict the target of a raid. Ground observers could then provide reports as the bombers crossed occupied territory and controllers could make a stab at directing fighters towards the bombing formations. Also, the German air-to-air radar interception system, known as *Lichtenstein*, was adapted to operate on longer wavelengths of between 3.7 and 4.1 metres, which acted as an antidote to the use of Window. German scientists also found ways of tuning in to the use of the 'Identification Friend or Foe' system used by the Allied bombers so that their own radar would identify the bombers as friends and not as enemy aircraft.

The electronic measures now in use in the skies over Europe were growing increasingly sophisticated. And of course, soon after counter-measures had been launched, then counter-counter-measures were developed. In the United States an immense amount of radar research was carried out at the Rad Lab in Boston, Massachusetts, where the counter-measures section had grown considerably in size. Here also, research was being done on perfecting the size and the shape of Window, known in America as 'Chaff', to maximise its effect. When the Americans used Chaff later in 1943, the aluminium strips were only a twentieth of an inch wide and one hundredth of an inch thick. They were even more effective in jamming the German Würzburgs. Machines for cutting the foil were built and brought to Britain. Hundreds of tons of aluminium were cut up, and in America consumers of Mars bars apparently had to do without their customary foil wrappers.

The disabling of the German ground radar defence system in the summer of 1943 was a victory of immense importance. It was the air war equivalent to the victories at El Alamein and Stalingrad, and of the defeat of the U-boat menace in the Atlantic. Like these other victories it did not bring about the immediate collapse of the enemy. But it was a turning point from which there was no going back, despite the development of counter-measures. From the end of July 1943, the RAF used Window on a regular basis. The strategic bombing offensive against Germany grew substantially. And it did so partly because the Allies had greater control over the skies through which the bombers had to fly.

Moreover, had Window and the other jamming techniques been used fifteen months earlier when they were ready for use, the lives of many aircrew would have been saved. At a conservative estimate, if the loss rate had been reduced from 6 per cent to, say, 3 per cent in the fourteen months following May 1942, approximately 1600 aircraft would not have been shot down and well over 11,000 aircrew would have been saved from death or captivity.[10]

We can only guess what would have happened if the Germans had in turn used their version of Window on bombing raids against Britain in 1943. Maybe more civilian lives would have been lost. Here we are entering the realm of one of the big 'what ifs?' of history. When the Germans did use *Düppel*, as they called their version of Window, briefly in January 1944, British counter-measures largely overcame its effectiveness. Certainly, the bombing of Britain by the manned aircraft of the Luftwaffe had largely run its course by then and it was not until the use of pilotless flying bombs with the V1, and ballistic missiles with the V2, from the summer of 1944 that the British people were driven back to their air raid shelters. By this stage a new generation of radar-controlled devices had been developed to help counter the V1. There was no defence against the V2. But that story belongs to another chapter of the radar war.

The Para raid at Bruneval had made a decisive contribution to the scientific war. The process of understanding how German radar technology functioned and how it could be blinded had been a long struggle. It had involved the brilliance of the photo intelligence teams in identifying the tiny specks on the French coast that proved to be radar installations; the genius of R.V. Jones in interpreting the pieces of evidence as he learnt them and in building up a detailed understanding of the German radar defence system; the heroism of John Frost and his Paras; and the skills of TRE in studying and calculating how the captured booty from the raid could be jammed.

In the autumn of 1943 Göring despaired at the success of the British radar scientists and he dismissed Kammhuber as head of the night fighter command. At one point Göring exploded with rage and frustration, proclaiming, 'In the field of radar they must have the world's greatest genius. They have the geniuses and we have the nincompoops ... I hate the rogues like the plague, but in one respect I am obliged to doff my cap to them.' He ended his tirade by saying, 'After this war is over I'm going to buy myself a British radio set, as a token of my regard for their high frequency work.'[11] It was a strange but fitting tribute, marking the enormous importance of the Allied victory in the radar war.

Epilogue

Several medals were handed out as a consequence of the Bruneval raid. The Royal Navy were particularly generous and three Distinguished Service Crosses were awarded, one to Commander Cook who had led the naval operation and had taken the tiny flotilla of landing craft in to the beaches to pick up the men, and one to Lieutenant Quick who had leapt into the water to connect a line from the landing craft stuck on the beach to the adjoining ALC. Two members of the MGB crew were awarded the Distinguished Service Medal and six sailors were mentioned in dispatches.

The army was less generous with its gongs. Major John Frost and Lieutenant Euan Charteris were both awarded the Military Cross (MC). This was a great achievement and well deserved for both men. The equivalent award for other ranks, the Military Medal, went to Sergeant David Grieve, who had screamed the war cry of the Seaforth Highlanders when he successfully attacked the Stella Maris, and to Sergeant McKenzie, who had fought in the same action. Both Lieutenant Young, who had led the attack on the Würzburg itself, and Corporal Jones of the Royal Engineers were mentioned in dispatches. To everyone's surprise, Lieutenant Vernon, the leader of the engineers, received nothing.

The RAF awarded a second DSO to Wing Commander Pickard for 'demonstrating his outstanding powers of leadership and organisation'. Although commander of the squadron of Whitleys, he had of course dropped the stick of Paras from his own plane in the wrong place and was, apparently, a little embarrassed to receive this distinction. But the RAF also gave the Military Medal to Flight Sergeant Charles Cox, who had 'volunteered' for the mission and who bravely succeeded in leading the dismantling of the Würzburg while under fire. Regimental Sergeant-Major Gerry Strachan, who was in hospital in intensive care, was awarded the French decoration, the Croix de Guerre. Intelligence scientist R.V. Jones was made a Companion of the British Empire for having suggested the raid in the first place.

In military terms, the huge success of the Bruneval raid had two major consequences. First, it put British airborne forces decisively on the map. Many had doubted the wisdom of diverting sparse resources into the Airborne Division. Despite the huge success of German paratrooper forces in May 1940, the failure of the first British Para raid in the south of Italy in early 1941 had shown up the risks of these operations and had tended to encourage the doubters. Bruneval was the first, striking success for British Paras. It would later be the first 'battle honour' of the Parachute Regiment.[1] The raid had shown the need for top rate intelligence and the virtue of good, careful planning. With two soldiers dead and six captured, a loss rate of 6.5 per cent was deemed acceptable for such a bold operation carried out behind enemy lines. General Browning was at last able to provide clear evidence of the Paras' value. The future of British airborne forces was now secure and it was never seriously challenged again. And, unknown in London, the Germans, too, had pointed out the courage and the daring of the Paras the first time they had come up against them.

Second, the raid was a triumph for the planning and the organisation of Combined Operations. Accordingly, one of the first to benefit from the success of the raid was the man who had helped to conceive the raid in the first place, the head of Combined Operations, Lord Louis Mountbatten. On 4 March, two days after the meeting with Frost in the underground war rooms, Churchill summoned Mountbatten to lunch at Downing Street. He approved strongly of Mountbatten's conduct at Combined Operations and told him so. What's more, the Prime Minister told Mountbatten that, rather than 'Adviser', he was now to be 'Chief' of Combined Operations and promoted to the rank of vice-admiral. In line with the principle of 'combined' forces, he was also to be appointed a lieutenant-general in the army and an air marshal in the RAF. This was indeed a remarkable promotion and no one other than the King held senior ranks in all three services. Mountbatten was delighted and wrote proudly to a friend that he was now 'the youngest Vice Admiral since Nelson'.[2]

It was a dazzling leap up the ladder, and a real sign of the Prime Minister's confidence in him. In addition, Mountbatten was to join the Chiefs of Staff Committee, even though he was so much younger than the other chiefs who met daily to direct Britain's war effort. For the men of Combined Operations this was a huge boost. John Hughes-Hallett later spoke of his 'exhilaration, almost exultation' at the elevation of his boss. 'At one stride our organisation had penetrated the very citadel of Power. We were now to work for a man with access to all the secrets.'[3]

Mountbatten enthusiastically wore the uniform of a vice-admiral in public. In a rare display of modesty, he failed to acquire the uniforms of a lieutenant-general and an air marshal, protesting that he did not have enough clothing coupons to purchase such outfits. But this marked a turning point for Mountbatten, the King's cousin. He would remain in the senior echelons of the military and political establishment. In 1944 he was appointed Supreme Commander of South East Asia Command and after the war he was made Viceroy of India where he oversaw the process of British withdrawal from the Raj and the creation of the independent states of India and Pakistan.[4]

Despite all the brouhaha, Bruneval was still only a small-scale raid. One month later a far bigger combined operation took place at St Nazaire. This large port on the western coast of France had the only dry dock on the whole Atlantic coast capable of repairing warships as large as the *Tirpitz*. The *Bismarck* had been heading there for repairs when it was sunk the year before. Churchill was terrified of a ship this size breaking out into the Atlantic to disrupt the sea lanes. Enormous resources were at the time being devoted to try to monitor and attack the *Tirpitz*, which was holed up in the fjords of northern Norway. To discourage it from trying to break out into the Atlantic, a commando raid was mounted supported by the Royal Navy.

But St Nazaire was a well-defended fortress with batteries of anti-aircraft weapons and naval guns. So the plan was to sail a line of vessels across the sand banks in the estuary of the Loire, taking advantage of an exceptionally high spring tide in order to get right inside the harbour. The ships would include an old First World War destroyer, HMS *Campbeltown*, packed with delayed-action explosives, which was to ram the gates of the dry dock. Commandos on board would land and head off to destroy a variety of other targets within the port. Other naval vessels, consisting of twenty Motor Torpedo Boats (MTBs) and MGBs, would arrive bringing in further commandos, each squad including demolition parties that once landed would cause further havoc around the port. The damage done, they would then withdraw on the MTBs and MGBs.

In the early hours of 28 March, the operation began with an RAF bombing raid on the harbour by Whitleys and Wellingtons, planned to distract the enemy at the critical moment. But cloud cover prevented most of the bombers from finding their targets and the local German commander became suspicious that something was up. Initially he suspected another parachute landing. The convoy of British vessels sailed into St Nazaire harbour with the *Campbeltown* flying the German naval ensign, but the ships were soon picked up by German searchlights and despite *Campbeltown*'s subterfuge came under intense fire. The vessel sailed on despite being hit and managed to ram the gates of the dry dock. The commandos on board disembarked and began to plant their explosives around the harbour. However, most of the vessels that were to take the commandos away were sunk and several hundred men were left stranded ashore. They fought on outside St Nazaire until they ran out of ammunition, when they had no alternative but to surrender.

By morning all was quiet in the harbour. A group of German officers and engineers came in to assess the damage. They were on board the *Campbeltown* when the explosives went off. In all, 360 men were killed in the huge explosion. The dry dock was damaged so badly it was put out of action for the rest of the war. Mission accomplished.

The success of the raid came at a high price. Of the 622 men from the Royal Navy and the commandos who took part, only 228 returned to England. One hundred and sixty-nine men were killed and 215 became prisoners of war. A total of eighty-nine decorations were awarded to members of the raiding party, including five Victoria Crosses, two of them post-humously. St Nazaire has gone down in the history of the commandos as one of their most heroic actions, as indeed it was. However, with a loss rate of more than 60 per cent, it was of a completely different order to Bruneval. It once again showed that daring and courage could not only inflict severe damage on the enemy, but that these raids had the consequence of drawing many enemy troops into France to reinforce the long coastline that faced Britain.

Only one man who had been on the Bruneval raid also took part in the St Nazaire mission. That was the German Peter Nagel, who had acted as translator for the Paras at Bruneval and did the same at St Nazaire. He was one of the many men captured at St Nazaire, but his disguise as Private Newman was so complete that the Germans never suspected he was of German origin. He survived captivity, returned to England and lived to a fine old age.

In October 1942, the Parachute Brigade was sent from Britain to North Africa. John Frost, who had been sent on a speaking tour to tell military audiences about the Bruneval raid, was promoted and became commander of the 2nd Battalion, which came to be known colloquially as 2 Para. Following the Allied landings in Morocco and Algiers in Operation Torch, Allied troops drove eastwards from north-west Africa. Meanwhile, Montgomery was advancing westwards from Egypt after his great victory at El Alamein. The idea was for the two forces to join up in Tunisia and to destroy Axis power in North Africa.

In Algiers, Frost and his men were told to wait for orders. It was clear that the British high command still did not really know how to use its airborne resources. And there was no one in the Allied headquarters with any experience of working with airborne troops. Eventually a plan was hastily drawn up for the 2nd Battalion to drop behind enemy lines near an airfield, then to march to a second airfield and destroy that, and then to meet up with advancing ground troops just outside Tunis for a triumphant entry into the capital.

Frost and his men jumped this time from American C-47 Dakota aircraft, which were far superior to the Whitleys. The men could sit in two lines and jump from a side door rather than having to lie across the fuselage and jump through a hole in the floor. Each Dakota took twenty Paras instead of half that number in the obsolete British bombers.

After several last-minute changes to the plan, Frost and the battalion landed at Depienne, south of Tunis, and set off for the airfield they were to capture at Oudna. When they reached it they were surprised to find it had already been evacuated. As their task had been to destroy aircraft and stores at Oudna, they were left without a mission. But there began a long and confused combat around the airfield and the surrounding rocky countryside. The whole operation had been ill thought through, and was woefully supported by an Allied headquarters that rapidly seemed to forget about the Para battalion stuck behind enemy lines – partly because the drop unfortunately coincided with a major new offensive by the Germans to the north that naturally focused the attention of the Allied commanders.

Effectively abandoned, almost out of ammunition, with many casualties that had to be left behind, Frost ordered his men to withdraw to what they thought was the Allied front line. Once again their radios failed to work properly, and in any case the batteries ran out after a day or so. A keen huntsman, Frost blew his hunting horn to direct the men. They moved at night when it was freezing cold, and in the daytime were harassed by enemy ground troops and strafed from the air by the Luftwaffe. The battalion marched for sixty miles across difficult countryside for five days and nights, constantly being harried by enemy forces with Panzers and armoured cars. Sheer guts pulled the survivors through. But 260 men were lost in the futile mission, killed, wounded or captured.[5] Philip Teichman, who had led C Company briefly before Frost, was among the dead, while several of the men who had taken part in the night raid on Bruneval were either killed or captured. Lieutenant Euan 'Junior' Charteris, the hero of Bruneval, led an advance party to try to find a way back to Allied lines and was killed while doing so. He had celebrated his twenty-first birthday but never reached his twenty-second.

When Frost and just half of the battalion found their way back to Allied lines, he was furious. Everything had been so well planned at Bruneval, but it was the opposite with Oudna. The mission had been put together at the last minute and lacked clear intelligence as to where the enemy were and in what numbers they were deployed. The battalion had been given no support and was left to fend for itself, with ammunition and supplies of every sort running out. Frost later called it 'perhaps the most disgracefully mounted operation of the war'.[6]

The battalion received reinforcements and remained in North Africa for several months of heavy fighting as ground infantry. In one of these actions at Tamera in March 1943, Lieutenant John Timothy captured a German machine-gun nest and two brand new MG 34 guns almost single handed. For this and other actions he was awarded the MC. The battalion took more than three thousand prisoners during the campaign, many of whom saying when they came in how terrified they were when they realised they were up against British Paras. Indeed, the Germans in Tunisia nicknamed the Paras from their crimson berets *Die Röte Teufeln*, 'the Red Devils'. It was a name that stuck.

When the invasion of Sicily took place in July 1943, airborne troops were used to seize key points behind enemy lines in advance of the forces that were landed on the beaches. The objective of the 1st Parachute Brigade was to capture and hold Primosole Bridge, the gateway to Catania. The 2nd Battalion led by Frost was to hold the high ground a mile to the south of the bridge. The drop, like that at Bruneval, was carried out at night. But this time it proved to be a disaster. The transport aircraft passed over the Allied fleet just after a Luftwaffe attack and were fired at by anxious gunners in the Allied naval ships. They were thrown off course by further anti-aircraft fire over the drop zone. More than half dropped their human cargos miles from the DZ, some men being told to jump up to thirty miles away on the slopes of Mount Etna. A dozen pilots could not identify the DZ at all and returned with the Paras still on board.

For the glider-borne troops the situation was even more tragic. Some gliders were released so far out to sea that they crashed into the water and hundreds of paratroopers drowned. John Ross, the second-in-command at Bruneval, was one of those dropped in the wrong spot and was captured. He spent the rest of his war in a PoW camp.

Frost found himself moving off with only a hundred men, less than a fifth of his intended strength. The paltry forces captured the bridge from Italian troops during the night, but were not strong enough to hold out against a fierce counter-attack by German parachute forces on the following day and the bridge was recaptured by the enemy. During the next night the ground troops who had landed further south joined up with the surviving Paras, but it took four days of bitter fighting and heavy losses before the bridge was recaptured and the advance on Catania could continue.

The whole airborne operation in Sicily had been a fiasco, for both the British and American paratroopers. Frost later described it as a 'humiliating disaster for airborne forces and almost enough to destroy even the most ardent believer's faith'.[7] However, although nothing much had gone to plan, the paratroopers had proved themselves once again to be tough and determined fighters and had shown their ability to cause chaos behind enemy lines, even when dropped miles from their intended DZ. The final verdict was, therefore, to continue with airborne operations. 2 Para was sent back to North Africa to recover and to be brought back up to strength. Frost was meanwhile delighted to welcome back to the battalion Sergeant-Major Strachan, who had apparently recovered from his bad stomach injury at Bruneval.

After spending some months fighting in Italy, during which Lieutenant John Timothy won a second MC, 2 Para was withdrawn to Britain at the end of 1943. A second division had been added to the 1st Airborne Division and General Browning was now in charge of an Airborne Corps. Despite the disasters in Sicily, it was clear that airborne troops were to be given a major role in the invasion of Europe when it came. But Frost and his men had to wait at home and follow the news of the invasion on the radio as other airborne units jumped on the night before D-Day. Their tasks were to secure the flanks of the landing beaches in order to prevent the Germans from mounting a rapid counter-attack while the invaders were still at their most vulnerable clambering ashore to establish a beachhead. On D-Day itself there were again problems with men being dropped in the wrong place, but American paratroopers performed well on the Cherbourg peninsula, and British Paras and glider-borne troops did a magnificent job at Pegasus Bridge and in capturing a large coastal gun battery at Merville.

Frost and 2 Para were held on standby as several operations following D-Day were planned but then abandoned. The situation on the ground was changing so rapidly that ops became redundant before they could be carried out. Their next and most famous action of all came in September 1944 in the operation known as Market Garden. This was a daring plan dreamed up by Montgomery to try to finish the war by

Christmas. Three airborne divisions, two American and one British, were to be dropped to capture three key bridges across canals in Holland approaching the Lower Rhine. Ground troops led by XXX Corps were then to smash through in a sixty-mile corridor and link up with the Paras, cross the Rhine, cut off the Ruhr industrial district and advance into northern Germany in a lightning blow. Frost and 2 Para were given one of the toughest jobs of all, to capture and hold the furthest road bridge at Arnhem.

A great deal has been written about the heroic but ultimately futile battle for the bridge at Arnhem.[8] The airborne commanders were worried that the DZs were in the wrong place and were too far from their objectives. And once again there were not enough aircraft to carry all the men needed in a single day. At the eleventh hour, aerial intelligence had spotted enemy armoured troops resting and refitting in the surrounding woods, but this vital piece of information was ignored.[9] So when Frost and his men finally reached the bridge, there were too few of them to defend their enclave from what proved to be an elite SS Panzer corps. The Paras were supposed to hold out for forty-eight hours, until the ground troops could fight their way through to relieve them. But problems with the advance of XXX Corps meant they never got through. The lightly armed Paras were completely outnumbered by the SS troops, who had plentiful supplies and were supported by heavy armour.

Frost's men held on amid bitter house-to-house fighting. Clinging on to the northern end of the bridge, they were isolated and surrounded, while once again their radios failed to work and provide a clear picture of what was happening elsewhere. With supplies of food and ammunition running out, with virtually no water and with the wounded stacked so closely together in basements that the medical orderlies could barely get around them, the SS commander invited Frost to surrender. 'Tell them to go to hell,' was his response.[10] But on the third morning, Frost was himself severely wounded. It was the end of the battle for him. In a truce later that day, he and the hundreds of other wounded were taken prisoner and removed to a hospital. The remainder of 2 Para fought on for another twenty-four hours until the German forces overran them.

John Timothy, by now a major in command of his own company, also took part in the Arnhem operation in a separate battalion. He soon found himself and his men fighting for their lives against far stronger enemy forces, equipped with heavyweight Tiger tanks which they could hear rumbling forward during the night. His company fought a brave rearguard action to enable the rest of the battalion to fight their way through to the road bridge. With his company reduced to only six men, he led an assault against an enemy strongpoint, managing to overcome it. For this he won his third MC in fifteen months. But he too was eventually captured and taken off to a PoW camp, Offlag VIIB in the east. There, he was taken for interrogation and found that his name was known to the Germans, still listed on a card index as a lieutenant, as the leader of *Rodney* at Bruneval. Conditions were Spartan, with meat served only once a week. With the Russians approaching, Timothy and his fellow prisoners were evacuated westwards. He managed to escape and eventually linked up with advancing American troops.[11]

Sergeant-Major Gerry Strachan was another Bruneval veteran to fight at Arnhem. Having been captured, he too spent the rest of the war in a PoW camp, Stalag XIII.

Frost, who took some time to recover from his wounds, spent a cold, hungry and utterly miserable winter in captivity until American troops liberated his prison camp in March 1945. General Browning had questioned before the operation whether taking the bridge at Arnhem was not a 'bridge too far' in Monty's ambitious plan, and it was this phrase that provided the title for the classic British war film made in the 1970s about the Arnhem story.[12] The part of Frost was played by Anthony Hopkins. Frost was a consultant on the film and, then in his sixties, found it strange to watch re-enactments of the battle being staged before his eyes with Hopkins playing his part. In the end, however, he quite liked the film, and no doubt the fame it brought him.[13]

Many of the Germans captured over the years had told the British Paras that they had no conception of what the fighting was like on the Eastern Front, so vast were the numbers involved and so bitter the battles. Hitler's ambition to conquer the Soviet Union in just six months following his invasion in June 1941 had nearly succeeded. As his armies rolled forward taking hundreds of thousands of prisoners, Hitler spoke of his 'crusade' against communism. He called the Soviet state a 'rotten structure' that when kicked in would soon come 'crashing down'. But in December 1941 the advancing German armies ground to a halt within sight of the Kremlin towers in Moscow. As the winter blizzards swept in, the Soviets launched a counter-attack with fresh troops from Siberia. The German army for the first time went into retreat. When the fighting season started again in the spring of 1942, Hitler launched a giant offensive to the south of the country. Its joint objectives were to capture the rich arable lands, the coal reserves and oil fields of the Caucasus, and to reach the Volga river and capture the model Soviet industrial city named after the country's leader, Stalingrad. Demands for manpower on the Eastern Front slowly began to consume the Wehrmacht and reinforcements were sent east until the Axis forces in Russia grew to 217 divisions by the summer of 1942.

One of the divisions transferred to the Eastern Front from France in May 1942 was the 336th Infantry Division, the unit that had defended the French coast north of Le Havre. The 685th Infantry Regiment, complete with its 1st Battalion under Major Paschke, was sent from the comfortable surroundings of the gentle Normandy countryside to the harsh and brutal world of the Russian front. Whether or not this was some sort of punishment perpetrated on the entire division for its failings at Bruneval is not recorded. It's difficult to see that blame could fairly be directed at a unit that had to confront a surprise night raid by British paratroopers, but it is entirely possible that the Nazi leadership would take no pity on a division that had failed to distinguish itself and had given the enemy a huge propaganda triumph.

Whatever was the case, on 14 May the 336th was transferred to Brittany and from there to Belgorod, 350 miles south of Moscow, where it joined the German Sixth Army commanded by General von Paulus. In the major offensive that summer, the division was involved in heavy fighting around the town of Rossosh in the Don basin in July and was so badly mauled that it was withdrawn from the front to recuperate for the autumn in Hungary. During this time the 685th was reformed as a Grenadier regiment and with the 336th returned to fight in Russia again at the end of the year.

The 685th Regiment found themselves fighting for their lives in Russia. By 1944, still as part of the 336th Division, they were fighting in the Ukraine and withdrew south to the Crimea and its capital, Sebastopol. The Red Army then advanced into the Crimean peninsula with thirty divisions and nearly half a million men. Hitler ordered his troops, based in the well-defended city, to hold the Crimea at any price. On 5 May the Soviets unleashed a huge bombardment, and after intense fighting day and night the German citadel capitulated after only five days. The German forces were annihilated, the Wehrmacht losing a hundred thousand men killed or captured. Some twenty-two divisions ceased to exist, among them the 336th.

The few men from the 685th Regiment who escaped were reformed into a new division, the 294th, before that unit was itself entirely wiped out in fighting in the southern Ukraine in August 1944. Very few of the men who had been based at the Hotel Beau-Minet or in La Poterie or elsewhere along that stretch of the French coast survived.[14] Fusilier Tewes, who had surrendered in the dugout on the beach at Bruneval, and telephone orderly Corporal Georg Schmidt, who had been taken prisoner in the Stella Maris, turned out to be the lucky ones. They were still alive in a PoW camp in England.

As a postscript to the annihilation of the German forces that had once guarded Bruneval, the German general in command at the time, Johann Joachim Stever, the ex-Panzer general, had been replaced as commander of the 336th Division in March 1942, a month after the Para raid. He had retired temporarily on grounds of ill health. But he recovered and like so many of his colleagues, he found himself by the summer of 1944 serving on the Eastern Front. Despite the severity of the fighting, he survived the long retreat across eastern Europe and returned to Berlin. Stever was no Nazi, and his lack of ideological commitment might have been one of the reasons for his demotion after the Blitzkrieg assault on France in 1940. However, as far as the Soviets were concerned, his position as a major-general in the Wehrmacht made him a war criminal. Soon after the end of the war, in May 1945, he was arrested by Soviet troops in Berlin. He disappeared and was never heard of again. Officially posted as 'missing' ever since, he was almost certainly shot in the back of the head, the favourite form of execution of the Soviet secret police, soon after being captured.

Of the British soldiers who had been at Bruneval and survived the war, Sergeant-Major Gerry Strachan, was liberated from his PoW camp and came back to Britain where he married his wartime girlfriend, Ivy, a corporal in the Auxiliary Territorial Service. He returned to his pre-war regiment, the Black Watch, and served in India during the final days of the Raj. However, he never fully recovered from the stomach wounds he suffered at Bruneval and, aged only forty-one, he died in 1948.

Flight Sergeant Charles Cox went back to Wisbech in Cambridgeshire where he opened a radio and television maintenance shop. He became a local figure well known for being able to repair almost all types of electrical equipment. But few locals knew of his role in dismantling the Würzberg on the cliff top, under fire, in 1942.[15]

John Timothy with his Military Cross and two bars could have stayed on in the army, but decided to go back to his former life at Marks and Spencer and spent the rest of his days rising through the ranks of the retail giant. He travelled the country with M&S and was manager of their Wakefield store for seven years.[16] John Ross, captured in Sicily, had spent much of the war active in the escape committees of the various PoW camps in which he was incarcerated. For this he was awarded an MBE. He returned to Dundee and became a successful solicitor after the war.[17]

Only 'Johnny' Frost stayed on in the army, becoming a legendary figure among British paratroopers. He rose to the rank of lieutenant-general and commander of the 52nd (Lowland) Division. Having retired in 1968 to take up farming in West Sussex, he led many annual reunions of veterans at both Bruneval and Arnhem, where every year Dutch children lay flowers on the graves of the British dead in the Commonwealth War Graves cemetery. Two roads in the vicinity of Bruneval have been named rue John Frost and in 1977, after *A Bridge Too Far* was released, the new road bridge across the Lower Rhine at Arnhem was renamed the *John Frostbrug*, the John Frost Bridge.[18]

2 Para remained one of the most famous units within the British Army. The battalion served in Palestine in 1946, took part in the seaborne landings at Port Said, Egypt, in the Suez Crisis of 1956, and was posted to what was then called the Persian Gulf in the early 1960s. The battalion was in the Far East for much of the next few years but was sent to Northern Ireland for the first of sixteen tours of duty in 1970. In August 1979, the unit suffered the worst single loss of life in Northern Ireland when the Provisional IRA killed sixteen men in a double ambush at Warrenpoint.

In the Falklands, 2 Para fought with great distinction, capturing many hundreds of Argentine prisoners during the battle for Goose Green and overwhelming a nest of machine-gun positions on Darwin Hill in the famous action on 28 May 1982. The battalion commander, Lieutenant-Colonel 'H' Jones, was killed leading this attack, for which he was awarded a posthumous Victoria Cross. 2 Para completed two tours of duty in Iraq in 2005 and 2007. The battalion formed the nucleus of the 16th Air Assault Brigade that fought in Afghanistan in 2008 and 2010. Heroes still emerge in 2 Para and soldiers carry on earning distinguished medals. The battalion continues to win further battle honours, although the first honour proudly listed in 2 Para's history will always, of course, be that of Bruneval.

The success of the raid at Bruneval in capturing enemy radar technology made a major contribution to winning the scientific war that was a key part of the Allied victory in the Second World War. In his volume in the Oxford History of England, A.J.P. Taylor wrote that it was Tizard, Watson-Watt and their associates that had 'laid the foundations for victory' with the development of radar.[19] After 1945, radar became one of the most important technologies of the second half of the twentieth century. It was used to assist civil aviation and helped keep the skies a safe place for travel despite the huge growth in numbers of aircraft over the decades. It is used in naval shipping of every sort, from small fishing trawlers to giant super-tankers, for navigation and safety. It plays an important part in weather forecasting and has been developed for a host of additional purposes never imagined by the early pioneers at Orford Ness and Bawdsey Manor, at Gema or Telefunken.

After the war R.V. Jones left the world of intelligence and returned to academia. He was appointed Professor of Natural

Philosophy at Aberdeen University, where he remained until his retirement in 1981. He did much important work on improving the sensitivity of scientific instruments, but his pivotal role in wartime scientific intelligence only emerged in the late 1970s after the stories of the extensive codebreaking operations at Bletchley Park were revealed. In 1994 he was made a Companion of Honour.[20]

In late 1945 a series of redundant army trailers full of mobile radar equipment were deposited in a muddy field in Cheshire and handed over to the care of Manchester University. Here an ex-TRE engineer, Bernard Lovell, began to develop an entirely new and dynamic use for radar. The equipment that had been used by anti-aircraft guns to detect enemy planes was now used to pick up radar echoes from the ionised trails of meteors, shooting stars, from the outer atmosphere of the earth. Slowly, and with better equipment, Lovell began employing the technology to study the moon and the planets. This was called radar astronomy, and the place where it started was Jodrell Bank.

By the mid 1950s, the transmitting element of conventional radar apparatus had been abandoned and, using the receiver alone, Jodrell Bank became the world centre of an entirely new science devoted to the study of radio waves from sources far away in the universe, called radio astronomy. Funding crises threatened the work at Jodrell Bank many times – on one occasion Lovell himself was threatened with imprisonment for supposed financial mismanagement. But the politics of the Cold War came to his rescue, and when he picked up signals from the missile that launched the Russian Sputnik in October 1957 Jodrell Bank instantly became world famous. With the

Americans showing massive interest in his work, the future
was secure.

Before long the huge, sensitive 250-foot receivers at Jodrell
Bank were picking up signals from objects unimagined when
the facility was established – from radio galaxies, quasars,
pulsars and masers to the residual radiation from the primeval
state of the universe. The techniques first developed on the
Suffolk coast were now used to penetrate the mysteries of
the universe and track objects billions of light years away from
our planet.[21]

In 1942, Robert Watson-Watt, who is often called 'the father
of radar', was knighted. After the war the British government
eventually awarded him a token £52,000 for his contribution to
the invention of radar. By the 1950s, he was spending most of
his time in North America as a consulting engineer. Despite the
award, Watson-Watt, like other wartime inventors, felt more
appreciated in the United States.[22]

In 1957 Watson-Watt was visiting the west coast. Late for a
speaking engagement, he put his foot down on the largely
empty freeway. What he did not know was that just ahead at
the side of the road was a policeman with a brand new radar
gun. The policeman recorded the speed of the vehicle, mounted
his motor bike, chased down Watson-Watt and told him he
had been caught speeding. Watson-Watt asked the cop how
he could prove what speed he had been travelling at, and the
policeman showed him the radar gun.

Cursing, Watson-Watt is supposed to have said, 'If I'd have
known it would be used for purposes like this I would never
have invented radar.'[23]

Acknowledgements

There are many people who helped with this book. As usual, I will start by thanking my colleagues at Flashback Television with whom I had the pleasure of making several television documentaries on radar, on airborne forces and on special operations. Particularly, I should like to thank Colin Barratt, Paul Nelson, Andrew Johnston, Hereward Pelling and Ian Bremner. I'm also grateful to Ann and Niels Toettcher, the current owners of Bawdsey Manor, for allowing me to explore their superb historic house. In addition, I would like to congratulate the Bawdsey Radar Trust who are doing excellent work in preserving and presenting the Bawdsey story. A 'radar tour', from Orford Ness to Bawdsey Manor, to Worth Matravers is a fascinating journey to make. Also, I'm grateful to my friend Trevor Kirkin for reading and commenting on the opening chapters.

Sadly, most of the men who took part in the Bruneval raid,

and those who were in the frontline of the scientific war, are no longer with us. But the records they left behind are marvellously rich. There are extensive reports and detailed summaries of the raid written at the time. British airborne troops had only been in action once before Bruneval, in southern Italy in February 1941 and that was a disaster. So the men on the Bruneval raid were like guinea pigs. The Airborne Division and the army as a whole wanted to scrutinise how the Paras would perform in combat, what problems they would face and how they would try to solve them. The key weapon they used was new; the communication systems they carried in packs on their backs were being tried out for the first time; the medical aids they would carry, even the canisters used for dropping their supplies, were all new and the senior officers wanted to know how they performed. Much was written in the weeks after the raid by those trying to learn the lessons of Bruneval. And today it is wonderful to read these accounts with all the vivid detail they reveal.

Like many of those who took part in the Second World War, when the Paras who had fought at Bruneval (and in all their other combats that followed) returned home after the victory in 1945 they wanted to forget about the war and to put it all behind them. There were new priorities to address and the challenges of settling down to peace-time life to face up to. But as they grew older and passed into retirement, many veterans wrote memoirs or were interviewed at length about their wartime experiences. Many of the men were extremely frank in these interviews. I have interviewed several wartime veterans over many years who will begin a story by confiding, 'Of course, I've never told my family this but ... ' That used to puzzle me until I realised that it is often a lot easier to tell something to a sympathetic stranger than to reveal it to loved ones, especially if the story has a dark side, something men would like to forget or that they still feel bad about. And many veterans felt a lot better for opening up about something they had not talked about for fifty or sixty years. They had got something that worried them off their chest. I used to call it 'interview therapy'. So many of the oral histories I have been able to refer to for this book are both open and honest. But as with all memories, the historian must be critical when reading or hearing them. Furthermore, they need a context in which to be understood and that comes from the original documents written at the time. It is the combination of original documents and later recorded memories or written memoirs that provides the raw material on which this book is based.

The core documents for the Bruneval raid are to be found in the National Archives at Kew and they are all listed in the endnotes. Additionally the Airborne Archive, part of the Airborne Assault Museum at Duxford, has a treasure trove of material relating to Bruneval, including unpublished memoirs, personal reports, documents, photographs and objects. I am grateful to Jon Baker and his supremely helpful staff. Their passion for and knowledge of airborne history make them ideal keepers of the Para flame. The Imperial War Museum has a wealth of material, ranging from the excellent interviews conducted by expert interviewers from the 1990s onwards, to the wonderful film and photographic records of the raid. I'm particularly grateful to Paul Sergeant and Jane Fish of the Film Archive for their help in tracking film material down. The

Medmenham Collection Archives, at RAF Wyton; the RAF Museum at Hendon; the Churchill Archives Centre at Churchill College, Cambridge; the Institute of Historical Research in London; and the BBC Written Archives Centre at Caversham have also given me access to some excellent and valuable material. I am grateful to the archivists and librarians in all of these establishments for their enormous help with my research. They are the people who keep the wheels of historical research turning, and all historians know how much we owe to them.

The first book about Bruneval by George Millar was published in 1974. Millar, himself a war veteran with a fine record, was able to meet many of the participants of the raid, for which I am of course immensely envious. His interview with Flight Sergeant Charles Cox really adds to the record of his story. Just when I was completing this book the massive tome *Raid de Bruneval et de La Poterie-Cap-d'Antifer* by Alain Millet supported by Nicolas Bucourt came out in France. It is a remarkable labour marking several years of fascination with the Bruneval story. I am indebted to Millet for the material about aspects of the French side of the story.

It used to be said that there was nothing much to be seen at Bruneval and the place was not 'worth a detour' as the old Michelin guides used to say. However, in June 2012 a splendid monument and a truly informative set of interpretative plaques in both French and English were opened at the site. Although much of the location where events took place is private property and so cannot be visited, the village of Bruneval is an unusual and fascinating place. Now the monument will add splendidly to every visitor's enjoyment and understanding of the events that took place there more than seventy years ago.

At Little, Brown I would like to thank Claudia Dyer and Iain Hunt for their professional and enthusiastic support of this project, and Linda Silverman for her work on the photographs. Many thanks also to Steve Gove for his thorough work on the manuscript. Behind them all, Tim Whiting has been from the start a great supporter and enthusiast for this book.

Anne has helped me and put up with me for the many months of obsession with Bruneval. My greatest thanks, as always, are to her.

Taylor Downing
February 2013

Notes

Guide to References

NA = National Archives, Kew
Airborne = Airborne Assault Archive, Duxford
Churchill = Churchill Archives Centre, Churchill College, Cambridge
Medmenham = Medmenham Collection Archives, RAF Wyton
IWM = Imperial War Museum, London
IWM Sound = Sound Records Archive, Imperial War Museum, London
IWM Film = Film Archive, Imperial War Museum, London
RAF = RAF Museum, Hendon
BBC WAC = BBC Written Archives Centre, Caversham

Chapter 1 – Radar

1 Ronald Clark, *The Rise of the Boffins*, p. 37; Robert Watson-Watt, *Three Steps to Victory*, pp. 110–12. In his account Watson-Watt says that when they picked up the signal of the aircraft nearby he cannot remember 'showing any detectable signs of excitement or elation', although this seems highly unlikely and he does refer to the fact that the phrase 'Britain an Island Again' later became a slogan for the radar research team; see p. 117. The receiver used in this experiment

is now on display in the Science Museum; see: http://www.science-andsociety.co.uk/results.asp?image=10306999&itemw=4&itemf=0002 &itemstep=1&itemx=3&screenwidth=1157

2 David Pritchard, *The Radar War*, pp. 14–22.

3 Watson-Watt, *Three Steps to Victory*, p. 94.

4 Robert Buderi, *The Invention that Changed the World*, p. 59.

5 Baldwin's only solution was a form of deterrence that would be more familiar to a later, nuclear age: 'The only defence is offence, which means that you will have to kill more women and children more quickly than the enemy if you want to save yourselves.' *Hansard*, 10 November 1932.

6 *The Times*, 8 August 1934; see also Taylor Downing, *Churchill's War Lab*, pp. 155ff.

7 A.P. Rowe, *One Story of Radar*, pp. 4–5.

8 NA: AIR 20/145, Memo from Hugh Wimperis to the Secretary of State for Air, Lord Londonderry; Ronald Clark, *Tizard*, p. 112.

9 J.A. Ratcliffe, 'Robert Alexander Watson-Watt', in *Biographical Memoirs of Fellows of the Royal Society*, 1975, pp. 549–68.

10 E.G. Bowen, *Radar Days*, p. 1.

11 NA: AIR 20/145; the memo is also reproduced in full by Watson-Watt in the Appendix of his *Three Steps to Victory*, pp. 470–4.

12 Watson-Watt, *Three Steps to Victory*, p. 126 or Rowe, *One Story of Radar*, p. 10

13 Watson-Watt, *Three Steps to Victory*, p. 126.

14 Orford Ness is now run by the National Trust and is still known as 'Suffolk's secret coast'. The remains of some of the buildings and the base of the transmitter towers can be visited; see http://www.nationaltrust.org.uk/orfordness

15 Bowen, *Radar Days*, pp. 8–9.

16 Bowen, *Radar Days*, p. 19.

Chapter 2 – Bawdsey Manor

1 Buderi, *The Invention that Changed the World*, p. 70; Clark, *Tizard*, p. 153.

2 NA: AIR 10/5519, p. 19; Watson-Watt, *Three Steps to Victory*, p. 145. Different accounts of the September 1936 trials are to be found in

Watson-Watt, *Three Steps to Victory*, p. 173, Bowen, *Radar Days*, p. 24–5 and Colin Dobinson, *Building Radar*, pp. 140–7.

3 The full story of the construction of the Chain Home system with its many setbacks is told in Dobinson, *Building Radar*, pp. 153–225.

4 Bowen, *Radar Days*, p. 27.

5 Clark, *Tizard*, p. 151.

6 David Edgerton, *Britain's War Machine*, p. 40.

7 Robert Hanbury Brown, *Boffin*, p. 22.

8 Bowen, *Radar Days*, pp. 69–70.

Chapter 3 – Freya and Würzburg

1 Watson-Watt, *Three Steps to Victory*, pp. 184–5.

2 Gema stood for *Gesellschaft für Electroakustische und Mechanische Apparate* (Company for Electro-Acoustical and Mechanical Apparatus).

3 Pritchard, *The Radar War*, p. 39. The actual grant was for seventy thousand Reichsmarks. As the Reichsmark was technically a non-convertible currency at the time, it's impossible to give an exact equivalent in pounds or dollars, but it was of the order of £10,000.

4 Taylor Downing, 'The Olympics on Film' in *History Today*, Vol. 62, No. 8 (August 2012), p. 25.

5 Pritchard, *The Radar War*, p. 49.

6 Max Hastings, *Bomber Command*, pp. 22–35.

Chapter 4 – Airborne

1 John Lucas, *The Silken Canopy*, pp. 13–66.

2 NA: WO 32/4157.

3 Lt.-Col. T.B.H. Otway, *Airborne Forces*, p. 3.

4 Leni Riefenstahl's film of Hitler in his Ju 52 arriving god-like through the clouds at Nuremberg for the 1934 Nazi Party rally opens her film *Triumph of the Will*.

5 Otway, *Airborne Forces*, p. 4.

6 Winston Churchill, *The Second World War*, Vol. II, pp. 38–9; Downing, *Churchill's War Lab*, pp. 102ff.

7   Otway, *Airborne Forces*, p. 21; Downing, *Churchill's War Lab*, pp. 93–5.

8   Raymond Foxall, *The Guinea Pigs*, p. 19.

9   Foxall, *The Guinea Pigs*, p. 20.

10 Otway, *Airborne Forces*, p. 23.

11 Foxall, *The Guinea Pigs*, p. 26.

12 Foxall, *The Guinea Pigs*, p. 27.

13 Otway, *Airborne Forces*, p. 32.

Chapter 5 – Early Warning

1   Dobinson, *Building Radar*, p. 227.

2   This phrase was used in a speech Churchill made to the workers at Bawdsey Manor when he visited the site on 20 June, and was remembered by Sir Edward Fennessy in Colin Latham and Anne Stobbs, *Radar*, p. 216.

3   Bowen, *Radar Days*, p. 93.

4   Dobinson, *Building Radar*, p. 283.

5   Dobinson, *Building Radar*, p. 284.

6   Leo McKinstry, *Spitfire*, p. 143.

7   Latham and Stobbs, *Radar*, pp. 3–8.

8   Bernard Lovell, *Astronomer by Chance*, p. 54.

9   Alan Hodgkin was later awarded a Nobel Prize in physiology and became President of the Royal Society and Master of Trinity College, Cambridge. For Lovell's later career see the Epilogue.

10 Lovell, *Astronomer by Chance*, p. 61.

11 Watson-Watt, *Three Steps to Victory*, p. 281.

12 For accounts of the Tizard mission see Downing, *Churchill's War Lab*, pp. 170–2 and Buderi, *The Invention that Changed the World*, pp. 27–37

13 James Phinney Baxter, *Scientists Against Time*, p. 142.

14 Lord Birkenhead, *The Prof in Two Worlds*, p. 211.

15 Dr J. Rennie Whitehead quoted in Colin Latham and Anne Stobbs, *Pioneers of Radar*, p. 61.

16 Lovell, *Astronomer by Chance*, p. 5.

Chapter 6 – The First Raids

1 Martin Gilbert, *Finest Hour*, p. 667; Downing, *Churchill's War Lab*, pp. 185ff.
2 Martin Gilbert, *The Churchill War Papers*, Vol. II, p. 370.
3 Gilbert, *The Churchill War Papers*, Vol. II, p. 559.
4 Gilbert, *The Churchill War Papers*, Vol. II, pp. 721–2.
5 Philip Ziegler, *Mountbatten*, p. 157.
6 Otway, *Airborne Forces*, p. 26.
7 Foxall, *The Guinea Pigs*, passim.
8 Antony Beevor, *Crete*, p. 230.
9 Gilbert, *The Churchill War Papers*, Vol. III, p. 722.
10 IWM Sound: 17182, John Timothy interviewed 18 December 1996; Harvey Grenville and John Timothy, *Tim's Tale*, p. 4.
11 John Frost, *A Drop Too Many*, p. 30.
12 IWM Sound: 29606, Tom Hill interviewed by Windfall Films in 2001.
13 IWM Sound: 18780, Macleod Forsyth interviewed 24 April 1999.
14 Richard Mead, *General 'Boy'*, p. 68.

Chapter 7 – Scientific Intelligence

1 R.V. Jones, *Most Secret War*, pp. 68–70.
2 Jones devoted some time in the post-war years to trying to identify the author of the Oslo Report. When he finally identified the scientist he was reluctant to name him. See Jones, *Most Secret War*, p. 71; R.V. Jones, *Reflections on Intelligence*.
3 Jones, *Most Secret War*, p. 42.
4 Churchill, *The Second World War*, Vol. II, p. 340.
5 Jones, *Most Secret War*, pp. 100ff.
6 Churchill: R.V. Jones Papers/NCUACS 95.8.00/B24/Report No. 13, 10 January 1942, p. 3.
7 *Sunday Times*, 29 June 1941.
8 Taylor Downing, *Spies in the Sky*, pp. 131–58.
9 The key reports were dated 17 July 1940, 14 August 1940 and 10 January 1942. They are all held in Churchill: R.V. Jones Papers.

Chapter 8 – Photo Intelligence

1 Downing, *Spies in the Sky*, pp. 82ff.
2 However, the WAAF officers still did not receive equal pay with their RAF colleagues; that only came many decades later. During the war a female photo interpreter was paid about two-thirds the rate of a male interpreter. See Christine Halsall, *Women of Intelligence*, p. 22.
3 Downing, *Spies in the Sky*, pp. 326ff and passim.
4 Medmenham: DFG 5794, CBS Papers, interview with Claude Wavell, 24 May 1956; Downing, *Spies in the Sky*, pp. 258–9.
5 Jones, *Most Secret War*, p. 236.

Chapter 9 – Combined Operations

1 Churchill, *The Second World War*, Vol. III, pp. 539–40.
2 Quoted by Mountbatten in John Terraine, *The Life and Times of Lord Mountbatten*, p. 85.
3 Ziegler, *Mountbatten*, p. 157.
4 M.R.D. Foot, *The SOE in France*, pp. 182–5.
5 Solly Zuckerman, *From Apes to Warlords*, p. 153.
6 Ziegler, *Mountbatten*, p. 164.
7 Mead, *General 'Boy'*, p. 73.
8 See Downing, *Churchill's War Lab*, pp. 87ff.
9 NA: CAB 79/17/23 and CAB 79/17/26 contain the rather anodyne minutes of the two COS meetings; correspondence about the raid from the Secretary to the chiefs between meetings is contained in AIR 8/867.
10 Martin Gilbert, *Road to Victory*, p. 78.
11 Gilbert, *Road to Victory*, p. 67.

Chapter 10 – Underground Intelligence

1 Gilbert Renault, *The Silent Company*, p. 5.
2 Renault, *The Silent Company*, pp. 38–9 and passim for the quotes that follow.
3 This Département is now known as Seine-Maritime.
4 *Guide Rouge de Michelin, 1939*.

5 This account and what follows is based upon Roger Dumont's account of his visit to Bruneval, recounted in Gilbert Renault, *Bruneval: Opération coup de croc.*

Chapter 11 – Training

1 Frost, *A Drop Too Many*, pp. 33–6.
2 Frost, *A Drop Too Many*, p. 38.
3 IWM Sound: 18780.
4 The designers were Major R.V. Shepherd and Harold Turpin. The name of the gun is an acronym made up of the initials of the surnames of the two designers, ST, followed by EN for Enfield.
5 The most celebrated stoppage of a Sten gun was in May 1942, when a Slovak soldier carrying out a British-equipped plot to assassinate SS deputy head Reinhard Heydrich pulled the trigger of his Sten at point blank range but the gun failed to fire. Another soldier threw a grenade which mortally wounded Heydrich.
6 IWM Sound: 27176, Geoffrey Alan Osborn interviewed in 2005.
7 Frost, *A Drop Too Many*, p. 41.
8 Pears later became part of Unilever, which now owns the painting and have loaned it to the Lady Lever Art Gallery in Liverpool where it is on display.
9 Airborne: 4D2 2.2.2, Commander F.N. Cook, private memoir of Operation Biting.
10 IWM Sound: 16727, Rev John Leonard Brooker interviewed 9 May 1996.
11 IWM Sound: 20365, Eric John Gould interviewed 17 June 2000.
12 IWM Sound: 17182, John Timothy interviewed 18 December 1996; Grenville and Timothy, *Tim's Tale*, p. 16.

Chapter 12 – Volunteers for Danger

1 This account is partly taken from Flight Sergeant's Cox report on Operation Biting in Airborne: 4D2 2.2.1, and partly from George Millar, *The Bruneval Raid*, pp. 33ff, based on an interview with Cox carried out in the 1970s.

2 Jones, *Most Secret War*, pp. 237–8.

3 Niall Cherry, *Striking Back*, p. 199.

4 Latham and Stobbs, *Pioneers of Radar*, pp. 43ff.

5 Millar, *The Bruneval Raid*, p. 36, quoting a letter from Frost.

6 See the entry on Peter Nagel in the Jewish Virtual Library at
   http://www.jewishvirtuallibrary.org/jsource/ww2/Peter_Nagel.ht
   ml. The quote is from an interview with Nagel's daughter.

7 Frost, *A Drop Too Many*, p. 42.

Chapter 13 – The Plan

1 Max Arthur, *Men of the Red Beret*, p. 22; interview with John Frost in
   1989.

2 Airborne: 4D2 2.2.1, 'Operational Orders for Operation Biting'.

3 NA: AIR 39/43.

4 The container of tools that was parachuted separately for the
   dismantling of the Würzburg consisted of the following: 'No. 2 Bag
   – 1 Claw hammer/1 Cold chisel/1 Hacksaw and spare blade/1 large
   screwdriver/1 long thin screwdriver/1 comb spanner/1 pair end
   cutting spanners/1 pair side cutting spanners/2 pairs rubber gloves/1
   roll copper wire/1 head torch/2 hand torches/1 shifting spanner with
   6 inch handle.' See NA: AIR 32/8.

5 Airborne: 4D2 2.2.2, Commander F.N. Cook, private memoir of
   Operation Biting.

6 NA: AIR 39/43, Cox's report.

7 One of the models still exists and is on display in the Airborne
   Assault Museum at the Imperial War Museum, Duxford.

8 Downing, *Spies in the Sky*, pp. 118–19, 259–60.

Chapter 14 – The Defenders

1 NA: AIR 32/8, Operation Biting: Airborne Division: Operation Order
   No. 1.

2 NA: AIR 32/8, Operation Biting: Airborne Division: Operation Order
   No. 1, Appendix I.

3 Frost, *A Drop Too Many*, p. 44.

Chapter 15 – The Drop

1 The Germans did not have this facility for meteorological prediction and so weather forecasting became an issue surrounded by security during the war. For this reason the BBC did not transmit weather reports on the radio and the newspapers did not carry weather forecasts, as it was thought they would give useful information to the enemy.

2 Airborne: 4D2 2.2.2, Commander F.N. Cook, private memoir of Operation Biting.

3 Frost, *A Drop Too Many*, pp. 47–8.

4 Airborne: 4D2 2.2.1, A.R. Humphreys, Reuters' correspondent on *Prinz Albert*, in Operation Biting – Personal Accounts.

5 Frost, *A Drop Too Many*, p. 48.

6 Frost, *A Drop Too Many*, p. 49.

7 NA: AIR 32/8.

8 NA: AIR 32/8, Appendix A.

9 RAF: *RAF Journal* Vol. 2 No. 5, 1944, p. 159.

10 NA: WO 106/4133, Biting – Personal Accounts.

11 *Guardian*, 2 March 1942.

12 Hilary St George Saunders, *The Red Beret*, p. 65.

13 Airborne: 4D2 2.2.1, Lieutenant Charteris Personal Report.

14 Airborne: 4D2 2.2.1, Lieutenant Charteris Personal Report.

15 IWM Sound: 18780.

Chapter 16 – Attack

1 Airborne: 4D2 2.2.1, Lieutenant Charteris Personal Report.

2 Frost, *A Drop Too Many*, p. 51.

3 NA: DEFE 2/101, Lieutenant Young Personal Report.

4 RAF: *RAF Journal* Vol. 2 No. 5, p. 160.

5 Cherry, *Striking Back*, p. 212.

6 Airborne: 4D2 2.2.1, Flight Sergeant Cox Personal Report.

Chapter 17 – Fire Fight

1 Airborne: 4D2 2.2.2, Commander F.N. Cook, private memoir of Operation Biting.
2 IWM Sound: 20365.
3 Airborne: 4D2 2.2.1, Lieutenant Charteris Personal Report.
4 IWM Sound: 29606.
5 Airborne: 4D2 2.2.1, Lieutenant Charteris Personal Report.
6 Literally this means the 'Deer's Antlers' and is an old cry of the Mackenzie clan inherited by the Seaforth Highlanders in the eighteenth century when the Mackenzies first raised the regiment.
7 IWM Sound: 29606.
8 Saunders, *The Red Beret*, p. 68.

Chapter 18 – The Ruddy Navy

1 Airborne: 4D2 2.2.1, Flight Sergeant Cox Personal Report.
2 IWM Sound: 17182
3 Airborne: 4D2 2.2.1, Flight Sergeant Cox Personal Report.
4 Airborne: 4D2 2.2.1, Major Frost Personal Report; Frost, *A Drop Too Many*, pp. 53–4
5 Frost, *A Drop Too Many*, p. 54.
6 Airborne: 4D2 2.2.1, Major Frost Personal Report.
7 IWM Sound: 18780.
8 IWM Sound: 20365.
9 Reminiscence by Donald Preist in Latham and Stobbs, *Pioneers of Radar*, p. 46.
10 They are both buried in the Commonwealth War Graves cemetery at Ste Marie, Le Havre.
11 IWM Sound: 18780.
12 Airborne: 4D2 2.2.2, Commander F.N. Cook, private memoir on Operation Biting.
13 Airborne: 4D2 2.2.1, A.R. Humphreys Personal Report.
14 Frost, *A Drop Too Many*, p. 55.
15 Alan Humphreys' reports were picked out by *Newspaper World* on 9 January 1943 as one of three sets of reports by Reuters journalists deserving special praise – the other two were Harold King for his

reports from Moscow and Arthur Oakeshott for his account from the Arctic convoys in 1942. See Graham Storey, *Reuters' Century*, pp. 225–6.

Chapter 19 – Aftermath

1 Alain Millet, *Raid de Bruneval*, pp. 278–80.
2 Millet, *Raid de Bruneval*, pp. 281–6.
3 Millet, *Raid de Bruneval*, pp. 287–97.
4 Today it is known as Lambinowice and is the site of the Central National Prisoner Museum.
5 Airborne: 4D2 2.2.2; also quoted in Cherry, *Striking Back*, pp. 380–2.
6 Frost, *A Drop Too Many*, pp. 56–8.

Chapter 20 – Good News

1 There were 23,000 households in the south of Britain with TV sets in September 1939. It took a long time for television to establish itself as a popular cultural form in the UK when it was re-established after the war. Even at the time of the London Olympics in 1948 only about 40,000 households in the Home Counties had sets and could pick up the signal from Wembley. The Coronation of 1953 gave a huge boost to the sale of television sets, but television only really became a mass popular pursuit with the coming of ITV, which rolled out across the nation from 1955 onwards.
2 Asa Briggs, *The War of Words*, pp. 141, 187. By 1942, 9,019,000 radio licences had been issued (Briggs, *The War of Words*, p. 666) and in most homes two to three people gathered around the wireless for the main evening news.
3 Richard Havers, *Here is the News*, pp. 116–17.
4 Briggs, *The War of Words*, pp. 75–84.
5 Havers, *Here is the News*, p. 72.
6 BBC WAC: HNB 28.2.42, 1 p.m. News.
7 BBC WAC: HNB 28.2.42, 1 p.m. News, p. 1. Each news item was typed on separate pages and many include handwritten approvals from the MoI controllers.

8 BBC WAC: HNB 28.2.42, 6 p.m. News, p. 1.

9 BBC WAC: HNB 28.2.42, Midnight News, p. 2.

10 The BBC began the war broadcasting in seven languages and ended it broadcasting in forty-five.

11 Renault, *The Silent Company*, p. 272.

12 Nicholas Wilkinson, *Secrecy and the Media*, pp.180ff.

13 *Sunday Times*, 1 March 1942.

14 *Observer*, 1 March 1942.

15 *Guardian*, 2 March 1942.

16 *Daily Sketch*, 7 March 1942.

17 IWM Sound: 18780.

18 IWM Sound: 29606.

19 IWM Sound: 18780.

20 Ziegler, *Mountbatten*, p. 171.

21 *In Which We Serve*, produced, directed, written and music composed by Noel Coward, co-directed by David Lean in his directorial debut; photography by Ronald Neame; featuring Noel Coward as Captain Kinross, Celia Johnson as his wife, Bernard Miles as Chief Petty Officer Hardy and John Mills as Ordinary Seaman Blake. Richard Attenborough makes his first screen appearance as a stoker who panics and runs away from his post. Two Cities Films, 1942; available on DVD through ITV Video.

22 IWM Film: BEY 222/01 and 02.

23 Quoted in Nicholas Pronay, 'The Newsreels: The illusion of actuality' in Paul Smith (ed.), *The Historian and Film*, p. 113.

24 See the British Universities Film and Video Council *News on Screen* database.

25 Gaumont British News is now controlled by ITN Source and the newsreel can be seen at http://www.itnsource.com/shotlist/BHC_RTV/1942/03/05/BGU408200005/?s=bruneval&st=0&pn=1

26 IWM Film: *War Pictorial News*, Issue 052, April 1942.

27 *School for Secrets*, produced by George H. Brown and Peter Ustinov; written and directed by Peter Ustinov; starring Ralph Richardson, Richard Attenborough, David Tomlinson and John Laurie. Two Cities Films, 1946; available on DVD through Simply Home Entertainment.

28 Grenville and Timothy, *Tim's Tale*, p. 64.

Chapter 21 – The Scientific War

1 Jones, *Most Secret War*, pp. 242–5.
2 Churchill: R.V. Jones Papers/NCUACS 95.8.00/B.31, Appendix III.
3 Jones, *Most Secret War*, p. 244. After the war Jones met General Martini, former head of the Luftwaffe Air Signals and Radar section, who explained this fully to him.
4 Jones, *Most Secret War*, p. 245.
5 Downing, *Spies in the Sky*, p. 260.
6 Lovell, *Astronomer by Chance*, p. 73.
7 Donald Preist, 'Memories of the Bruneval Raid' in Cherry, *Striking Back*, pp. 387–8.
8 Jones, *Most Secret War*, p. 297.
9 Albert Speer, *Inside the Third Reich*, pp. 283–4. For the detailed damage assessment report after the raid, see Downing, *Spies in the Sky*, pp. 204–5.
10 Based on figures for the number of sorties from May 1942 to early July 1943 in Hastings, *Bomber Command*, Appendix A, pp. 426–7, with an average crew of seven men in a Halifax, Stirling or Lancaster heavy bomber.
11 Buderi, *The Invention that Changed the World*, pp. 208–9; Jones, *Most Secret War*, p. 386.

Epilogue

1 There was some argument about whether Bruneval qualified when the Parachute Regiment was first allocated its battle honours in 1956. The officer distributing the honours thought the regiment had proposed too many and needed to cut back its list. He suggested Bruneval 'was only a small scale raid' and he was 'doubtful whether it should be included'. Airborne: Misc: Letter Lt General Lathbury to Col Coxen, 2 July 1956. Nevertheless, the Parachute Regiment insisted, and so it was included and is still held with great pride.
2 Ziegler, *Mountbatten*, p. 170.
3 IWM Film: LOC 60. John Hughes-Hallett spoke these words in an interview for the Rediffusion Television series *The Life and Times of*

Mountbatten (1969), Episode 5 'United We Conquer'; also quoted in Ziegler, *Mountbatten*, p. 170.

4 Mountbatten continued his naval career and went on to become First Sea Lord in the late 1950s and Head of the Defence Staff in the 1960s. He was assassinated by the IRA while on holiday boating off Mullaghmore on the Irish coast in 1979.

5 Otway, *Airborne Forces*, p. 80.

6 Quoted in Arthur, *Men of the Red Beret*, p. 65.

7 Frost, *A Drop Too Many*, p. 185.

8 For example Martin Middlebrook, *Arnhem 1944: The Airborne Battle*; William Buckingham, *Arnhem 1944*; Robert Kershaw, *It Never Snows in September: The German View of Market Garden and the Battle of Arnhem, September 1944*; Lloyd Clark, *Arnhem: Jumping the Rhine 1944 and 1945*, and many others.

9 Downing, *Spies in the Sky*, pp. 318–19.

10 Frost, *A Drop Too Many*, p. 253; the story was that a sapper who had been captured by the Germans was sent back to Frost with the suggestion he should meet the German commander to negotiate the surrender of the Paras. The sapper was Sergeant Halliwell, who had helped with the dismantling of the Würzberg radar at Bruneval. Halliwell said he did not want to have to go back and tell the SS commander to 'go to hell' and so Frost let him remain, reckoning that if he never returned the Germans would get the message that the Paras were not ready to surrender.

11 IWM Sound: 17182; Grenville and Timothy, *Tim's Tale*, pp. 47–63.

12 *A Bridge Too Far*, directed by Richard Attenborough; written by William Goldman based on the book by Cornelius Ryan; produced by Joseph Levine; starring Dirk Bogarde, James Caan, Michael Caine, Sean Connery, Edward Fox, Anthony Hopkins, Gene Hackman, Hardy Krüger, Laurence Olivier, Robert Redford and Maximilian Schell. A Joseph E. Levine Production for United Artists, 1977.

13 Frost, *A Drop Too Many*, pp. 253–5.

14 See: http://www.lexikon-der-wehrmacht.de

15 Charles Cox died in 1995.

16 John Timothy died in 2011.

17 John Ross died in 1993.

18 John Frost died in 1993.

19 A.J.P. Taylor, *English History 1914–1945*, p. 392.

20 R.V. Jones died in 1997.

21 Lovell, *Astronomer by Chance*, pp. 105ff; Bernard Lovell died in 2012.

22 Frank Whittle, the inventor of the jet engine, was another. The British government had given him an award of £100,000 but he preferred to spend most of his time in North America.

23 Robert Watson-Watt returned to live in Scotland in the 1960s and died in 1973.

Bibliography

Primary Sources – Unpublished

The National Archives in Kew contain the core official documents and reports on the raid and all the minutes of the War Cabinet and of the Chiefs of Staff Committee.

The Airborne Assault Archive at Duxford contains copies of several documents along with memoirs, photographs and other objects relating to the raid. Also held here are many of the Personal Reports written within a few days of the raid.

The Imperial War Museum holds a collection of interviews with members of C Company of the 2nd Parachute Battalion, as well as the film and photographic records relating to the raid.

The Churchill Archives Centre at Churchill College, Cambridge, contains the papers of R.V. Jones.

The Medmenham Collection Archive includes private papers and documents relating to the Central Interpretation Unit at RAF Medmenham. Extracts from documents and photographs from the collection are reproduced by courtesy of the Trustees of the Medmenham Collection.

The BBC Written Archives Centre contains records of all BBC radio news bulletins during the war.

All of the above are referenced in the notes.

Primary Sources – Published

E.G. Bowen, *Radar Days*. Bristol: Adam Hilger, 1987.

Winston Churchill, *The Second World War*, 6 vols. London: Cassell, 1948–1954.

Major General John Frost, *A Drop Too Many*. London: Cassell, 1980; republished Barnsley: Pen & Sword, 1994.

Martin Gilbert, *The Churchill War Papers*, Vol. II, *Never Surrender May 1940–December 1940*. London: Heinemann, 1994.

Martin Gilbert, *The Churchill War Papers*, Vol. III, *The Ever Widening War 1941*. London: Heinemann, 2000.

Harvey Grenville and John Timothy, *Tim's Tale: A Wartime Biography of Major John Timothy*. Privately published by Lulu Press.

Guide Rouge de Michelin 1939. Paris: Michelin, 1939.

Robin Hanbury Brown, *Boffin: A Personal Story of the Early Days of Radar, Radio Astronomy and Quantum Optics*. Bristol: Adam Hilger, 1991.

R.V. Jones, *Most Secret War*. London: Hamish Hamilton, 1978; republished London: Penguin, 2009.

R.V. Jones, *Reflections on Intelligence*. London: Heinemann, 1989.

Bernard Lovell, *Astronomer By Chance*. London: Macmillan, 1991.

Gilbert Renault, *The Silent Company*, translated by Lancelot

Shepherd. London: Arthur Barker, 1948.

Gilbert Renault, *Bruneval: opération coup de croc*. Paris: Editions France Empire, 1968.

A.P. Rowe, *One Story of Radar: An Account of the work of the Tele-communications Research Establishment*. Cambridge: Cambridge University Press, 1948.

Sir Robert Watson-Watt, *Three Steps to Victory: A Personal Account by Radar's Greatest Pioneer*. London: Odhams Press, 1957.

Solly Zuckerman, *From Apes to Warlords*. London: Harper & Row, 1978.

Secondary Sources

Max Arthur, *Men of the Red Beret: Airborne Forces 1940–1990*. London: Hutchinson, 1990.

James Phinney Baxter III (Official Historian of the Office of Scientific Research and Development), *Scientists Against Time*. Boston: Little, Brown, 1946.

Antony Beevor, *Crete: The Battle and the Resistance*. London: John Murray, 1991.

Lord Birkenhead, *The Prof in Two Worlds – The Official Life of Professor F.A. Lindemann, Viscount Cherwell*. London: Collins, 1961.

Asa Briggs, *The War of Words: The History of Broadcasting in the United Kingdom*, Vol. III. Oxford: Oxford University Press, revised edition 1995.

William F. Buckingham, *Paras: The Untold Story of the Birth of the British Airborne Forces*. Stroud: History Press, 2008.

Robert Buderi, *The Invention that Changed the World*. London: Little, Brown, 1997.

Niall Cherry, *Striking Back: Britain's Airborne and Commando Raids 1940–42*. Solihull: Helion, 2009.

Ronald W. Clark, *The Rise of the Boffins*. London: Phoenix House, 1962.

Ronald W. Clark, *Tizard*. London: Methuen, 1965.

Colin Dobinson, *Building Radar: Forging Britain's Early-warning Chain 1935–45*. London: Methuen, 2010.

Taylor Downing, *Churchill's War Lab – Code Breakers, Boffins and Innovators: The Mavericks Churchill Led to Victory*. London: Little, Brown, 2010.

Taylor Downing, *Spies in the Sky – The Secret Battle for Aerial Intelligence during World War Two*. London: Little, Brown, 2011.

David Edgerton, *Britain's War Machine: Weapons, Resources and Experts in the Second World War*. London: Allen Lane, 2011.

M.R.D. Foot, *The SOE in France: An Account of the Work of the Special Operations Executive in France 1940–1944*. London: HMSO, 1966.

Ken Ford, *The Bruneval Raid: Operation Biting 1942*. Oxford: Osprey, 2010.

Raymond Foxall, *The Guinea Pigs: Britain's First Paratroop Raid*. London: Robert Hale, 1983.

Martin Gilbert, *Finest Hour: Winston S. Churchill 1939–1941*. London: Heinemann, 1983.

Martin Gilbert, *Road to Victory: Winston S. Churchill 1941–1945*. London: Heinemann, 1986.

Christine Halsall, *Women of Intelligence: Winning the Second World War with Air Photos*. Stroud: History Press, 2012.

Max Hastings, *Bomber Command*. London: Michael Joseph, 1979.

Richard Havers, *Here is the News: The BBC and the Second World War*. Stroud: Sutton Publishing, 2007.

Paddy Heazell, *Most Secret: The Hidden History of Orford Ness*. London: History Press, 2010.

Colin Latham and Anne Stobbs, *Radar – A Wartime Miracle Recalled by the Men and Women who Played their Part in it for the RAF.* Stroud: Sutton Publishing, 1996.

Colin Latham and Anne Stobbs, *Pioneers of Radar.* Stroud: Sutton Publishing, 1999.

John Lucas, *The Silken Canopy: A History of the Parachute.* Shrewsbury: Airlife, 1997.

Leo McKinstry, *Spitfire – Portrait of a Legend.* London: John Murray, 2007.

Richard Mead, *General 'Boy': The Life of Lieutenant General Frederick Browning.* Barnsley: Pen & Sword, 2010.

George Millar, *The Bruneval Raid: Flashpoint of the Radar War.* London: Bodley Head, 1974.

Alain Millet (avec la participation de Nicolas Bucourt), *Raid de Bruneval et de La Poterie-Cap-d'Antifer: Mystères et Verité.* Bayeux: Heimdal, 2012.

G.G. Norton, *The Red Devils: The Story of the British Airborne Forces.* London: Leo Cooper, 1971.

Lieutenant-Colonel T.B.H. Otway, *The Second World War 1939–1945, Army: Airborne Forces.* London: Imperial War Museum, 1990 [originally published confidentially by the War Office in 1951 as part of a series of books written to 'preserve the experience gained during the Second world War'].

James Owen, *Commando: Winning World War Two Behind Enemy Lines*, London: Little, Brown, 2012.

David Pritchard, *The Radar War: Germany's Pioneering Achievement 1904–45.* Wellingborough: Patrick Stephens, 1989.

Nicholas Pronay, 'The Newsreels: The illusion of actuality' in

Paul Smith (ed.), *The Historian and Film*. Cambridge: Cambridge University Press, 1976.

Hilary St George Saunders, *The Red Beret: The Story of the Parachute Regiment at War 1940–1945*. London: Michael Joseph, 1950.

Albert Speer, *Inside the Third Reich*. London: Weidenfeld and Nicolson, 1970.

Graham Storey, *Reuters' Century 1851–1951*. London: Max Parrish, 1951.

A.J.P. Taylor, *English History 1914–1945*. Oxford: Oxford University Press, 1965.

John Terraine, *The Life and Times of Lord Mountbatten*. London: Hutchinson, 1968.

Julian Thompson, *Ready for Anything: The Parachute Regiment at War, 1940–1982*. London: Weidenfeld and Nicolson, 1989.

Nicholas Wilkinson, *Secrecy and the Media: The Official History of the United Kingdom's D-Notice System*. London: Routledge, 2009.

Philip Ziegler, *Mountbatten: The Official Biography*. London: Collins, 1985.

Index

390